In My
Father's
House

Dorothy
Allred
Solomon

IN MY
FATHER'S
HOUSE

Franklin Watts
New York   Toronto
1984

Library of Congress Cataloging in Publication Data

Solomon, Dorothy Allred.
    In my father's house.

    1. Solomon, Dorothy Allred.   2. Mormons
—United Stated—Biography.   I. Title.
BX8695.S755A33 1984   289.3'3 [B3]   84-11964
ISBN 0-531-09763-3

Lines from the song "Vaya con Dios" by Inez James,
Buddy Pepper, and Larry Russell, copyright © 1953,
1981 by Beachaven Music and Jarest Music.
Reprinted by permission.

Author's Note

Certain names have been changed.
Otherwise, the facts are as I remember
them, or as research yielded.

I acknowledge that truth indelibly carves
itself on the face of reality, yet we each
perceive the etching in our own way.
All I can claim for the pages within is
the honest presentation of my vision
and experience of the truth. I know that
others have their version, equally valid.
I invite them to share it with the world.

This book is dedicated to my families, large and small.

In My Father's House

"In my Father's house are many mansions: if it were not so, I would have told you. I go to prepare a place for you."

St. John 14:2

Prologue

In October of 1890 the church of Jesus Christ of Latter-Day Saints approved a manifesto abolishing the practice of polygamy. Hundreds of Mormon marriages were thereby dissolved, thousands of children bastardized, and innumerable hearts broken.

Thirteen years later, my grandfather, Byron Harvey Allred, Jr., gave up his holdings in Star Valley, Wyoming, and boarded a train with his wife and children, bound for a polygamist-refugee colony in Mexico. In Logan, Utah, the family paused to pick up Grandfather's fiancée, Mary Evelyn Clark, an eighteen-year-old girl who would become his second wife and, eventually, my grandmother.

As they chugged toward Mexico, Grandfather hovered over the young woman, alternately anxious and grateful. As she was traveling to meet him, a taxi driver had tried to rape her. There had been a big scene with police and locals, with two young girls venturing forth to confess the perpetrator's abuse of their virtue. The scandal had shaken everyone deeply, and Grandfather praised God that things hadn't been worse. Clearly Satan was trying to pervert their celestial cause, Grandfather reasoned.

While Grandfather comforted Evelyn and rejoiced in their narrow escape, his first wife, Charlotte, wrestled with her seven children and her feelings. She had promised to accept the Principle of Plural Marriage wholeheartedly, to be obedient to the wishes of her husband and the secret instructions of Church authorities. But after days of sleeping upright and persuading her fidgety children to do likewise; after days of rocking back and forth in the narrow car, enduring her husband's attentions to a younger, cooler woman; after days of vacillating between her commitment to live polygamy and her commitment to the life she had known, Charlotte's nerves must have writhed like maggots, gnawing at her resolution and strength. While laying over in the hot, dry border town of El Paso, Charlotte dreamed something so vivid, so prescient, and so horrible that Grandfather recorded it in his journal: "She dreamed that I was faithless to her, that I deserted her while crossing a muddy river in which [our children] Ezra and Othello were lost . . . and that in her great struggle to save them, I would not come to her assistance."

Grandfather explained that the nightmare came true in all aspects but one: "Never for one second . . . in my hard life was I indifferent to my darling wife's suffering and sorrow."

Grandfather joined his father and mother, who had also entered plural marriage. They all set up residence in Colonia Dublan, a village of extremes, where expatriate Mormons busied themselves building adobes, irrigating gardens, and cultivating bright flowers in clay pots while gun-toting Mexican rebels lolled in the sandy shade of the church ogling shy, prim Mormon girls. The black-clad patriarchs and their wives had sacrificed property, society, and U.S. citizenship to keep the Principle alive without breaking the Twelfth Mormon Article of Faith, which promises allegiance to the government, and now they were as dazzled by the refraction of the desert sun as by their uncompromised religious ideals. The stark land appropriately backdropped the unyielding remnant of Mormon polygamists.

Two weeks after their entrance into Mexico, Othello, the baby of Grandfather's family, died of meningitis, fulfilling part of Charlotte's nightmare. Three days later, another part of the phantasm came true—at least in Charlotte's eyes—despite Grandfather's claim that he never ignored her suffering. Grandfather, Charlotte, and Evelyn hitched up the wagon and carried a sealed envelope to the president of the Latter-Day Saints Mexico Mission, Anthony W. Ivins, in Colonia Juarez. The document, signed by Mormon Church President Joseph F. Smith, gave permission for the three to be sealed in plural marriage. Ivins performed the ceremony as he had numerous others since his appointment to the Mexico Mission, although in later years he would become one of the Principle's major detractors, labeling fundamentalists who clung to polygamy "adulterers" and "outlaws."

The journey back to Dublan brooded along as though no transition could be made from the short funeral procession the day before. Grandfather and Grandmother Evelyn were discreet; Charlotte, her eyes red and her face gray, dabbed inside her sunbonnet with a handkerchief; but when they stopped to view the distant hills, she nodded her appreciation. She had found the strength to take Evelyn's hand and to give her to her husband, just as Sarah, sorrowing in her childlessness, had given Hagar to Abraham. And when President Ivins asked, "Do you, Charlotte, willingly give this sister in eternal marriage to your husband?" Charlotte had murmured perhaps her only words of the day: "I do."

As if stricken by realization of his undue haste, Grandfather became ill on the journey home. When able to travel again, he invited Charlotte to vacation with him in the verdant mountains southwest of Dublan. Evelyn spent her honeymoon tending the children at home.

A few months later the last part of Charlotte's dream became bleak reality. In the typhoid-stricken community Grandfather buried his oldest son, Ezra. Losing the cornerstones of his family shook Grandfather's faith in the Church as deeply as the tragedies shook Charlotte's faith in her husband. Grandfather had been promised by a priesthood bearer, a trusted Church elder, that the boy would live, and now Ezra's body lay six feet beneath the shifting sands of Chihuahua. "I was wild and dumbfounded," Grandfather wrote. "I wished I could have died without witnessing this. Had God broken His Word? Was there really a God? Were those who claimed to hold His Priesthood imposters?"

Grandfather, reared to believe in divine revelation from God to man, to trust in the Church authorities, and to exercise the power to heal by the laying on of hands, now quaked with doubt. A few days after Ezra's funeral, days without sleep or food, he lay beside Charlotte, trying to focus his distraught feelings. Charlotte, in her stupor, could offer him no consolation. He felt utterly isolated, beyond her reach and beyond reaching out to touch her. As he regarded his hollow-eyed wife, it seemed he watched a mirror of his own vandalized soul.

Then a vision came over him. He later recorded it in his journal: ". . . the side of the room seemed to vanish. I saw . . . a beautiful soft light approaching . . . I saw my boy in all the beauty of health and strength. . . ."

He described Ezra's radiant smile and a heavy golden chain that the boy extended, saying, "See, Father, not one link is broken."

This vision or dream restored Grandfather's faith in God, in a resurrection, and in his church. On the basis of "personal revelation"—a Mormon belief that God communes with individuals—

Grandfather drew on dreams and visions throughout his life to give meaning to his reality. Like Joseph Smith, Jr., who had founded the Mormon Church after a visitation, like Moses or Martin Luther or Christ, Grandfather clung to his intensely personal communion with God until the voice of conscience shouted down all other voices of the world.

Joseph Smith's ministry had begun at fourteen when he knelt in prayer, responding to James's exhortation: "If any of you lack wisdom, let him ask of God, that giveth to all men liberally, and upbraideth not; and it shall be given to him." Young Joseph sought to know which church was true, and was overcome by a vision—a visitation from God the Father and His Son. Thereafter, Joseph joined none of the existing churches but waited for further revelation. Over the next years he reportedly experienced visitations from an angel called Moroni, who led him to a set of golden plates hidden in nearby Hill Cumorah. The plates were said to contain the ancient history of North America as set down by prophets of God. Translated, these became *The Book of Mormon*—the foundation of Joseph's new church and a companion to the Bible in witnessing to the divine sacrifice of Jesus Christ.

In 1831 the Church of Jesus Christ of Latter-Day Saints was formally established, basing its doctrines on the literal truth of the Bible, *The Book of Mormon*, and a set of revelations received by Joseph Smith as "Prophet, Seer and Revelator" that became known as *The Doctrine and Covenants*. (Additional scripture, *The Pearl of Great Price*, would follow.) The name of the new church reflected a belief in the imminent second coming of Christ and the restoration of His priesthood upon the earth. The promised millennial reign of peace and love would be ushered in by "saints"—members of the Church.

Among the many revelations documented by Joseph Smith was a "New and Everlasting Covenant" of marriage, a contract between men, women, and God that would insure the eternal progress of the souls "sealed"—bonded by priesthood authority for time and all eternity. This marriage covenant addressed the Principle of Plural Marriage, known also as the Law of Abraham, which in the words of the 132nd section of *The Doctrine and Covenants* "was ordained . . . before the world was."

The Mormon Principle of Plural Marriage held the same promise for patriarchs as that made by God to Abraham in Genesis. Since Mormons regard themselves as descendants of Israel (either in spirit or in fact), they too deserved to "father . . . many nations," to be "exceeding fruitful," and to bless the world with "seed as the stars of heaven and as the sand . . . upon the seashore." Church leaders would later justify the Principle as: promoting a charitable attitude; granting an opportunity for true cooperation; permitting men to build family kingdoms over which they would reign through all eternity, producing endless lives and building up the kingdom of God; and giving the many souls who waited in the spirit world an opportunity to achieve their "mortal estate" before the destruction and resurrection of the earth.

But controversy surrounded polygamy from its inception. Joseph Smith introduced the Principle to only a handful of Church authorities in the early 1830s, several years before the Covenant was set down in a formal revelation in 1843. It was practiced secretly and surrounded with rumor. Detractors of the Church said that Joseph Smith invented his revelation about polygamy to temper a volatile affair with young Fannie Alger and to save himself from the fury of his wife, Emma. Others insisted the revelation was divine, like all the revelations forming the foundation of the young church: if the Principle was false, then all was false. Still, scandal raged; even Church members whispered that Emma threw one of Joseph's plural wives down the stairs on discovering that the young miss was pregnant and that she turned the Alger sisters out into the cold when she caught them with Joseph. "Gentiles" (as Mormons call outsiders) needed little prompting to believe the worst. Already incensed by the Church's political power and troubled financial history, mobs dogged the Church from one settlement to another, looting and burning Mormon homes, and even murdering, until the outrage culminated in the assassination of Joseph Smith in the jail at Carthage, Illinois.

The ravaged church licked its wounds across the Great Plains to remote Utah, where polygamy, touted as a plan for man's deification and celestial glory, could be practiced openly.

Second Church President Brigham Young promoted polygamy with fervor, taking twenty-seven wives himself and declaring to his brethren in a rather infelicitous figure of speech, "We must gird up our loins and keep this Principle."

Since he had risen from his sickbed in a covered wagon to look over the Salt Lake valley and declare, "This is the place," the desert had indeed blossomed "as a rose," thanks largely to the Mormon Church and to Young's role as Utah's first governor. He had transcended the splintering effect of Joseph Smith's death and had taken the reins of power to clarify and implement church hierarchy.

In addition to President Brigham Young, who was Prophet, Seer and Revelator, the Church was ruled by the twelve apostles, who served as special witnesses to Christ, and a group of authorities who supervised the Church structure, including missionary efforts and membership. The body of the Church was divided into stakes (roughly comparable to dioceses), supervised by a stake president and high council, which contained a number of wards (like parishes) each led by a bishop. On the bishops fell direct responsibility for the spiritual and material welfare of each Latter-Day Saint.

In the mostly salt and sagebrush wasteland of Utah, such responsibility was immense, especially considering that the desert, the Indians, and the crickets did their best to disrupt the Mormon end of the food chain. So Brigham Young invoked the United Order previously established through *The Doctrine and Covenants:* "For if ye are not equal in earthly things, ye cannot be equal in obtaining heavenly things." Under this system each saint consecrated his time, his property, his crops, and his money to the Church. The bishop stored all goods in his warehouse, then distributed the wealth according to need. This way, Brigham Young promised, Zion would prosper and the scripture would be fulfilled: "There shall be no poor among them."

The abundance of polygamy, the cooperative effort, and the United Order produced a vitality that lured settlers and prospectors headed for the lush ground and gold fields of California. Rather than brave the Salt Flats, they stayed in Zion, though they were doomed to be strangers among the Mormons. But gradually, Zion lost its isolated freedom. Entrepreneurs and politicians complained about the formidable force of the Mormon Church, focusing on the most peculiar practice of a peculiar people. Polygamy was under fire again.

As the U.S. government held out the carrot-on-a-stick of statehood, it exerted increasing pressure to eradicate polygamy from Utah Territory (it was said to be, along with slavery, one of the "twin relics of barbarism"), and the Mormon bloc of votes grew, including the franchise of women who usually voted as their husbands dictated. At last the Edmunds-Tucker Act (and others) stripped Mormon polygamists of franchise, lands and possessions, and personal freedom. Church authorities, forced into hiding, were discovered by "peeping Toms" and imprisoned. But third Church President John Taylor warned the Church to stand its ground, predicting that "one backward step . . . and the time will come when the greatest enemy of the Principle is the Church itself." After Taylor's death, the push for statehood intensified. In 1890 the Church finally capitulated, signing the manifesto and releasing the congregation from an unpopular doctrine that caused its believers more grief and harassment than any other aspect of the religion.

Although my grandfather had descended from two generations of the Church's proud and overt polygamous epoch, he had not intended to live the Principle. He was devoted to his childhood sweetheart, Charlotte. The couple had been present at the October conference when the manifesto was read and sustained by the congregation, releasing them from any obligation to live the Principle. In years to come Grandfather recorded that he had been out of the room burping the baby when the sea of hands went up affirming the manifesto; he looked on his absence as enormously significant.

For the time being, Grandfather turned his prodigious energy to making a secular success of his life. He farmed, he taught school, and he entered Wyoming politics. Then he turned to lawyering, which became a forum for his strong opinions and his theatrical gifts. (He was a great Shakespeare lover and named several of his children after characters from the plays.) Grandfather's intercourse with the law taught him much about man's criminal nature. After exposure to fraud, incest, and murder, a kind of cynicism began to flourish and with it a talent for telling lewd tales. Then suddenly, as if lightning had struck his little arbor of secular success, Grandfather was called on a mission to preach Mormon doctrine in Indian Territory. While on his mission, Grandfather met one Loren C. Wooley, former bodyguard of Church President Taylor, who believed that "honest and true" men were still obliged to live "the fullness of the gospel"—including polygamy.

Wooley reported that in 1886 he had eavesdropped on a most unusual conversation while guarding Taylor in the West Jordan home where he hid from U.S. marshals and dodged "peeping Toms." Seated just outside Taylor's bedroom, Wooley heard voices and saw a brilliant light emanating from the door. Alarmed because no one was allowed in or out, Wooley dashed outside to check the windows, which were bolted fast, the curtains drawn. The mysterious conversation continued far into the night. Briefly wondering if the Prophet had been hiding out too long for his own good, Wooley listened carefully; three distinct voices reached his ears. At dawn President Taylor emerged from the room and called everyone in the house together. In the presence of thirteen witnesses he pointedly refused to sign the manifesto outlawing polygamy that had recently been drafted for his signature by Apostle George Q. Cannon. Taylor then sat down and wrote a revelation—the subject of the conversation of the night before, according to Wooley—denying any document that would abolish "the New and Everlasting Covenant." Transcriptions of the revelation existed, Wooley claimed, in Taylor's handwriting! True, Church officials could not afford to acknowledge the document, but they knew it existed.

Wooley convinced Grandfather that he must search his soul about the Principle. On returning to his unsuspecting Charlotte, Grandfather was a changed man. He had repented of his salacious stories and abandoned his secular ambitions. Now, he wrote, he was filled with a yearning to "serve the Lord." This spiritual wave rose to a new crest when his father's plural wife, "Aunt" Johanna, rose in testimony meeting and predicted Harvey was destined for apostleship in the Church. Then one night Grandfather dreamed that he met a lovely blond woman in a southland near a river and that he took her by the hand and called her Evelyn.

A year later he actually met my grandmother on the steps of the Star Valley Wardhouse. Flustered by this materialized dream, he made something of a fool of himself, blurting inanities to her parents, forgetting to be civil to her, and then, realizing his blunder, returning to grasp her hand with an enthusiasm that embarrassed everyone.

He embarked on the delicate business of courting Evelyn without actually courting her. After all, he was a married man, and polygamy was against the law; he couldn't afford to visit Evelyn at her parents' home, bringing her flowers and love letters. Besides, he had no right to woo Evelyn without his wife's consent if he adhered to the precedent set by Sarah in "giving" Hagar to Abraham. But he didn't want to burden Charlotte with knowledge of his love for another woman unless he could ascertain that his affection for Evelyn was reciprocated.

Whispered discussions with Church elders confirmed his suspicions; some members in good standing still privately practiced polygamy. At last he mustered the courage to express his affection to Evelyn, who demurely accepted it. Grandfather, ever one to wear his feelings on his sleeve, was pained by her coolness. Later he discovered that Evelyn had received another proposal that day—from the Star Valley stake president, who also had plural marriage on his mind.

Grandfather's contact with sensitive, complex situations had only sprouted. Charlotte Pead had grown up in a family that, like many Mormon households, regarded plural marriage as an outmoded or corrupt doctrine that only provided an excuse for perversity. When Charlotte learned of her husband's plan for a multiple family, she found herself in philosophical quicksand. Her mother, hawk-eyed for any threat to a woman's power, had warned her this would happen. Charlotte's life became a nightmare of vacillation, of making up her mind for or against the Principle, and then changing it in the next week or day or hour.

Grandfather was not immune to her feelings. "When I would let my mind dwell on dear Lottie's grief, I would feel that I could not possibly carry this matter any farther, and many times in my depression, I would firmly resolve that I would put an end to it all—that I was not fit to live this great law, calling for such heart-ache and sacrifice."

But as a good Mormon wife, Charlotte upheld Church tradition, believing her eternal welfare depended on her husband. Besides, she had been exposed to countless Mormon doctrines, variously expounding that men holding the high priesthood of the Church would be, in the words of Apostle Orson Pratt, "condemned if we do not enter into that principle." So Charlotte suppressed or reversed her objections and wept in secret. When Grandfather sensed her grief, he faltered and threatened to call everything off. But she came to him, black-bound book in hand, and read that the Lord had said, "I reveal unto you a new and an everlasting covenant; . . . if ye abide not . . . then are ye damned."

In addition to Charlotte's lapses of jealousy and suspicion, Grandfather had to deal with the ambivalence of his Church superiors. On the one hand were men who vehemently denounced polygamy, calling those who lived it "lawless" and "sinful." On the other hand were respected Church leaders who had obdurately maintained and even expanded their plural families since the manifesto, some who had hidden in the Allred home because they might be betrayed to the law by their closest brethren.

Finally Grandfather journeyed to the Salt Lake temple. After interviews with the Church presidency, he came away with a sealed letter of instructions to the Mexico Mission president. Thus he found himself in a disease-ridden desert with two families dependent on him, bereft of his property and his good standing as a U.S. citizen. Besides losing two sons of his first family, he and Evelyn lost their first son to unpredictable seasons and poor shelter—pneumonia. Then Charlotte (who, as Grandfather wrote, was "in the family way again") was stricken with dropsy. She wavered between disorientation and death for many weeks. A churchwoman who had observed Charlotte's failing health was inspired to suggest a bizarre treatment. So great was Charlotte's faith in her "sister's" prescription that she daily swallowed one of the gray millipedes that lurk under boards and dead weeds, took it alive and wriggling in a teaspoon of water. In three days she recovered her health.

But disease and desert winds did not drive Grandfather from Mexico. Not even marauding Mexican revolutionaries scared him away. It was infighting among the Mormon colonists over bogus land deals that pushed him out. He could no longer live in a lawless desert. He left with his father's curse rather than his blessing, a vituperation that "God will punish you if you leave."

Soon after my father was born in 1906 Grandfather took steps toward departure. In 1908 Church authorities at last granted their approval, warning him that he was on his own with the law. He crossed the border with two wives and two families, and in that single swift step from Ciudad Juarez to El Paso he became an outlaw.

His dilemma did not last long, for it seems that his father's curse descended. In Idaho, Charlotte died under the rough hands of a drunken doctor while giving birth. Her twins lived just long enough to be named and blessed, then also died. Grandfather was a monogamist once again. Grandmother Evelyn, scarcely twenty-four years old, became mother to eleven children.

In the next years his father's family was chased across the border by Pancho Villa. Within a year of their crossing, his father, mother, and only full sister died, as if the designation of criminal was too poisonous for their rarefied spirits.

The Byron Harvey Allred, Jr., family became members in good standing of the Idaho branch of the Church, where they raised their children much as in any devout Mormon household: with a lot of hard work, a lot of confusion, a lot of church meetings, and a lot of love. The Principle of Plural Marriage gradually became a mere backdrop for the way their lives together had begun.

Some fourteen years later, having served in the Idaho legislature for a good span, Grandfather ran for the U.S. Senate. His nomination was all but guaranteed when Church authorities telegraphed that he must withdraw from the race because of his "odious background"—his brief sojourn in polygamy. Grandfather threw down the nomination and trekked to Canada with his family, where he sulked with the weather for three years, then returned to begin a book in defense of the Principle. He married a third wife, and on publication of his book, titled A *Leaf in Review*, he was excommunicated from the Mormon Church. All his fine spiritual ambitions netted Grandfather the title of "apostate" rather than "apostle" from his brethren in the Church.

My father, who had grown up in an ostensibly monogamous environment, was deeply loyal to the Church and devoted in his calling as Long Beach Stake Genealogical Society president, a prestigious church position for a twenty-seven-year-old man. He heard about Grandfather's book from his older half-brothers and tried to dissuade him from such rashness. He wrote Grandfather a long letter, accusing him of "kicking aginst the pricks" of ordained authority. Grandfather calmly defended his point of view, quoting from his book: "I have at last arrived at a milestone in . . . life where I . . . fear . . . facing the consequences of a violated conscience through continued silence, far more than . . . the displeasure and abuse of mortal man."

My father, Dr. Rulon Clark Allred, fasted, studied scriptures, and prayed for guidance. In the nearly twenty years since he had been baptized he had known that he must be accountable, that he alone would answer to God for the life he led. He followed the Church-ordained policy of seeking a personal revelation until he gained a testimony of "the fullness of the gospel."

From the moment he began serious study of the Principle he was regarded askance by his beloved Church. His bishop ordered him to stop studying Church scripture. His stake president accused him of apostasy. His wife accused him of lust, and after an extended, bitter quarrel she took their three children to visit an old boyfriend in Idaho.

My father did not pursue her, though he later said that his heart was breaking. In five years' time he took five wives and moved them from house to house, fleeing law enforcement officials and Church spies. The official Church had hired detectives and assigned members to infiltrate the scattered group of fundamentalists with the purpose of gathering information that would insure excommunication and imprisonment. In 1945, when thirty-three men and women were convicted of conspiracy to teach plural marriage, a Church spokesman proudly claimed: "Among witnesses for the prosecution are men who have been appointed by the Church to search out the cultists, turning over information . . . to the prosecution. . . . these . . . have been appointed by the Church to do all they can to fight the spread of polygamy."

Despite the loss of his Church standing, his first family, and his good citizenship, despite his status as a felon, my father became a shaman, regarded as a physical and spiritual healer by thousands. People reeled with shock when this venerated man was gunned down in his medical office on May 10, 1977.

How could it happen in the City of Zion—Salt Lake City— where life revolves around religion? Young lives are marked by baptisms, patriarchal blessings, seminary graduations, priesthood appointments, temple endowments, missions. Mature lives are gauged successful according to upward movement in the Mormon hierarchy. The religion is so pervasive that it dominates social life and career options. One ambition of good Latter-Day Saints is to attain such material greatness that they can make a significant contribution to Church coffers through their tithes and offerings. For the especially devout Latter-Day Saint, Mormonism is a total way of life. He wants no more from the world than to spend his life in Zion's tight, yet ever-expanding circle beneath the auspicious light of the Church. Outsiders come to the valley and experience the culture shock of foreigners. Yes, Salt Lake City is a place where people habitually sacrifice in the name of God.

Like his brethren in the official Church, my father believed in personal sacrifice. He also believed that we live on "the Saturday night before Christ's millennial reign"; he devoted himself to bringing as many souls into the world as possible, going about it as if all the awaiting cherubim depended on him alone. Thirteen years after his decision to live the Principle, I was born, his twenty-eighth child, daughter of his fourth plural wife. Like my brothers and sisters (forty-eight of us at final count), I was born into a family of spiritual bluebloods, into a Church divided by its most centrifugal principle, into a nation that overrules its own Constitution, into a world that whispers its own doom.

And so I have invoked translation to save me from my paradoxes, to rescue me from a shadowed, outlaw world of secrecy and suspicion into a brighter sphere of truth and life. For like my grandfather I have come to that milestone where the violations of silence give way to the vibrations of speech.

Chapter

1

In the days before I knew that someone plotted to kill my father, before I knew that my family was in danger of being dispersed, before I knew that the authorities were trying to put my parents in jail, and before I understood that spies had been planted in the religious group my father led, we lived peaceably on a twenty-acre farm in south Salt Lake County, Utah.

Peaceably and, for all I knew, in perfect accord. I was surrounded by playmates and solicitous adults. I knew that my father loved me, and like most others in our sprawling family, I worshipped him.

In those early 1950s, when the Korean "police action" sputtered and someone named Harry Truman was president, my father's household was mostly oblivious to the tumultuous world beyond the veil of poplar, pine, and black walnut trees that protected us from prying eyes.

The mothers said—in all earnestness—that the world would be a far better place if my father headed the nation, and added that he might have been president of The Church of Jesus Christ of Latter-Day Saints and even president of the nation if only he hadn't been born of polygamous refugees in Mexico and then chosen to live the Principle of Plural Marriage himself. And so we spent an inordinate part of our young lives secretly yearning for the comforts sacrificed to society, circumstance, and God's law. When we mourned another season without new bicycles or were stung by a neighbor child's taunt of "Plyggie, plyggie, worse than a niggie," our father would console us in stately tones:

"We haven't the money or the public regard of our neighbors, but we have each other. And we have something far more precious than riches or fame. We have the knowledge that we are right in what we believe."

With such encouragement to count our blessings, we'd soon forget the world of Mammon with its wicked ways and revel in our own white house with its surrounding buildings and expansive grounds.

My father rarely spoke of world events, but when he did—usually while towering over his congregation of fundamentalist Mormons—he thundered that the communist threat to freedom only proved we were living in the "Last Days" and that prophecy was being fulfilled before our eyes. As he warmed to talk of tyrants and of how Satan had infiltrated all the world, threatening even the land of the free, he strode up and down the dismal concrete meeting hall, his silver-blond hair transformed into a beacon by the Sunday sunlight, his lanky form dignified even in agitation.

My father was a naturopathic physician, an old-fashioned doctor who made house calls for people too sick to come into his office, who delivered babies—including his own vast brood—at home, and who often accepted a bushel of apples or help with the rickety plumbing as payment for his services. He often mixed his priesthood power to heal by the laying on of hands with his scientific knowledge. He had a witch doctor's understanding of herbs and natural potions, a shaman's ability to move his patients to faith in the Great Physician to Whom he attributed all his healing powers.

We were as surrounded by Mormonism as by our mountains in the Salt Lake Valley—nearly 360 degrees, eclipsing our view of any other way of being. I was three-and-a-half years old on that fall day in 1952 when I first noticed the shadows impinging on our province of light. My father returned from a baby case at dawn. The slam of his car door awakened me, and I heard his feet crunch gravel as he moved toward the barn. I was out of bed in an instant, forcing on my shoes and racing for the door.

"Just a minute, young lady." My mother sent me to dress, then delayed me further, insisting that I have my face washed and hair combed.

"We want to look our very best for Daddy," she reminded me, stuffing my arms into a sweater. Then I was outside, the chill damp air stinging my eyes and cheeks as I stumbled down the steps of the gray house where I had been born.

As soon as I was old enough to walk, a plethora of older brothers and sisters had taught me to count, marching me up and down those concrete steps that my father had laid. He had built the frames and smoothed the cement sometime during the polygamy trials of

1944 that had sent him to prison, the time the mothers referred to as "when Daddy went away to college."

Two hundred steps from the back porch of the gray house stood a big red barn, a dark, wonderful womb of hiding places and sour animal smells, of bristly ropes and slivery sticks of wood, of mangers and grain bins and rusty tools. We twenty-odd children headed for this beloved retreat to laugh and sing at our own echoes, to join in our most raucous games, or to secrete ourselves in its comforting corners when we wanted to be alone.

In the early morning no one played in the barn, for there was work to be done. The barn doors, flung open, released air saturated with urine and musty hay. By the time I reached the barn that morning, my oldest brother, Saul, and Aunt Henni's Isaac, both nearly fourteen, were scooping out stalls and filling the mangers. My father balanced on a one-legged stool, the shiny pail fixed between his knees. He patted old Bossy's flank and spoke soothingly as he curled his long fingers around her teats, sending a gentle tintinnabulum to the rafters as the first jets sang into the pail.

"When your daddy was a boy," my father said, his voice soft and private as Bossy's udder, "I loved to watch my father milk, too. I learned as soon as my hands were strong enough. Want to try?"

I sucked my breath and leaned forward, nearly upsetting the stool as I grasped the firm, hot teat. I squeezed gently and no milk came out. I felt my face prickle red.

"Like this," my father whispered, setting his hand over mine. We pulled together, and as a long, steady stream bubbled into the pail, an answering stream of delight bubbled in me. I smiled into my father's eyes and he hugged me to him. For that moment, no one else lived but my father and me. The barn suddenly became a palace of light.

"By the time I was baptized, I could herd cows and milk them, could plow and harrow and plant and harvest. Do you think you'll be able to do all that by the time you're eight years old?" he asked.

I giggled. "Daddy, I'm a girl."

He shrugged. "That's no excuse." And he set to telling about his boyhood—when he was twelve and his little horse, Fleet, had thrown and dragged him, bouncing his head off rocks until his spirit left his body and gazed over the wide world like an eagle tethered to the sun. It was then, he said, that he realized he wouldn't die when his body did but would live on to reclaim his estate on the morning of the First Resurrection.

— *17*

Then he told of Canada, where his father had moved in hope of finding other true saints, where cold struck so deep that great limbs cracked and fell, where he walked a mile to the woodpile in the bitter twilight and was chased by wolves.

"I learned something then," he told me. "I learned that it does no good to be ruled by fear. Far better to keep your good sense and have faith in the Lord. When a person's time comes, it's the will of God and there's no use resisting it."

He turned and spoke up so that the boys could hear. "I remember when I was about your age, fourteen, and all the other fellows were wrapped up in girls and baseball. They made fun of me and nicknamed me 'Elijah' because I was so zealous in my church duties. But I stuck to my guns, and after awhile they came around and began to include me. I hope my sons will profit from my experience and have the courage to stand proud in their beliefs when people mock them."

My father turned and gazed expectantly at them. Saul stood silently, examining the prongs of his pitchfork; I could see the angry muscle working in his cheek. But Isaac nodded and went on shoveling manure. It was always that way: Saul thinking and doubting and asking questions until my father reminded him before all the priesthood that only "an adulterous generation" would ask for signs; and Isaac always agreeing, accepting, supporting anything my father said. The two boys had the same light hair, the same high forehead, the same spare jawline. Yet Isaac smiled readily, his face open and glowing as my father invited him forth to sing, his golden voice pouring music like honey over our hearts, song after song from the repertoire he practiced with my mother. And Saul sat watching, his mouth closing over a jagged line of teeth, his jaw tight, his voice deep and reluctant, his eyes burning with candor and barely harnessed anger. They looked alike, yes. But their temperaments contrasted like dark and light.

My father stripped the last drops of cream and hung the stool on its peg. Then, with a backward glance at Saul, he caught the full pail in one hand and my hand in the other.

"Come on, Princess."

We emerged into the clean, sharp air. He stopped to polish his black oxfords against his pantlegs. Manure stuck stubbornly to the soles, despite all his stomping and scraping.

We crunched across the yard to my Grandmother Evelyn's cottage, a one-room dwelling with windows on three sides and a single door facing north. It stood adjacent to the gray house, and sometimes when Grandmother needed help she'd reach through her rear window with a cane and rap sharply on my mother's bedroom glass—quick, impatient taps like the drumming of her fingers on the card table when she played pinochle.

The door opened immediately. Grandmother stood like a tall, cool pine overlooking the compound, ignoring me.

"Good morning!" my father called cheerily and kissed her withered cheek. Still she did not smile.

"How are you today, Mother? That kidney troubling you this morning?"

"I'm fine, just fine," she retorted, and pressed her lips together as if irritated by his reminder of her infirmity. She had been dour and intimidating for as long as I could remember.

I waited as my father poured milk into a porcelain basin on Grandmother's bare table. On the old dark bureau by the door was a double portrait of Grandmother and my grandfather, Byron Harvey Allred, Jr. She had been beautiful then, when she married him at the age of eighteen, her face light and sweet and smooth as powdered sugar. My mother said we inherited our blond hair and fair skin from her. But now her hair was white and her face cragged with old hurts.

Grandfather Harvey died long before I was born, and for years I tried to imagine him from that portrait on the bureau—high forehead balanced by a forthright jaw, eyes glimmering with amusement despite the old convention of sober portraits, ears strangely Pan-like. That morning I noticed a faint white scar bridging his straight nose.

"How did Grandfather get that scar?" I asked Grandmother.

"Children should be seen, not heard," she said abruptly and turned away. Afterward, as we headed across the yard, my father told me how my grandfather had been cutting wood with some of the brethren and an axhead flew off its handle and sliced off Grandfather's nose.

"It was hanging by a little flap of skin, like that," he said, pinching thumb and forefinger together.

Sunday school stories of tarring and feathering of Church leaders and of gunshots at the Carthage Jail swarmed in my head. "Did they do it on purpose?"

"No, dear, it was an accident. When blood spurted from your grandfather's face, the man who owned the ax called to the other brethren. They formed a prayer circle and administered to him. Within seconds, the blood slowed to a trickle, and in a few days, there was only a white scar to show what had happened. Faith is the strongest medicine in the world, faith and the priesthood."

I squinted up at him. "You mean it just grew back together?"

My father nodded solemnly. "That cut on your hand that Daddy bandaged yesterday? If you had enough faith, it would be completely healed by now. The scriptures promise that we can grow limbs as easily as a lizard grows a new tail, if only we will have enough faith."

I examined the cut, which still hurt, and wondered why I couldn't make it better. In the years to come I was to think of Grandfather's scar again and again; that faint, ragged line seemed to symbolize everything I longed to believe about our way of life that was counterbalanced by heavy promontories of reality.

Perhaps a hundred feet from Grandmother's cottage loomed the white house, where Aunt Gerda, Aunt Rachel, and Aunt Lisa lived with their children. The front of the white house faced westward, a bland, tree-shaded facade for curiosity-seekers who stopped on the highway. But its back seemed almost human, regarding the rising sun through paint-specked windows, its benevolent, crinkled stucco smiling on our games of kick-the-can and tag.

My father and I entered the cool, dark cave of the white house's milk room, and he carefully poured the warm, frothy milk into steel pans, where the cream would rise and later be skimmed by Aunt Gerda. I could hear her banging pots in the kitchen and wondered if today she would call out to my father, "Breakfast, Rulon! Time to sit down!" Then a kiss good-bye and he'd go to her. But today Aunt Gerda didn't get him, and we returned to the gray house, stopping on the back porch to listen as meadowlarks called from the pasture.

"Hear that? They're singing, 'Utah's a pretty little state.' " He mimicked them almost perfectly.

I smiled up at him and sang it back. Then he pointed out each of the mountains of the Wasatch: Olympus, Twin Peaks, Lone Peak, and far south, the white tip of Timpanogos where, he told me, the daughter of a great Indian chief stretched across the mountain crest. She knew that the daughter of a chief must marry no one but the lord of the mountain, and so she sacrificed herself to him.

"That is how it should be for my daughters," he said. "You must save yourselves for only the best men. I have traced our lineage to the Tudor kings. And we are spiritual royalty, too. Our bloodlines go back to Ellison, son of Joseph who was sold into Egypt. Did you know that?"

All I knew was that I didn't really want to die for anyone. I decided then and there that if I sacrificed myself for someone, it would be my father. I certainly wouldn't lie down on a stony, cold mountain and die for anyone else . . . except, perhaps, my mother.

When we went inside to the warmth of baking biscuits, my father shouted, "Good morning!" as if to awaken any lazy soul still sleeping. From the beginning he spurned indolence in his homes, for he bore his burden of seven families and the burdens of others who came to him for help as well.

My mother scurried between the table and stove, her long chestnut hair whipping out behind her. My father stopped her and took her in his arms. "Hannah, darling," he murmured, and they kissed a long time, until I tugged at my mother's housecoat, whining, "I'm hungry, Mama."

She flushed and slowly drew away. "I must get breakfast, Rulon darling." But she smiled at him a while longer, her hazel eyes soft and liquid as a doe's.

In a few minutes, my mother's twin, Aunt Henni, strode in. Her long brunette hair, like my mother's though not so auburn, was carefully netted. Her white nurse's uniform, crisp as her manner, fitted a figure also like my mother's: maternal yet spare somehow, in the jut of collarbone and angular wrists. She was ready to accompany my father to his office.

"Why are babies always born just before dawn?" she yawned and sat down long enough for the food to be blessed. Then she gulped her Postum and, announcing "I'm fasting today," disappeared into her bedroom.

Aunt Henni was usually drawn and shaky after a nighttime baby case, but my father seemed fresher than when they left, exuding a jubilant energy that filled the house. Birth energy, I came to think of it, a spiritual light that danced like sunbeams across the breakfast table.

"How did it go, Rulon?" my mother queried softly.

"Beautiful! Just beautiful! Sister Ruth was a good girl, a brave little mother. And what a giant she had—eight pounds, fifteen ounces! I believe we're bringing a race of supermen into the world these days!"

Aunt Henni reappeared in the doorway, purse in hand. "My

Isaac was at least that big. Of course, he was a month late." She watched my father eat. "I'm always so grateful when the baby's born and the mother's all right," she said finally. "I still can't forget that Marks baby."

My father's face darkened and he stared fixedly at his oatmeal. Usually, he could take care of problems; if the infant were tongue-tied or club-footed or the mother especially weak, my father came home and gave special praise to the Lord in his morning prayer that he had been given the knowledge to correct such things. Sending group members with complications to the hospital caused trouble for our people. Besides lacking records of birth, health insurance, and an attending physician registered with the hospital, our people were singular in their mistrust of drugs and surgery and medical men. But the Marks case had been beyond anyone's help. The mother had labored so long and hard she nearly died. And the baby was stillborn. My mother had tried to explain the deep chill that settled over our household the morning after.

"A baby was born dead, and the mother is so bitter. She blamed the baby's death on your daddy, even though the poor little soul passed away a week before she went into labor. The whole thing nearly broke his heart. You saw how gray he was, and his hands were like ice."

Throughout the day, family members had worn long faces, and the mothers seemed edgier than usual. Aunt Gerda ordered the children to get out of her house, and Aunt Lisa burst into tears for no reason.

But today my father tossed me in the air before he put on his shiny black secondhand suitcoat and gray felt hat. Then, lifting my mother off her feet, he whirled her around the kitchen. "Someday I'll take you honeymooning again, darling," he whispered as she squealed.

Aunt Henni strode down the hall with her raincoat on. "We're late for prayers," she announced.

My mother lugged me to the white house parlor where we met for prayers each morning, the seven mothers and their children kneeling northward to face the Salt Lake temple in a daily reminder of our everlasting ties with the official Mormon Church. My father said the prayer, and we repeated after him in unison:

"Help us to live in love and harmony."

"Help us to live in love and harmony."

"Open the temple doors to the worthy Saints."

"Open the temple doors to the worthy Saints."

"Hasten the day when the blood of the righteous will cease to cry for vengeance upon the wicked."

"Hasten the day when the blood of the righteous will cease to cry for vengeance upon the wicked."

Then there was much kissing and hugging before my father could make his way to the green Hudson, black grip in hand, and drive away with Aunt Henni as he did every day but Sunday. I stood in the yard with my mother, waving until they turned onto the highway, out of sight.

Later that morning, I found my mother breaking bread into bits. "Why are you fixing the sacrament today?" I asked.

She laughed. "This isn't for sacrament. It's stuffing. Brother Musser is coming for dinner tonight. He has something very important to say to us."

Brother Musser was the leader of our group, which had members all over the West. Everybody loved him and looked to him as the final authority on any matter. Many people believed he was a prophet.

All day the preparations for dinner went on. The folding doors between the white house parlor and dining room were thrown open to form one giant room stretching the length of the house. My father returned from his office before noon and set long planks on sawhorses that the mothers covered with variously shaped tablecloths. Aunt Gerda's pink dishes and red goblets crowded against Aunt Navida's Wedgwood. All the mothers bustled in the vast high-ceilinged kitchen, bumping hips and elbows. They shooed me outside.

Outdoors, the day shimmered cold and bright, with wild geese calling to the tame ones rippling our pond. In a corner of the yard near the chicken coops, my brothers, ten-year-old Jake and eight-year-old Danny, sat over buckets, their blond heads bobbing, their flannel sleeves rolled to the elbows, their pocketknives in hand, and their fingers covered with bloody feathers. I ran to them, knowing that something terrible had happened.

"Wanna help?" Danny gave me a cocky grin and jabbed the smelly, half-plucked carcass in my face.

"You killed them!" I wailed. "They were my friends!"

"They were your Easter pets," Danny chortled. "Now they're my dinner." He kept smiling that tight, teasing smile, watching me cry.

Jake blew on his red hands to warm them. "Daddy told us to do it," he said softly, his blue eyes full of sympathy. "Now go help Mama so you don't have to watch."

Sobbing, I ran to my father. "Why did you tell them to kill my ducks?"

He stopped raking leaves and sighed as I buried my face in his coat. "Why didn't you shoot those instead?" I pointed overhead at the wild birds passing over the south pasture.

My father patted my head and looked above, smiling mildly. "Once I'd have been glad to, Angel. But Daddy doesn't hunt anymore."

"Why not?" I snuffled. Hunting strange ducks seemed far preferable to killing my Easter presents.

"Brother Musser told me that a man of God must not kill anything. Now stop crying. Your Easter ducks were raised for this purpose."

He turned back to rake the lawn. Hurting all over, I ran to the barn and hid in a deep corner of the hayloft where I could cry without being teased. I blamed Brother Musser. I blamed Danny for laughing about my ducks. But deep down I knew who was to blame. It was the first time I had seen my father do something hateful in the name of God.

To cheer me up, my father and mother took me along when in the late afternoon they went for Brother Musser.

"You must be quiet, darling. Brother Musser still hasn't recovered from his stroke," my mother whispered as my father helped the older man down the steps of his stately red-brick house.

Brother Musser had a soft white crown of hair, a stiff white moustache, and big shining eyes. Earlier, my mother explained that my father made a small hole through his ear to cure the cancer that once grew there. My father had mixed up an old Indian remedy in a bottle lid and dabbed it on Brother Musser's ear, where it burned through skin and flesh. My father threw the bottle lid away, and the cancer never came back.

With an hour before dinner, there was time for a short drive into a nearby canyon to see the autumn leaves.

"How I love the mountains this time of year!" my father exclaimed. "They lift a man's soul to the clouds."

We climbed a narrow highway with no guardrail along the cliff edge. My father was paying more attention to Brother Musser than to the road, craning his neck and nodding toward the back seat.

He was telling a joke about the colorful Mormon Church apostle J. Golden Kimball.

"You know Brother Kimball had an addiction to coffee," my father said, and turned to see Brother Musser nod. "One time he was on the road with two pious Word of Wisdom-perfect brethren, and they stopped at a restaurant for refreshment. Brother Kimball promptly ordered his usual, and one of the brethren leaned forward and whispered, 'Why, Brother Kimball, I'd rather commit adultery than drink that cup of coffee.' " My father paused and indulged in a tight little grin, tasting the punchline before he let it go. "Then Brother Kimball replied, 'Hell, who wouldn't!' "

My father threw his head back and hooted. Brother Musser chortled and choked. My mother smiled behind her hand.

"Mama!" I whispered. "What if Daddy drives off the cliff?" My palms were wet.

My mother smiled. "Don't worry, honey."

But my father chattered on. "Look, that cliff face has the features of an Old Testament prophet." Then he showed us the difference between spruce and pine boughs and pointed out a deer and two cottontails.

"He isn't watching," I whimpered. "We'll get hurt."

"Now, hush," my mother said firmly.

"Don't you trust your daddy, dear?" My father smiled. He turned and winked at Brother Musser.

"I would if you'd watch where we're going," I piped.

Brother Musser chuckled from the back seat. "You're going to get trouble from this one, Rulon."

My father flushed, and for a moment the car was very quiet. Then my father carefully turned the car around. I hung white-knuckled onto the door until we were safe against the mountain and headed for home.

When we arrived at the white house, stuffed celery, dishes of cranberry sauce, and baskets of hot rolls crowded against name-cards set at each place to include everyone, even the children. I sat beside my mother and begged for a sip from her red goblet.

"You wouldn't like it."

"Please," I wheedled.

"It's wine. Good Mormons don't drink liquor or wine."

"You're drinking it!" I accused.

She flushed. "The Word of Wisdom is a law of moderation. We mustn't use tobacco, but your own daddy smoked a cigarette in my ear to stop its aching. It's all right to use these things sometimes."

"Then why can't I taste it?"

She sighed and held the goblet to my lips. My mouth puckered. "It's awful! Why are you drinking that stuff?"

"Shhh! Because Brother Musser is here, and it's a very special dinner. Something like the Last Supper, where the apostles drank wine with Jesus."

Brother Musser, stationed at the head of the table, and my father at the other end, kept a ripple of laughter running up and down the line of women. But the two men across from me sat grim and cold as two folding chairs. I hadn't seen them for a long time and asked my mother who they were.

"Members of the council," she whispered. "One is Brother Musser's son. The other is Aunt Navida's brother."

The last time I had seen the men, a much larger group had assembled in a long, low hall built entirely of concrete. Voices echoed hollowly as people rose and spoke, their faces twisted or wet with emotion. Brother Musser had stood a few minutes before the meeting's end and announced that he had just received a revelation: my father was called by heaven to assist him as first counselor, although many members of the council outstripped him in years and experience in "the Work."

Mouths had hung open. Faces contorted. Eyebrows knit like thunderclouds. My father's brothers and a handful of others nodded silently or gazed serenely amid the protest. Almost every fundamentalist family in the state was present or represented at the meeting. The "call" to head the remnant of the Principle was no trifling matter.

Brother Musser indicated that he would anoint my father immediately and asked for silence. But one man jumped up and pointed at eight or ten men who faced the crowd. "These are the true council!" he boomed. "And I'll kill the first man who says otherwise!"

Murmurs of dissent flew like dirt clods thrown by family friends and patients my father had healed. Hate became something palpable. My mother jerked upright and murmured, "This is the spirit of the Lord?"

Tightly wrung faces surrounded us. A woman at the piano beat her lap with her fists, lips pressed together as though something terrible might fly out of her mouth.

Then Brother Musser had stood and the room settled.

"Come stand here, at my right hand, Brother Allred."

My father stepped forward. Although much taller than Brother Musser, his head and shoulders bowed and tears dripped to the floor.

Since that meeting only part of the group remained loyal to my father, meeting with us in our living room or in my Uncle Andrew's garage. Some people thought the falling away was just as well. My mother said it was wrong how some of the councilmen arranged marriages for their young people. "Everyone has a right to fall in love, like I did with your daddy. I know that's not how the brethren in Short Creek believe—they think they know what's best for everybody." She was speaking of the small settlement near the Utah-Arizona border where Brother Musser had married her to my father.

Most of the people who now boycotted my father's meetings dressed differently: the men in black suits and the women in severe contrast to my mother and aunts, who used some makeup and rolled up their old-style garments with their long sleeves and legs to conform to the fashions. The official Church had long since cut back the white garment worn at all times under one's clothing to remind temple-goers of their covenants to protect them from evil; even the sacred markings had been altered. But the fundamentalists wore the original pattern, just as Joseph Smith had given it.

Brother Musser had urged his followers to wear the garment in modesty, fitting in with the world without sacrificing convictions.

"We must not make a mockery of the Lord's work," he said.

But the other group wore fundamentalist Mormonism like a badge: severe buns, long skirts, black suits, faces scrubbed and plain, persisting in old-fashioned dress even for the children.

And now two of the men sat at our table, grimacing and shifting in their chairs as my father and Brother Musser joked with the mothers and children. Aunt Sarah leaned toward my mother and muttered that one of the men had tested the windowsills for dust.

"Can you believe how smug?" Aunt Sarah said. My mother rolled her eyes and nodded.

"Don't worry," Aunt Sarah whispered. "I wiped the sills just before they came. Remember, cleanliness is next to godliness!" She winked, and the two women smiled behind their hands.

After dessert, my father and uncles stood in a half-circle near the piano and sang choral arrangements of Brother Musser's favorite hymns. Then, after some quiet talk, Brother Musser stood. His moustache was stained red at the tips, and one of his hands was pinched against his body, trembling. I wondered why only half his mouth moved as he spoke.

"This trouble of authority has gone on long enough, brethren," he declared. "It's time to get the matter settled." Brother Musser's voice, which usually creaked like an old rocker, rang loud and clear.

"Brother Pedderson," he said, "I call on you to be my witness." Aunt Navida's brother sat up straight. My mother's hand flew to her heart. The room hushed as Brother Musser motioned to my father to stand beside him. He put his good hand on my father's shoulder. "At the age of twenty-seven, I was called to take a second wife and charged by Church President Lorenzo Snow to 'help keep the Principle alive.'

"When I was forty-three, I was ordained with the sealing power of Elijah to perform plural marriages. Sometime later I was ordained a patriarch and high priest apostle and ordered to see that 'never a year passed that children are not born into the covenant of plural marriage.' " He stopped speaking for a moment and wiped his moustache. A chair scraped. Everyone was watching him, and he sagged a little, reaching out for my father's arm to steady himself.

"I have served this people as long as I was able. Now a call has come from the Other Side. It is time for someone to fill my shoes."

The room buzzed suddenly. The two dissident councilmen leaned forward, one of them holding up a hand like a policeman stopping traffic. But Brother Musser's voice grew even louder, each word reverberating like a bell. "Brethren, I want you to bear witness. Brother Rulon is my first counselor. I'll tell you again, once and for all: when I go, he will take my place as head of this priesthood. If this council cannot uphold him, I will appoint a council that will."

Then Brother Musser's voice broke and he began mumbling to himself as he felt for his chair. My father's head was bent, eyes squeezed tightly shut and fists clenched at his sides. Bits of manure still clung to his black oxfords.

Flushed with anger, the two councilmen jumped up and walked quickly toward the front door, their voices hissing. Some of the mothers were crying; others were laughing and talking excitedly with each other. Brother Musser sagged in his chair, looking drained and weary. My mother led me toward the door.

As we left, the councilmen stood stiffly at the doorway, two statues staring back at Brother Musser.

"Doesn't mean a thing," Brother Pedderson muttered as we passed. "He's drunk!"

"Hasn't been in his right mind since the stroke," the other councilman said. "And you can bet Rulon took full advantage of those house calls to keep him off his rocker!"

My mother gasped. Then she marched me through the door without nodding or saying good-bye to the two men.

Walking home through the chill darkness, my mother took a deep breath. "I don't suppose we'll see Aunt Navida's brother again."

"Aunt Navida will be sad."

She nodded. "Such hard feelings. Did you hear what they were saying? That Brother Musser was drunk! He only had one glass of wine, like the rest of us. They've already accused him of being senile and befuddled by his stroke! The nerve!" She sniffed. "As if Brother Musser isn't just as much an instrument of the Lord as he was ten years ago. The Lord doesn't let strokes and senility stop Him anyway."

She spoke, as she often did, as though I was one of the grown-ups. At the time I thought it must be because I was as smart as a grown-up. Later, I realized her manner was another indicator of her profound loneliness.

As I got into bed, I asked, "Why can't we just be friends with them? Jesus said to love everyone."

She stared out the window. "We love them, all right. That's what makes it so hard." She pushed her hair off her forehead. "Your daddy doesn't want to be the leader. He cried when Brother Musser gave him the blessing and said he didn't feel worthy of such a big responsibility. But Brother Musser insisted. Finally, when the council got so angry, your daddy got on his knees and begged to be released. But Brother Musser said the choice had been made on the Other Side, by the priesthood in heaven. And he said your father would be damned if he didn't accept the calling. So he did."

"What will happen now?"

"Brother Musser will choose a new council, just as he said. The others are rejecting a revelation from the Lord."

I felt proud of my father, yet sick inside. "Are they mad at us, Mama?"

"Mad enough that some of the brethren threatened to kill your father. Not the men you saw tonight—but others in the group. That's why Brother Musser came to dinner tonight: to tell the brethren once and for all. Now there's no changing it. It's in God's hands."

Then she left, and I was alone. My heart was beating hard and I wanted to run down the hall after her. I thought of my father and wondered who wanted to kill him. When I tried to close my eyes and sleep, I saw my ducks, half-plucked and bloody. Then, eyes wide and smarting in the dark, I remembered the scar on Grandfather's nose. The cut on my hand still hurt, even when I sucked on it. At last I got out of bed and stared out the window, my bare feet splayed on the hardwood floor seeming to join with the chill of the fruit cellar beneath and with some deeper, older, darker winter than any I could remember. Suddenly I shuddered violently and pressed my face against the cold pane. There, in the ghostly bulk of the white house beneath the cold, clear starlight, stood my father, alone.

Chapter 2

Although we were reared to treasure truth and "cling to the light," our way of life was filled with secrets. The grown-ups, while urging us to "catch the sunshine" and frequently reminding us in song that "Jesus wants me for a sunbeam," maintained remarkable obscurity, which in later years they justified as screening life's stark realities so that we could better enjoy childhood. They also obfuscated information that could start trouble with the authorities and shielded us from any knowledge that would compromise our unlimited adoration of them, my father in particular. And so as we rehearsed the Ten Commandments and Christ's Higher Laws, we also imbibed an unspoken code of secrecy that was maintained, wittingly or unwittingly, until we were curious enough to question it.

I'm not certain just when I sensed my father's relationship to the other women who lived in the compound—the "aunts" who passed out cookies or tended me when my mother went away, who hugged or scolded me as though they had a perfect right to take my mother's place.

At first the "other mothers," as my father referred to them, were simply the mothers of my playmates—the score of blond children who also called my father Daddy.

But I had watched my father: He kissed Aunt Sarah with his eyes closed just as he kissed my mother. He went downstairs to Aunt Navida's apartment in the gray house and sat down to dinner with her children. Sometimes he came out of Aunt Henni's bedroom in the early morning with only his temple garments and bathrobe on. And during Sunday school, when I was cozy on his knee, one of the other mothers had pushed her little girl forward, saying, "It's time to give someone else a turn, Dorothy Jeanne." But full understanding of the situation did not hit until the day

Aunt Navida's Tommy and I decided we would be married when we grew up.

"You can't marry Tommy." My mother smiled into the bathroom mirror, twisting her long chestnut hair into a chignon.

"Why not? He's a boy."

"He's your brother. Brothers can't marry sisters."

"My brother? Saul and Jake and Danny are my brothers. Tommy isn't your boy."

"But he is your daddy's boy." She looked at me and pursed her lips. "I guess it's time you knew your daddy is married to Aunt Navida."

"He's married to you!"

"Well, he's married to Aunt Navida too. And to Aunt Henni and Aunt Rachel and Aunt Sarah and Aunt Lisa and Aunt Gerda."

How unfair! I watched her stick hairpins into the soft figure eight of her hair for awhile. "Is that why Tommy calls him Daddy?" For the first time, I suspected that "Daddy" might not be my father's first name.

"Of course."

"Did you marry him first?"

She shook her head. "Aunt Gerda did."

Another cheat! My mother should have been first. I pressed my cheek against the woodwork until it hurt. "Do other people have lots of wives?"

"In the early days of the Church, many people lived the Principle. But then the manifesto was accepted. Now most people in this part of the world have only one wife. It's called monogamy."

"Then why does Daddy have so many?" My voice strained against a stuck place in my throat.

"Because it's God's law. We have to live it."

"It isn't fair," I muttered.

My mother abruptly pulled down her chignon. "This hair! I wish your father would let me cut it." Then she turned to me with a little smile. "If your daddy had settled for one wife, you wouldn't be here, darling."

I went outside and stood in the yard, watching for my father's green Hudson. I needed to talk to him. At last his car rumbled along the lane.

"And what did my princess do today?" my father asked, lifting me into his arms.

I had held back my tears until I was safely within his bearhug. Now I sobbed,

"I was going to marry Tommy. But Mama says I can't. Can I marry you?"

He grinned, his gold fillings glinting in the afternoon sun. "Someday you'll grow up to be a fine woman like your mother, and your own young man will come along. Then you won't think twice about leaving your dear Daddy."

I clutched his neck. "No, I won't! I'll never leave you and Mama!" Then I saw he was carrying me toward Aunt Navida's basement apartment. I stiffened and drew away.

"Are you going to eat supper with Aunt Navida again?"

"I believe it is her turn."

"Are you married to Aunt Navida?"

His eyes went wary, the pupils hard as little rocks. "Yes . . . ," he said at last.

"And to Aunt Henni and Aunt Gerda and . . . all the others?"

He cupped my chin in his hand and his eyes bored into me. "Yes, but you must not tell anyone. Especially not strangers."

He had never looked at me this way! I didn't want to hear anymore about it.

I put my hands on his thin cheeks and pouted. "Do you love Aunt Navida more than you love me?"

Instantly, his expression changed. He groaned and laughed at once, throwing his head back and rolling his eyes. Then he clicked his lips against his teeth as he did before speaking at meetings. "Each of the mothers is a jewel in Daddy's heavenly crown. Each is special. Your mother is a ruby. Aunt Navida is a sapphire. And you— you are a star hurled from the sky. I'm counting on you to shine for others, to bring light to the world."

Then he set me on the top step. "Daddy must say good-bye now," he said firmly and turned to go into Aunt Navida's apartment. I hoped she wouldn't be home.

To my delight, headstrong Aunt Navida was not at home to my father that night. She had scheduled him for her anniversary, later in the week, so she turned him away. In a few minutes he appeared at our door.

"Can I invite myself to supper, girls?" my father asked, grinning sheepishly at my mother and Aunt Henni.

"Of course!" My mother's face glowed as she hurried to set another place at the table. Aunt Henni began to make rice pudding, one dessert that agreed with my father's ulcers. She even put raisins in it.

Halfway through supper, my father disappeared down the hall into the bathroom. A moment later we heard him retching.

My mother's hand flew to her heart. "I hope the cream gravy wasn't too rich."

Aunt Henni waved her words away. "Don't be silly. He had a terrible day. A hundred interruptions. People wanting to talk about anything and everything, just dropping by without an appointment. And now this mix-up with Navida. I suppose they had a tiff about it, too."

My mother sighed. "I wish the other girls weren't so hard on him. Either that or they could save their complaints until *their* night with him."

"That'll be the day—in the millennium," Aunt Henni muttered.

"Shouldn't you be lying down, Rulon?" my mother asked when he returned to the table. "I hope it wasn't what you ate."

My father shook his head and smiled wanly. "No, dear. It's this confounded stomach of mine. After all the weeping and wailing and gnashing of teeth that went on today, it's taken a fit. I simply must learn that you can please some of the people some of the time, but not all of the people all of the time."

"Come on, Rulon," Aunt Henni said, standing. "Lie down on my bed. You should rest, at least until home evening."

He followed her down the hallway to her room.

At our weekly home evening, something for everyone was offered—from religious lessons to fairy tales, from card games to hymn singing. It was the one time when only a matter of life and death could coax my father from the white house parlor where all his families gathered at seven o'clock sharp.

My mother dried her hands on her apron and untied it as we all crossed the yard. Other mothers stood in the white house kitchen, pajamaed babies flung over an arm or being nursed to sleep as the mothers chattered. Eventually the little ones would be eased into one of the bedrooms, where they'd sleep wedged between other babies on the big double bed.

As usual, we began by singing a hymn, "In Our Lovely Deseret, Where the Saints of God Have Met," one of my father's favorites. Although pale and shaky from the ulcer attack, he stood with the rest of us and sang loudly.

When we were seated—the mothers on the long sofa against one wall and we younger children clustered around our father, on the arms of the secondhand easy chair losing its stuffing or Indian-style at his feet—he called us to be silent. Even the toddlers hushed as he asked soft-eyed Annette, Aunt Rachel's ten-year-old, to "open with prayer." My family began all gatherings, whether a dance or a party, a meal or an afternoon quilting session, with prayer.

Then my father asked who had a part on the program. Aunt Gerda unbuckled a black case and hefted her red-and-white accordion over a broad shoulder. Besides being the oldest and first married of the mothers, Aunt Gerda was most imposing, almost as big as my father, with a largesse of personality to match her girth. Having "invited" all the other mothers into the family, Aunt Gerda seemed the quintessence of magnanimity, a great soul actualizing her first wife's position according to the Law of Sarah. She towered like a mountain with rolling foothills of flesh above us children, her gray-shot brown hair bristling around a plumpish face and jutting jaw, enhancing an impression of irrepressible vigor.

Aunt Gerda would barge around her large white kitchen, beating out homemade noodles, scrubbing two loads of laundry, and stretching a quilt before going to her secretarial job in town. "A bundle of energy," my mother called her, pointing out that much of Aunt Gerda's drive came from an impulse to do good as well as from an overactive thyroid.

Despite its methodical quality, Aunt Gerda's accordion music always infused us with some of her energy, and we tapped our toes and hummed along as she played.

Then Aunt Henni rose to give the lesson. She stood with arms folded and lips pressed together, her nostrils flaring slightly, until the fidgeting stopped. Then her gaze softened and she spoke in the honeyed voice she usually reserved for my father's patients.

"Tonight we're going to learn a song. Songs are nice to sing, but more importantly, they teach us lessons." Aunt Henni was always talking about teaching lessons. Sometimes she said, "Someone should teach you a lesson." Other times she said, "I oughta box your ears." Either way she said it, I was more inclined to listen to her commands than to my mother's gentle pleas. It was she who taught me to love scripture, to explore ideas, and to be self-confident.

— 35

"The song we're going to learn teaches us that we must not say things that hurt others. The Lord has commanded us to 'love one another.' "

Aunt Henni nodded at my mother, who played the opening chords on the piano. Then Aunt Henni waved her arm in time as she sang in her strong alto:

Angry words, oh let them never
From the tongue unbridled slip
Let the heart's best impulse ever
Check them ere they soil the lip.

As we all sang the words, I felt funny inside. Why was Aunt Henni teaching us not to say angry words when *she* spoke them?

Still, I sang:

Love one another
Thus said the Savior
Children obey the Father's blessed command.

When we had finished singing, Aunt Henni's eyes sparkled approval, and my father nodded, though his eyes were closed in thought. "Thank you, Mother Henni. A lesson we must strive to remember." Then, opening his eyes and glancing around he said, "Isaac dear, will you favor your Daddy with a solo?" And Isaac stood while my mother played to the opening phrase of "O My Father." His rich tenor stroked us all to a sweet, ethereal sleepiness.

O my father, thou that dwellest
In the high and glorious place,
When shall I regain thy presence,
And again behold thy face?

Gradually my father's face relaxed and his cheeks took on some color. After a long silence, he motioned us younger children to gather closer. I found my usual place on his knee, and he recited "The Cremation of Sam McGee," his voice wailing and whining and drawling and at last ghosting through the rhyme. Then he launched into his own winter story of the wolves in Canada, of how he ran from the quiet thunder of their paws and sensed the pant and drool of their pointed snouts, and of how, while racing across the clearing toward the brightly lit dugout window, he fell and lost his load of wood, cutting his cheek on a stump's edge. And then, when our hearts were nearly still with dread—though he sat before us, as alive as our senses—he told the happy ending: that the wolves did not get him, and his father did not scold him for returning empty-handed, and his mother had kept a plate of supper warm for him.

While he regaled us, dark-haired, dark-eyed Aunt Rachel prepared refreshments, her faintly moustached mouth pursed and her short, lumpy frame jiggling as she served up applesauce cake made with wholewheat flour and raw sugar—the way my father instructed us to eat for our health. But when Aunt Rachel baked for her family, she made rich white bread of angelfood texture from refined sugar and flour, adding plenty of butter and eggs. It was her only extravagance; her apartment was sparely furnished and her children dressed in bare necessities. My mother theorized that by the time she spent her grocery allowance on such ambrosia for her family of ten, she had no funds to provide a more comfortable life. Aunt Rachel often seemed to resent my father's and the other mothers' zeal, the overlong meetings and prayers and debates. Bored by abstractions, she reveled in the sensate world and knew things about people from gestures and expressions rather than from words. Thus she was painfully aware that others scorned her apparent simplicity. There was a frightened, needy quality about Aunt Rachel that I would later associate with orphans and abused children. Now, as she served me, her mouth sank in a sad smile, and I felt a twinge of guilt that my own life should be so happy. And then the dark feeling passed, unrecognized.

As we ate, my father brought up a serious matter. He reminded everyone to keep the pasture gate that led to Cottonwood Creek closed at all times.

"The creek is cold and higher than usual," he said. "We don't want to lose another of our babes to the water."

Instinctively everyone turned to look at Aunt Lisa, the youngest of my father's wives, scarcely half the age of Aunt Gerda when she married. Everyone knew she still grieved for little Marie, her oldest daughter, who had drowned in the pond while only a toddler, because she had asked that no one wash away the tiny mudprints on the basement window. Marie had played there the day she drowned, patting the glass and waving at her mother, who darted inside and asked one of the mothers to keep an eye on the children while she cleaned my father's office. My father was due to return from a mission with the Mexico Lamanites (as Mormons call Indians), and Aunt Lisa wanted everything spick-and-span for· him.

No one seemed to assign blame for Marie's death. If Aunt Lisa harbored resentment, it remained her deep secret. She often recited her predictive dreams that she would lose Marie, if not to the drowning, then to an automobile accident or a disease. The matter was closed, along with the tiny grave, with only occasional wistful references to Marie.

Of all the mothers, Aunt Lisa was perhaps the most certain of the exclusive righteousness of the group. But rather than being calcified by her narrow views, she remained curiously youthful, as though her rigidity and conviction preserved her individuality, like tree roots gripping the land, staving off erosion. Always welcoming the challenge of connecting old with new, she decried Christmas and Easter as pagan holidays and substituted the Prophet's birthday and the anniversary of the Mormon Church.

"Well, we all know who leaves the pasture gate open," drawled Aunt Sarah in response to my father's warning. Her voice was calm, but she was plump and fiery, and now she shot one of her pointed looks at my brother Danny. "These young rascals who've inherited their father's passion for fishing." She clicked her tongue. Her expression remained stern, but a smile played at the corner of her mouth. Aunt Sarah, with her auburn hair, quick wit, spitfire temper, and scathing honesty kept one blue eye fixed on celestial bliss, the other on reality. She was the one adult in our compound who refused to take everything seriously. She usually saw people as they were, without the tincture of idealism. Her big soft arms later became a refuge when my own mother's seemed too frail for the bulk of my problems.

Now Danny studied the patches on his knees, as if hoping we would forget that Aunt Sarah had her gaze fixed on him. How strange to see our cocksure Danny embarrassed. He was the one who laughed when my mother spatted him with the butter paddle, the one who dared Aunt Sarah to catch him before he reached the swamp, where she'd never follow.

"Enough said," my father sighed. He was pale again. Most of his cake remained uneaten. "Do we have a closing number?"

The mothers gathered at the piano, six of them standing in a semicircle, arms strung around each other's waists. My mother sat at the keyboard and played the opening strains of "I'll Take You Home Again, Kathleen."

There was some bustle as Aunt Gerda and Aunt Navida vied to determine a starting note. I had heard muted talk of tensions between them, both women mature and efficient, crack secretaries and natural rivals. Then the mothers' voices melted in perfect harmony. Although both Aunt Gerda and Aunt Henni were tall women, Aunt Gerda dwarfed Aunt Henni's spareness, but their strong alto voices were evenly matched. Willowy Aunt Navida, whose spectacles hid traces of earlier beauty and gave her a waspish look, sang soprano alongside the shorter, rounder prettiness of Aunt Sarah. And sandwiched in the middle were the "runts" of the family, shorter than the others and perhaps stunted by early marriage. But Aunt Lisa's youthful voice sprang with conviction to uphold Aunt Rachel's soft, slurring second soprano.

Suddenly I noticed tears rolling unchecked down my father's cheeks.

"Does your tummy still hurt, Daddy?" I whispered. He did not answer.

The mothers also wept, all but Aunt Gerda, who frequently stated in her quick, clipped way, "I spent all my tears in Forty-four."

As the song ended, I slid off my father's knee and went to my mother. "Why is everyone sad?"

My mother dabbed at her eyes and put an arm around me. "Don't worry, darling. We always cry when we sing that song."

My father blew his nose with a loud honk. "Beautiful, girls. Just beautiful. Thank you."

"Why?" I whispered to my mother. "Why do you always cry?"

"It reminds your daddy of his first wife, Aunt Susan. Someday she'll return to him—Brother Musser promised. But we're missing so much in the meantime."

"I though Aunt Gerda was Daddy's first wife."

"Shh. Yes, I know. Gerda was married before any of us here, but Susan was first. She and your daddy had four children. I've never even seen them."

A mother, brothers, and sisters never seen. I felt dark inside, a small hole growing bigger, darker.

"Didn't you want to see them?"

"Susan doesn't want anything to do with us. She left your father because of the Principle, because he believed he must take more wives. He tried to send Christmas and birthday presents, and he wrote lots of letters to them, but all came back unopened. Now hush up and kneel down. Time for prayer."

I scarcely heard the prayer for thinking about Aunt Susan—a mother I had never met, a mother who left my father and wouldn't read his letters, a mother who could make my father and the mothers cry but didn't want a thing to do with us.

I was already feeling sick to my stomach when my mother told me I couldn't sleep in her bedroom (as I usually did to save bed space) because my father would spend the night with her. I moaned. It was just one cheat too many.

"I don't like sleeping upstairs!" I cried as we went into the gray house. "There's a wolf in the cubbyhole. Danny showed me its tail."

My mother stooped beside me. "Darling, that's not a wolf. It's an old fox stole someone bought at the thrift store. It isn't even alive."

I just sobbed harder.

"Shall I ask Aunt Henni to let you sleep with her this once?"

I shook my head. I'd rather sleep with Danny and listen to his scary stories than crowd into bed with Aunt Henni and her only daughter, twelve-year-old Amanda, who bristled every time I turned over. I stumbled past the cubbyhole and settled on the bed, staring out the window and listening to my brothers as they worked in the barn. Then the night grew still except for a yelping dog and the cries of a peacock in Cheaseman's aviary across the highway.

I blew on the cold pane and drew on it. The moon glinted on dry, frosty grass sprouting at the window edges. Suddenly, Danny was on the bed beside me, tickling me until I screamed. He smudged off the foggy window with his sleeve while I tried to get my breath.

"See that star up there? That's the North Star, the one seamen use to find their way home. And you know who lives there?" His voice filled the air with whispery magic.

I shook my head. Danny let silence pool around us.

"The City of Enoch," he finally said in a superior voice.

My father said we must love each other no matter what, but sometimes it was hard with Danny. Like when he laughed about my ducks. Like now. Even if he was a boy and eight years old, he didn't need to act like he knew everything. He'd been baptized and he'd gone on his first Boy Scout overnight camp, and last Wednesday Daddy took him to priesthood meeting. It was bad enough that he got to do so much, but then the way he flaunted it! My four-year-old heart could scarcely endure its pangs of envy and outrage at his superior expression, so pious yet teasing.

"Oh, you don't even know what the City of Enoch is, do you?" he smirked. "That's right, they only tell the men. Someday you'll have to ask your husband."

Only the men could know! Another cheat in a day full of them!

"Tell me, please tell me. I can't wait until I'm married!" I couldn't bear secrets. Secrets were like Aunt Henni's room, waiting to be explored but forbidden to my touch. How could I ever learn everything, know everything, as my father taught is our purpose on earth, if people were always keeping secrets? I thought of the secrets I had learned that day, about the mothers and my father, about Aunt Susan who didn't love us. I thought of my father's eyes, going hard as two BB pellets, saying I must not tell anyone, especially strangers. Maybe I didn't want to know secrets after all. Leave them to the grown-ups.

But Danny cleared his throat. "Enoch walked with God. He was so good he was translated. He didn't die or anything, God just scooped him and his family up and put them on the North Star."

"Who said?"

"Daddy."

"Mama says Daddy is closer to God than anybody. Will he be translated?" I murmured. Would God translate all of us along with him? I imagined a crystal city peopled with transparent, radiant beings.

Danny's eyes narrowed. "Aunt Henni says the City of Enoch was where the Gulf of Mexico is now. And now it hasn't got a bottom."

"No bottom? How could it not have a bottom?"

Danny shrugged. "Berna and miles of ocean, I guess. Like a really, really deep hole of water that never ends."

I shivered, slipping beneath the covers, my mind picturing dark, bottomless places—secrets that were never told or never understood but became darker and bigger as time went on. Like the secret of Aunt Susan. Like the secrets inside me. When Danny was snoring, I knelt, hunched inside the covers, and prayed to go to the North Star where there would be no secrets, and a long, long way from the Gulf of Mexico.

It was even harder to keep the secrets than I had expected, for I always felt their black, bulky weight inside me. However, the mothers—especially my mother and Aunt Henni—and my father often chuckled about the stories they arranged for nosy neighbors and prying strangers.

"You're my brother-in-law," my mother laughed, "so you must be my children's uncle."

My father then instructed us to tell anyone who asked that the man tending horses or raking leaves was our uncle and we had no idea where our father might be.

So came my initiation into the torsion of "Mormon logic," a process of rationalization evolved in the early, polygamous years of the Church to deflect persecution. The trick with Mormon logic was to obscure the truth without actually lying. Unfortunately, we sometimes had to tell outright lies, for as children we'd not yet learned to manipulate the truth into superficial meanings that took an opposite course in reality.

One day, as I picked grapes from the vines weaving through the driveway fence, a man in a dark blue suit and hat drove up and poked his head out the window.

"All those kids your brothers and sisters?" he asked, pointing to the group of children in the orchard.

I caught my breath, thinking of my father's warning about strangers. I remembered how the grown-ups worried recently, when one of Aunt Rachel's children told a school friend about our family.

I stared at the man for a moment, then dropped my gaze. "No," I said. I shoved a cluster of grapes into my mouth so I couldn't answer any more questions, and hurried, flushed and trembling, to the barn, where I waited until the stranger backed out of the driveway. I watched awhile longer, afraid he would return, and remembered my father told us we should be proud of our family.

"You aren't just half-brothers or half-sisters. We are all one, all one family."

And he said we shouldn't be embarrassed about the way we lived. "There's no need to be ashamed of the gospel of Christ," he had proclaimed and had read a passage from the Bible to prove it.

But the dark flush I felt was shame, the same feeling I got when I stole cookies from my mother's cache in the linen closet. I had lied. I tried to think of what I could have said without lying. But one way or another, everything I might have said felt like a lie.

That evening, during dinner, I asked my mother, "Why do we have to lie to people about the family?"

My mother flushed and stammered. "Well, of course you must always tell Mama and Daddy the truth. But some other people . . ." She glanced around as if searching for the answer among the dishes on the table. Then her eyes rested on my father. "Rulon dear, will you explain it to her?"

My father didn't look up from the trout he was filleting. "We must sometimes disobey a lesser law to keep a higher one." He said it like he was reading from a book.

My forehead felt tight, and I didn't ask any more questions. But Aunt Henni tucked her food into a corner of her mouth. "Brother Musser said so himself. Even the leaders of the Church had to lie to the authorities and break the law of the land to live the Principle. Now, can we get on with supper?"

I still felt I had missed something. The Principle was the way we lived; I couldn't change that. But telling the truth or not was a problem I faced every day.

In the years ahead the problem grew. The secrecy that separated our family from the rest of the world pressed us back on each other until I felt crowded and trapped. The mystery maintained within the family preserved an illusion of intimate space that made me feel stifled and excluded. As I grew older, I came to equate secrecy with lying, privacy with conspiracy. And I learned that it wasn't always easy to tell the truth, even when it had nothing to do with the Principle of Plural Marriage.

Chapter

3

In my father's house there was a pecking order. Everyone pretended that it didn't exist, that all was equal as stipulated in the United Order. In explaining why we should turn our earnings over to him, my father said the United Order and the Principle went hand in hand, that one could not work without the other. He promised to divide the total according to need, as Brigham Young had done in the early days.

But inequity thrived nonetheless, in a thinly disguised caste system among my father's wives.

Long before I was actually told, I sensed the immense importance attached to each wife's place in the family. The system was partly based on the sequence of marriage to my father. But weak or selfless personalities suffered despite the verbal emphasis on Christian love in our household. The more dominant women strutted and thrived, for they stood with impunity on "the letter of the law," a typifying attitude for our Old Testament culture. Some wives pecked all the others, some pecked only those more insecure than themselves, some pecked no one, and some lacked energy even to scratch.

Aunt Rachel's children were thin and sickly. My father didn't believe in immunizations—"Their effect on the human organism is incalculable," he said—so some of his children sniffed and measled and mumped their way through childhood, while others, like myself, basked in perpetual health. The other mothers said Aunt Rachel's children were sickly and small because she had them so close together that they missed out on nourishment both before and after being born.

One day when I was playing near the garden with Aunt Rachel's Leora, she told me tearfully that my father had decided that she should live with Aunt Gerda, because Gerda didn't have enough children, and Rachel had too many.

"She makes us call her Mother. She's not my mother," Leora hiccupped. "We have to ask before we can go upstairs to visit Mother. Even Mother says so."

My chest felt thick and heavy as she made me promise not to tell anyone.

When I first intuited the power associated with a first wife's status, I grieved over my mother's place far down the list as fourth of my father's plural wives. I knew, for instance, that a first wife went more places with her husband. Aunt Gerda accompanied my father to all his professional meetings, to her children's school programs, and to neighborhood gatherings. The other wives went to school programs alone or with sister-wives and couldn't acknowledge my father if they saw him there. Occasionally, on birthdays or anniversaries, my father took his other wives out to a movie, but always looking over his shoulder, fearing he'd run into someone who knew him.

During the months of my father's parole from the Utah state prison, Aunt Gerda, as the legal wife, was the only one allowed to live with him. They rented a small apartment behind a market and enjoyed a monogamous sojourn except for weekends, when my father came back to the white house to visit his children for a few hours. During his parole Aunt Gerda, who had waited for twelve agonizing years to be fulfilled in the Principle's major purpose, at last conceived a son, Tyrone. The monopoly granted her by the authorities at last seemed sustained by the hand of God.

When parole ended and the mothers quilted together in the white house kitchen, Aunt Gerda stabbed the material with her needle.

"Oh well, who wants whipped cream every night? Then it isn't special anymore."

Aunt Sarah looked up. "I'd trade places with you in a minute, Gerda," she said. "I'd love to have whipped cream every night."

Despite her apparently blasé attitude and the advent of two more sons, Bennie and Heber, Aunt Gerda continued to display a fondness for whipped cream—if not every night, then as often as possible.

When I asked my mother about Aunt Gerda's favored status, she said, "Some say the Law of Sarah gives the first wife dominion over the other wives because Sarah in the Bible gave her hand-maid, Hagar, to Abraham. But Gerda wasn't slated to be the first wife. Rachel was engaged to your father before Gerda even met him. And besides, I don't believe in that first-wife notion, there's not a word of scripture to support it. We all have the same rights, first or last. Still . . . some people in the group see it the other way. . . ." She paused and smiled to herself. "Especially the first wives."

Aunt Gerda had married my father in her late twenties, when other Mormon women might have pined into spinsterhood. But she had trained her efficient nature into a secretarial career that maintained her independence throughout life. In retrospect Gerda claimed that she always knew she would marry a man with other wives, even though the Principle was revealed to her only weeks before she entered it. When Brother Musser performed the cere-mony, he promised my father, "This woman will give you all the wives you deserve." Gerda took Brother Musser's pronouncement literally and soon recruited Henni (who sang beside her in the Hollywood ward choir) into my father's family.

In the early days at the white house when all the women lived together, Aunt Gerda ran my father's family like a drill instructor. She owned ideas on everything from proper budgeting to meal planning, from entertainment to family routines. Soon she estab-lished the wives in a schedule: Each woman took a week in the kitchen, preparing meals, cleaning cupboards, and scrubbing dishes. Another week she'd be "kitchen helper"—setting tables, drying dishes, and cleaning the dining room. Other weeks eased by with only a bathroom or stairway to worry about, leaving time for her to sew or decorate her bedroom or spend special time with her children.

But for years Gerda had no children. Time hung like a shroud around her. Even though Brother Musser had promised in a bless-ing that she would someday become "a mother in Israel," the waiting became more difficult as she neared middle age. Her executive temperament yearned for a means of expression and surfaced in relationship to the younger wives, whom she often treated like children. Some of these young women bore babies more quickly than they could handle them, while Gerda, who was fully pre-pared for the peculiar type of matriarchy demanded by the Prin-ciple (being supremely independent and happy to raise children her own way), was blessed with no tiny charges.

In addition, Gerda found the other women veritable teenagers, who knew next to nothing about domestic management. Some of them had to be shown everything. Gerda would mold them into respectable housewives or know the reason why not.

"Check with Boss Two," the other mothers reminded each other before opening a jar of strawberry jam or planning an evening with my father, for one of my father's colleagues had dubbed my father Boss One and Aunt Gerda Boss Two, although in fact the positions interchanged.

Once my mother returned from visiting her own mother in southern Utah just in time to celebrate her anniversary. My father invited her to a movie, but Aunt Gerda broke in. "The family went to a show last night. We can't afford another movie." One of the other women (probably Henni or Sarah) told Gerda to mind her own business. Then everyone stood and gaped. No one had actually rebelled against the pecking order before.

"You need to understand," my mother said in defense of Aunt Gerda, "we older girls had to help raise the younger wives. Rachel, for instance, had just turned fifteen when she married your father."

Aunt Rachel, with her short, squat frame, looked as though a giant hand had held her down during the crucial years when full growth is usually achieved. Even her face had a pushed-together look, nose edging toward her chin when she smiled and mouth slightly sunken, as though its usefulness diminished as years went by. Even when I was small, she appeared considerably older than her years, yet something undeveloped and childlike dominated her personality. She had been pretty enough before marrying and had caught the eye of more than one patriarch, old and young, in the Short Creek community that spawned her.

Although Short Creek frequently showed up in the newspapers—in 1935, in 1944, and again in 1953 as federal and local authorities conducted "polygamist roundups"—the residents led a primitive life in adobe or slat-board cottages with dirt floors, raising their own food and inventing their own institutions as best they could.

Without adequate schooling or social life, Aunt Rachel spent a lackadaisical youth. Her twin sister had died when she was nine, her mother when she was eleven. Her father's first wife, who had no children of her own, took Rachel and eight siblings under her wing. But Aunt Rachel's father, John Y. Barlow, Joseph Musser's predecessor, fretted about his oldest daughter. Unlike most of his community, she displayed an indifference to religion and a disturbing earthiness that someone "from the world" might have called sensual. And the way her dark eyes flashed and darted when the young men flirted with her. . . . John Y. felt his daughter should be married and the sooner the better.

When he met my father, he knew immediately where Rachel's security lay. Newly free of his first wife and thirty years old, Rulon appeared to be the perfect mate for John Y.'s young, love-hungry daughter. The doctor had been seasoned by the hardship of his first marriage (to Susan) and humbled by the heartache of separation. Now he rendered a fatherly compassion toward group members. Meeting the world head-on and grappling with Church leaders for a testimony to call his own had earned him self-respect and the high regard of the Short Creek commune. And he would soon be established as a healer among them. John Y. arranged the betrothal, as was the custom of Short Creek patriarchs, who supposedly knew the will of God not only for themselves but for other people as well. Although Rachel immediately agreed, the marriage was set for a couple of months hence, when my father's divorce from Susan was final.

Then my father met Aunt Gerda.

Gerda knew from the start that God intended the young doctor for her. Undisturbed by his former marriage and his engagement to Rachel, Gerda arranged to date him. She confessed her testimony of the Principle, letting it be known where she felt she belonged; a conversation with John Y. and my father decided that Gerda would preempt Rachel's marriage date by three days to become the first and legal wife.

Afterward, they told Rachel she was too young, unprepared for the responsibility of meeting the world as the doctor's wife. Aunt Rachel, never overly articulate, took in the explanations without a murmur. The only sign of what burrowed in her heart showed in her large, dark eyes, where the spark diminished and after a time went out altogether.

My mother testified to Aunt Rachel's sense of betrayal: "Once or twice Rachel confided that the whole thing hurt her. She used to come and visit while I was doing the ironing, sensing that I understood better than those with plenty of energy because of my poor health. I've had trouble keeping up with Henni since we were six and I came down with rheumatic fever. And then sinus trouble when I was fourteen. And now these horrible nerves . . . and depressions." She sighed. "Anyway, I don't blame Rachel for being hurt. I don't know who insisted that Gerda be the first wife, whether it was your father, or John Y., or Gerda herself. Maybe Rachel was too young to be the legal wife. But she could have enjoyed the special place of a first wife—whatever that is—without being the legal wife, you know."

I, too, visited with my mother as she ironed, listening to fairy tales or stories of her girlhood and, as my curiosity grew, to the family histories. I watched her sprinkle the clothes, then roll them, then test the iron with a spit-dampened finger. Then I stared, wanting the wrinkles of my confusion to become as smooth as the white shirts my mother ironed for a dollar a basket.

"What happened when you met Daddy?" I asked my mother as she creased a collar. "Did you fall in love all at once?"

She nodded, smiling. "When I heard Dr. Allred was to speak at our cottage meeting, I expected a short, stooped graybeard, anything but this tall, blond, handsome young man who spoke so eloquently about the gospel! Henni and I talked about him all the way home, but neither of us dreamed we might marry him someday. Even though he bore his testimony of the Principle that night, it just never occurred to us that he might take other wives. He had married Gerda only the night before. And then, we were so young, only sixteen. . . ."

She paused, staring into space and half-smiling. "Gerda says she knew from the minute we met we would be his next wives."

"And were you?"

"Yes . . . well, after Rachel, who was married two days later. You see, my father was sick with tuberculosis and couldn't work, so he spent most of this time studying scripture. One book that convinced him that the Principle is true was A Leaf in Review by your other grandfather. Soon my parents and your daddy became good friends, and he came to our house for Christmas dinner. That was when he asked my parents if he could marry one of their girls."

"Which one?" My heart thudded expectantly, for at the time I had only wondered about which of them had been first.

The iron smoked and my mother snatched it up, leaving a small brown boat on the white cover. Her face flushed and she glanced at the clock. "Goodness! The bread should have come out of the oven five minutes ago!"

In the rush of turning out the steaming bread and preparing

supper, my questions about the marriages of my mother and Aunt Henni waited for a time.

But only for a time. I longed to know which of the two had married my father first, perhaps because my father and other members of the family often treated them as a single entity. When my father gave books to each of the other mothers, he usually gave a single volume to "My Twins." When grocery allowances were distributed, my mother and Aunt Henni shared their allotment. And while each of the other mothers had her own quarters, Aunt Henni and my mother shared the gray house and consequently all their mornings and evenings with my father.

One anniversary my father whimsically took my mother to see five different features in three movie houses. They arrived home at four in the morning to be confronted by Aunt Henni's tormented face. "Where have you been?" she demanded. "I've been out of my mind with worry!"

When making decisions, such as who would have how many bushels of pears for canning, Aunt Henni spoke up for herself and my mother. And although my mother did the bulk of cooking, cleaning, and child tending while Aunt Henni worked at my father's office, the two of them went grocery shopping the same morning every week throughout their lives, Aunt Henni driving them in the green Hudson. My mother didn't bother to get a driver's license because Aunt Henni arranged to take her every place she might reasonably go. When major family arrangements were negotiated, Aunt Henni took the floor for "the twins" while my mother sat quietly by, her hazel eyes deep in thought.

But in our gray house, the differences between the two were vivid. My mother, preoccupied with house, children, and piano, sometimes didn't make her bed until noon, but Aunt Henni's bedroom was always clean and neat as a showcase: floor shining with fresh wax, bedspread blinding white, dresser dusted, and closet door closed. I loved to go into that place where everything was so carefully ordered—like the willow groves beyond the creek where animals couldn't graze or sully its fresh green. But I was forbidden to go into Aunt Henni's room while she worked. Sometimes she let me come inside to watch as she dressed for work. The bureau drawers opened and closed—too quickly. I glimpsed handkerchiefs and gloves, jewelry chests and boxes of stationery. I longed to touch her beautiful things, to memorize their order, to peer inside the bottom drawer, under the bed, in the closet.

"Why don't you have nice things like Aunt Henni?" I asked my mother.

"I have little children instead of nice things." She smiled. "Now that Amanda and Isaac are older, Henni can keep order and work all day too." Then she explained that Aunt Henni's lovely belongings were part of her reward for working so hard in my father's office. "The patients appreciate what she does for them and they bring her gifts."

One day, when I was playing dress-up and had tired of my mother's depleted store of costume jewelry, I crept into Aunt Henni's room. I opened the top drawer and gaped. Lipsticks stood in rows like toy soldiers, and earrings lay in a shimmering pool. Delicate lace handkerchiefs piled up like summer clouds. These beautiful things made the world seem so fine a place to be—I wanted them! My mother didn't have such things, and it wasn't fair. I stared at my face in the dresser mirror, at the ugly way my lower lip protruded when I was unhappy. Hadn't my father said I was his princess, that I should wear a crown? I decked my chest and forehead with necklaces and fumbled with the hand-tooled earrings from Mexico. I dabbed perfume from one of the pretty vials on the dresser-top and smeared bright lipstick over my mouth. Then somehow I dropped the tube on Aunt Henni's frost-white rug. I gasped, doubling over in terror. She would know! I shoved the jewelry back into the drawer and ran to hide under my mother's bed.

My mother was furious. "It will never come out! Never! What on earth will I tell Henni?"

I refused to cry or say I was sorry, feeling it served Aunt Henni right for having such nice things and all day with my father too. When Aunt Henni came home, she stood over me, a hand on one hip, her face like stone. "Why don't you get into your own drawers?"

When she had gone, I climbed inside my toy drawer and got stuck there. I yelled until my mother came to see who was dying. When Aunt Henni found out, she laughed. And I had to laugh too, in spite of myself.

A singular event, my mother's anger over the rug. She never spanked me, rarely lost her temper, and devoted the better part of her spare time—time she might have spent at her beloved piano—to making dresses with ruffles, lace, and ribbons for me. She told me stories and poems as she ironed or kneaded bread. She invited me to make cakes and cookies, to play dolls and house, and she drew paper dolls and pictures to suit my whim. Her only daughter, I had been named after her favorite doll, and when I was with her, my life was a series of games, one make-believe after another.

In fact, the whole family pampered me—all but Aunt Henni. Once I grew past the stage when my willfulness could be regarded as "high spirits," she stopped bringing me treats from work, perhaps because I had grown to expect them. "Don't whine," she'd say. "Can't you be patient?"

As she came upon me where I often sat, on the top step looking out over the compound, her rubber-soled nurse's shoes muffling her purposeful step in much the same way she masked her purposeful manner with a ready smile, she would brush past me. "Move, Dorothy Jeanne. You shouldn't make people walk around you."

In the office she was a model of efficiency but had the gentle touch of one gifted with healing. Some of the patients preferred her even to my father for the massages and special treatments. She was briskly warm as autumn sun, always inquiring after patients' families and soliciting reports of their health.

But she could be as impatient and opinionated as my father. When someone challenged the Principle or another idea she held dear, her eyes blazed, her nostrils flared, and she began to talk with her arms—sharp, cutting movements, as if she were trying to divide the world in two.

One night, after Aunt Henni had read to us from *The Book of Mormon* and the other children had gone upstairs, I asked, "Who married Daddy first? You or Mama?"

She glanced up. "I did." Her chin lifted.

"But Mama is oldest!" I had learned that much long ago. My mother had been eight minutes older, a blue baby. The nurse put her in the oven to keep warm while Aunt Henni was being born.

"Well, I married him first." Aunt Henni's voice was far away, as if she spoke from a tower.

"If you hadn't married him, Daddy would have married Mama anyway. Wouldn't he?"

She smiled tightly, her nostrils flared. "That's a silly question. I did marry him."

"Well, he would—wouldn't he?"

She shrugged. "Maybe not. When your father asked for my hand in marriage, my father said if he wanted to marry one of us, he'd have to take the other one too."

As her words sank in, my heart clenched like a fist. I stared at her.

"If it hadn't been for me, you probably wouldn't be here." Aunt Henni smiled. She reminded me of the barn cat licking the milk pail of its rind of cream. Then she turned back to her scriptures as if I weren't really there after all. My feelings changed that day; I realized that there was a price tag attached to having a second mother.

One hot June evening my mother took a bath. She didn't let me come in as she usually did. Suddenly she shrieked. Aunt Henni came running and helped my mother into the bedroom. A couple of minutes later my father rushed past me with his doctor's grip in one hand. I hovered about the bedroom door, listening. A soft moan reached my ears. Aunt Henni came out of the room, nearly knocking me over. Her white uniform rustled just as it had when she left for work that morning. She was carrying a wad of linen and the porcelain basin.

"What's wrong with Mama?" I shrilled, my heart pounding.

"Nothing. She's just having a baby. Now go outside and play."

Aunt Henni smelled strongly of disinfectant, and her voice told me she meant business.

When she went back to the bedroom, I returned to peer through a crack in the door. I glimpsed my mother's unbobbed hair, spread across the white pillowcase.

"Stay calm. Just relax," I heard my father say gently. He reached forward and stroked my mother's forehead. Then his white coat blinded my view.

A minute or two later there was an angry yell. I was shocked. There really was a baby.

"Well, there," my father cooed. "I don't blame you for yelling. This world is no picnic."

The next time Aunt Henni came out of the bedroom she was holding him. "Your baby brother," she said proudly and held him down for me to see. He was covered with white down and streaks of blood. Aunt Henni didn't send me away, so I followed her to the kitchen.

She cradled him in one arm and filled a saucer with olive oil, warming it on the stove for a few seconds before she took him to the table. "Isn't he beautiful?" she breathed, her eyes glistening.

But something in the twist of her smile made me remember

— 53

what my mother told me: that we must be patient and understanding with Aunt Henni, that Aunt Henni prayed every day and fasted regularly to be blessed with another baby. For thirteen years since Amanda's birth, and even though my father promised her another child in a special blessing, Aunt Henni had waited. My mother said the waiting was hard. Maybe my mother had said nothing to me about the new baby because she knew I would talk about it all the time, a reminder to Aunt Henni of the one she waited for.

With an arm beneath my new brother's weak, wrinkled neck, she sponged away the soft white wax and massaged fragrant olive oil into the creases of his jerking red body. The odor itself made me feel wide open inside, for the consecrated oil was also used to seal blessings on people's heads and to anoint the sick.

"Can I hold him too?"

She didn't answer for the pins in her mouth as she put a binder around the green stub of the cord. Then she dropped something in his eyes. He howled.

"It's silver nitrate, to keep babies from going blind. Our people don't need to worry about it, but it's the state law and we don't need any more trouble with the authorities than we already have." She turned him over and rubbed his back. "It's very hard to be born. The baby goes through as much as the mother."

My heart jumped. "Is Mama all right?"

"She's fine. But don't bother her. She needs to sleep." Aunt Henni wrapped a blanket around him.

"Now, come sit here on the couch if you're going to hold him. Don't breathe on him. Hold his neck."

I sat holding him as though he were the finest heirloom crystal in Aunt Gerda's china closet.

"Your daddy says he'll be named Stephen, after the disciple," Aunt Henni said, squeezing my shoulder. And our eyes met, shine for shine, smile for smile.

My mother let me watch as she nursed him, her breasts heavy and full as sun-hot ripe tomatoes in the garden. But her face was long, her eyes red, and she rarely smiled since the baby's birth.

"What's wrong, Mama?" I asked.

Her voice was thin and she shrugged. "I don't know. I guess I don't feel special anymore."

I didn't know what to say, so I wandered outside. My older brothers and sisters were cutting spinach at "the Japs," as we naively called our gentle neighbors, or cleaning cages in Mr.

Cheaseman's aviary for twenty-five cents an hour. The peacocks scolded as my brothers moved about the cages. "Help! Help!" the birds cried, a sound that also seemed to come from my heart.

I went back into the house. My mother was sitting on her bed, crying. Aunt Henni led me away. "Go outside," she whispered. "Your mother isn't feeling well."

I felt numb and frightened. When Aunt Henni left in the green Hudson to do the grocery shopping alone, I went inside to my mother. A question was gnawing at me.

"Mama, what if Daddy decided I should live with someone else, like Leora has to? Would you let them take me away from you?" My throat was tight.

Her eyes filled. "Darling, no one is going to do that." Her voice was low, ashamed. "Please don't worry. Mama has enough on her mind right now."

My mother's nervous illness became a critical part of our lives, but for years no one made a connection between her failing health and the pecking order. The patriarchs—my father and Brother Musser—eulogized the arrangement. They said the Principle gave women greater freedom—a half-true statement, for polygamous women had more time and support for individual pursuits than their monogamous counterparts. But men and women both seemed blind to the unrest and suffering born of constant comparison and subtle competition.

"Every woman has the right to motherhood," Brother Musser wrote before he died in 1953, citing proof of the Principle's divine nature and unlimited benefit to women.

My father reasoned that women outlived and outnumbered men due to wars and stress, and said women needed to flock together for companionship beneath the shepherding of a good man.

The issue of eugenic breeding, which had been promoted by the early patriarchs of the Church, was another of my father's defenses of the Principle. He frequently reminded us that this law, designed to "raise up a righteous seed unto the Lord," guaranteed that as bearers of the seed we measured brighter, more capable, and more beautiful than other people. But we must not shirk our responsibility, part of which entailed accepting the order of things without criticism or question.

My father often reminded us how blessed we were to be assured of good parents and a strong, broad base for our family. "Look around you!" he boomed. "The American family eroding everywhere! Divorce epidemic! But you children don't need to fear losing your loved ones. Even if your mother died, you'd have six other mothers to take care of you."

And so it was in my father's house, a pecking order best symbolized by twinness—an intricate interdependency of personalities, of dominating and dominated, of extrovert and introvert. Aunt Rachel, who lost both her mother and her twin while very young, found both mother and twin in Aunt Gerda. While Aunt Gerda hostessed in the white house parlor and kept strict order, Aunt Rachel bore children, tolerated their noise and dirt, yet maintained a youthful kind of rebellion in her soul. Aunt Rachel warned the children that scouring powders would age their hands, but Aunt Gerda taught them to plunge their fingers into hot dishwater. Aunt Rachel fed the children hunks of hot white bread dripping with honey, but Aunt Gerda gave them bitter Brigham tea and thin slices of whole wheat. Aunt Rachel lolled with the half-naked children on mattresses tossed on the bedroom floor and talked with them as though they were small adults, but Aunt Gerda brusquely pinned and twisted them into the sturdy new clothes she was always making, and spoke to them in reprimand.

In a similar way, my mother bore children, pursued domestic bliss, played the piano with a virtuoso's touch, and got sick, while Aunt Henni delivered children, pursued a career alongside my father, led the singing with her strong alto, and stayed healthy. Together they were two halves of a whole—Moses and Aaron, the spirit and the letter of the law.

Chapter 4

Through much of my early childhood, I resented being a girl. My longing to be a boy began on a day when I was two, almost three, and my brothers were trooping home with me across the golden fields after a long fishing jaunt, slogging through swamps, sidestepping meadow-muffins and cow-pies, picking cockleburs and thistles from our stockings, until at last we reached the bridge across Spring Run. Home was still a pasture away, so my three brothers stopped to relieve themselves, three sprinkling arcs drubbing into the creek. My full bladder also ached, so I slipped down my pink silk undies to make my own golden arc. Instead I filled up my shoes. My brothers hooted, and I was furious in my embarrassment, swinging wildly at them and sobbing.

As time went on, my resentment grew; enveloping anger about priesthood secrets, covetousness for pocketknives and basketballs, rage that Danny could pin me to the rug and hold me there, jealousy that my brothers went to special meetings and on fishing trips with my father. Girls could not go on these exclusive excursions. Moreover, girls were expected to learn at an early age the dullest of domestic skills—dishwashing, fruit bottling, sock darning. Girls must stay close to home, docile and uncurious. The life of a boy, with its rank smells of sour worms and barn manure, its damp and dirty attire, its bruises and black eyes, seemed far preferable to the safe, boring world of women. I wondered about a God and parents who would conspire to put me in this cage, this prison of femininity. But little did I know in those days what my brothers went through. . . .

One might assume, as so many outsiders have done, that rearing a son to become a polygamous patriarch involved nothing more than some lessons in womanizing plus some secrets on keeping energy up. In reality the boys' lessons in womanizing were abysmally

absent, but the secrets of an energetic life dominated male education. Such secrets had only indirectly to do with virility and directly to do with vitality; they involved the principles of faith, repentance, and keeping God's law, so that a young man's progression
to godhood could be eternally ensured.

Pursuit of godhood. That glittering goal, at once an accursed
journey and a blessed pilgrimage, possessed my brothers' lives from
the moment they discovered that they were becoming rather than
being, from the moment that simply living was not enough—for
surely God could not perform his marvels through protégés in dirty
tennis shoes and T-shirts, nor would He wish to smell like swamp
and rainbow trout. God must ever present himself in Sunday slacks
and starched white shirt and didn't mind if His tie choked. Moreover,
He must always have Sunday school manners, never yelling or
running or pulling girls' hair or telling dirty jokes. For, as the boys
were often reminded, "the natural man is an enemy to God."

Pursuit of godhood was difficult for ordinary scab-picking boys
like Saul and Jake and Danny, especially since my mother delighted in their good health as much as she was appalled by the
formidable force of their energy.

Even mild-mannered, evanescent Isaac had to have the natural grit more or less scoured away. Once, when he caught a cat by
its tail and let it fly into the pond, Aunt Henni boiled out the back
door, firmly grabbed Isaac by the leg and let him fly into the pond.
"Now you know how it feels," Aunt Henni declared, searching the
mud for Isaac's new socks.

The natural boy, when pitted against his mother's attempt to
civilize him, often won out: When Saul declared that if he had to
practice the piano one more time he would kill himself with the
butcher knife, my mother impressed him into no more piano lessons. But when my father got involved, the contest shifted. He not
only expected the boys to master their natural passions, he retal-
iated with something similarly primal when they did not. One fast-
Sunday, Danny, newly baptized, sauntered toward my father, who
was conferring with the brethren under the trees. Although it was
an hour until dinner, and no baptized saint was supposed to eat
until an eighteen-hour fast had been accomplished, Danny smugly
munched on a biscuit. "Where did you get that?" my father asked,
interrupting the conference. "Mama gave it to me," Danny retorted. "I told her I was hungry." Whereupon my father delivered
a swift kick to the seat of Danny's pants. Treated thus, before all

the brethren, Danny became the core of a most unflattering example whereby others might discipline their sons.

Like boys in the official Mormon Church, my father's sons participated in Boy Scout activities: dens and troops of youngsters taught to honor God, nature, and country by troop leaders who, in this case, believed in the Principle. These leaders had distinguished themselves in various ways, often in their support of my father; yet despite the common theological threats, some warped radically into private systems of belief.

Jake's leader was Edward Balboa, a short, red-haired, pale-eyed Scot whose religious center revolved around flying saucers. An obscure contingent of Mormons had long held onto an apocryphal prophecy that the City of Enoch would soon return to save us from self-destruction, descending in spaceships from the North Star. During camp-outs in the primitive Uintah Mountains, the boys set beside the flickering campfire and watched the stars and and moon brightening. Inevitably, Balboa began to speak of the mysteries of the great universe, waxing rhetorical. "Even now the citizens of Enoch are watching us from the moon. They can see everything we do—everything wonderful and everything dark and dirty."

Many a Boy Scout camp was spent searching the night skies for fleets of spaceships bearing special knowledge and enlightened beings who would set the world in order and who, through magical osmosis, would transmit the lessons of mutual respect, tolerance, and Christlike love that we as yet had failed to receive from our earthling brethren.

One night the talk turned to whispered horrors and tales of evil. "The Gadianton Robbers performed their satanic rites at this very spot," Balboa proclaimed, eyes closed, arms outstretched. "Feel their presence here. Such devilish things they performed—cutting beating hearts from breasts, raping virgins, drinking blood to seal their diabolical oaths." Whereupon Balboa wrapped his short frame in his bedroll and promptly began snoring. The young boys lay wide awake and terrified, waiting for the ghost of Gadianton to ascend and murder them all in their bivouac.

Not all the Boy Scout leaders were so colorful. Some possessed good common sense and an understanding of nature that rivaled my father's. Saul's leader, Dean Brady, could name every tree in the Wasatch National Forest, could spot elk and cougar tracks, could explain the use of every herb. Dean Brady was a survivalist. He knew how to make whistles and flippers from green willow, knew which green tops had edible roots, which berries would kill you. He could construct a lean-to of pine boughs in less time than most men could pitch a tent. He taught the boys how to catch fish on a dry fly and then wet their hands before releasing them back to the stream. "It's OK to eat these beauties when we need to. But I've got no truck with people that waste God's bounty," he said.

Through Dean Brady, Saul's respect for nature deepened into an abiding passion that would influence the rest of his life. Not the least of these influences was a regard for his own natural thought processes that could not be smothered by the doctrines he was daily taught. Like Dean Brady, who often argued with my father about the essential nature of free will, Saul had ideas of his own, ideas that were often in conflict with my father's practices.

An early run-in with my father set the seal of rebellion on Saul's character. When only ten years old, Saul took the initiative to find a job harvesting spinach with our Japanese neighbors. True to the United Order policy whereby my father gathered in everyone's earnings and distributed according to need, Saul turned his wages over to my father, who said he would see that Saul's money was saved for "a rainy day." When bicycles went on sale, Saul approached my father, hoping that he too would hear the thunder, since the new junior high school was out of walking distance. But the funds were gone, and my father made no apology for the fact. Saul felt he'd been lied to and cheated.

Isaac, on the other hand, embraced such self-abnegation while very young and malleable. One night, when all the families lived together in the white house, chocolate pudding was served for dessert. Isaac, only five years old at the time, complained that his dish held less than that of the other children. Aunt Henni admonished him not to be greedy, but Isaac continued his plaints until she slammed down her spoon.

"All right! You want more pudding? You'll eat every pudding here." So Isaac commenced eating some fourteen puddings while the others gazed on in awe. As his stomach grew fuller, his face grew redder. Soon he was sick, sick of pudding and sick of himself. He learned very young what it means to surfeit on one's own desires.

A willingness to serve in obedience was essential to fully taking the next step in a fundamentalist boy's life. At the age of twelve most boys were ordained deacons in the priesthood and thus became God's representatives on the earth. As deacons they were to teach and preach the gospel, expound on scripture, exhort people to pray, and be able to recite the thirteen Articles of Faith. Rare was the twelve-year-old boy who could perform all these responsibilities in good faith, but ready or not, in a year or two he was moved on to become a teacher, which entails visiting people in their homes and encouraging them in "the Work." By the time he had turned sixteen, he was ordained a priest, eligible to baptize and to administer the sacrament, a full-fledged agent of the Lord in practice and, it was hoped, in spirit.

Obedience, like a huge umbrella, protected a young man from too much life experience and therefore from the continual need to make choices. Once he had made the choice to magnify his priesthood, he must only follow the rules and God would take care of him. Like all umbrellas, this one could obscure vision of sky, sun, stars, and other people.

Some boys felt their advent into the priesthood to be a solemn responsibility and took it upon themselves to be good examples. Others, like Saul, felt themselves impressed into a system of service they could not wholeheartedly support. Whether the young man matured in the order of things, with his priesthood covenants intact, or fostered his individuality separate from the religious group, the weekly priesthood meetings provided an opportunity to ponder what it means to be a man.

Saul and Isaac had always treated girls with gallantry, deference, and a special kind of tenderness. Saul championed our cause in barnyard games, and Isaac was always there to hold and kiss us better when we had bruised our shins or our hearts. Perhaps their special feeling for females grew out of the tender relationship each had with his mother. Saul vowed he'd someday treat his wife the way he'd like to see his mother be treated, defending her health and her feelings against any who would violate her.

The oldest boy in a polygamous household was accorded immense responsibility, for on the many nights when my father was not at home, Saul became my mother's companion, a surrogate father for us younger children, and (once he held the priesthood) the head of her household. Aunt Henni counted on Isaac to conduct meetings and family prayers and included both him and Saul in family decisions that my father wasn't around to make. All the intimacy my mother might have bestowed on a monogamous relationship was thus endowed on her children, particularly her oldest son. To be given such sobering duties one night and then to be treated like a child when next my father spent the night at home must have been confusing, at least.

Later in his life my father ventured publicly that sex is "a gift from God, to be enjoyed with restraint." Despite his apparently wholesome attitude toward sexuality he became most uncomfortable as his boys and girls grew up and approached him in natural curiosity about the subject he knew so well: where babies come from. Perhaps he could not bring himself to reduce something he considered sacred to the purely clinical terminology of a physician. Or perhaps he reasoned that the more ignorant his children, the more chaste they would be. From the time his children reached puberty until they were safely married, he assiduously avoided intimate conversation with them.

But something moved him to charge Samuel Hampton, the deacons' leader, with the responsibility of sex education in Wednesday night priesthood meetings. Saul later described how Hampton, newly married and profoundly embarrassed to discuss such a forbidden subject, stuttered from one general announcement to another, his long white fingers trembling, smoothing his tie, rattling keys in his pocket, raking his thick brown hair. And then all the announcements had been read and my father nodded at Hampton and quietly slipped out the door.

Hampton cleared his throat half a dozen times. The boys sat up, alerted that this was not going to be a typical doctrine and testimony meeting.

"You young men who have been wondering about sex . . . ," he began. The boys sat up straighter. "You need to know that it is for procreation—nothing else. It isn't for fun or for sport or to make you feel good, like some out in the world believe. It's for procreation." This remark out, Hampton began to act like a caged animal, pacing the room.

"You may not believe it right now, but it is quite natural to want to kiss a girl." Most of the boys believed it, since they had been encouraged from babyhood to kiss everyone—mothers, father, sisters, brothers, even cousins.

"And then, when you kiss her, it's quite natural to want to touch her breast." Blushes rose in the room.

"And then," blurted Hampton, "it is quite natural to want to complete the sex act." This out, he pulled out his handkerchief and wiped his forehead.

Only the most astute and intuitive of the boys had any notion of what was being discussed, except that they were supposed to want to touch girls somewhere they instinctively avoided.

Hampton had called for a volunteer to give closing prayer, when he remembered the most critical information of all: "Oh! And of course, you will do none of these things until you are married, sealed for eternity by the priesthood. Also, you must never, never abuse yourselves. Save your seed for the Lord's work and your wives."

Fortunately, growing up on a farm, plus repeated exposure to home birth, enhanced Saul's and Isaac's understanding significantly. While they were very young, perhaps eight or nine, they deliberated over the sudden appearance of a new calf, remembered that Bossy had been enormously fat and now was thin, and theorized about the birth process.

"I don't know," Saul muttered after a few moments of musing. "It's gotta come out somewhere." He lifted Bossy's tail, then quickly dropped it.

"I know where it comes from," Isaac stated.

"How? How do you know?"

"I just do."

"Two minutes ago you said you didn't know either," Saul argued. "Were you holding out?"

"No," Isaac said serenely. "I've had an inspiration."

"Well?" Saul blurted. "Aren't you going to tell me?"

"That line of hair along the cow's belly—see it? It just unzips and the calf falls out. And then daddy or somebody has to zip it back up again."

Some days later, my father sent for Ruckhaus's bull. Cal, the oldest of the Ruckhaus family of seven boys, stood by to witness and report to his father about the bull's performance. Saul had long admired Cal Ruckhaus, two grades ahead of him in school. Saul imitated his basketball style and coveted the easygoing manner in which Cal made and kept friends, so he followed him down to the pasture. Isaac soon joined them. My father came out of the white house and waited around for awhile, saying little, moving impatiently from one foot to the other, alternately eyeing his wristwatch and the grazing bull.

"Haven't even noticed those two lovely ladies, have you, you stupid beast," he muttered. Then he took note of Saul and Isaac straddling the wooden fence. "Stick around, boys," he called. "You might learn something." And he abandoned the pasture to keep a nine o'clock appointment at his office.

When at last the bull began pursuing our thin, nervous Jersey, Red, the boys' hearts thumped and their stomachs knotted. They rubbed wet palms against their jeans and watched, astonished, as the brazen bull mounted poor Red. A hot mix of excitement, disgust, and disbelief stirred in Saul's chest. And an undeniable rush of joy—the joy of imminent knowledge.

"What's goin' on?" Saul said huskily.

Cal snorted. "You don't know? They're mating. That's how a cow gets a calf."

After a long minute Saul decided he could not pass up this opportunity to know more. "Where does the calf come out?" he asked.

Cal Ruckhaus hooted. "You stupid plyggies." Then he spat. "Comes out the same place it's goin' in."

Saul watched for a minute longer, then nudged Isaac. "Unzipped."

Isaac blushed furiously.

Cal folded his arms and took a man's stride. "Yep. That's how animals do it. That's how they get their babies. It feels good, too."

The two boys stole a look at each other, having already surmised as much. The brays and grunts, the tenacity and force of the bull, the heat and intensity of the energy could not be ignored.

Cal eyed them. "You know, your parents did the same thing to get you."

"No!" Isaac yelped.

"Yep," Cal said smugly, rocking back on his heels. "Even you holier-than-thou plyggies."

"I don't believe it," Isaac shouted. "My mother and father would never act like that!" And he strode toward the house.

Cal Ruckhaus laughed again. "Sure they don't," he called after Isaac. "You came from a cabbage patch, right?"

Saul felt the blood creep into his face and with it an uncomfortable certainty that what Cal Ruckhaus said was true: the white garments parted in strategic places; their bodies were of flesh. Despite the white energy of the spirit, despite the force of the priesthood, despite the refinement and discipline of his parents, despite the grand scheme of the Principle to "raise up a righteous seed unto the Lord," Saul sensed that they were subject to animal impulses, to animal behaviors just like the bull and the cow. And he sensed that as Cal had said, it felt good, too.

Ignorance persisted, however, and Saul's dim awareness of how little he knew made him reluctant to date. Perhaps his caution could be traced to the time a girlfriend refused to go swimming with him in the river after school, though they had done so before. He pressed her for her reasons.

"I want to know what's going on. Is it that you don't want to be with me?"

"That's not it, you dummy. I can't go, don't you see? I'm having my period!"

Saul watched her, dumbfounded.

"Menstruating. You know, when a girl bleeds."

He caught his breath. "You're bleeding? Will you be all right? Maybe you'd better sit down."

She shook her strawberry blond head in frustration.

"No, I'm fine." Then her small features softened. "You really don't know, do you. . . ." And she told him about a woman's body and the monthly flow.

Saul went home and slammed his books on the table. "I don't believe it!" he shouted. My mother watched, tense and quiet, from the counter where she was kneading bread. Saul swallowed, and the muscle in his cheek throbbed. "As if it isn't bad enough that we're so different—Daddy with all these wives and kids so that people wonder what in the Sam Hill we're up to—but we have to be stupid too!" He spat each word like poison. "Sixteen years old and I still don't know about menstruation. So where do I have to learn it? From a *girl*—a girl I wanted to date!"

My mother hugged herself and shook her head morosely. Her eyes were brown puddles of shame. She said nothing.

"It isn't fair for me to learn these things from the kids at school, Mama. I thought I already knew everything I had to know. I thought I could count on Daddy to tell me anything I hadn't figured out by myself. Why wouldn't he tell us, Mama? Didn't he think we'd need to know someday? I mean, we can't stay at home and be children forever, can we?"

My mother just shook her head and stared at the floor.

"Good grief, didn't he think we could be trusted? After all, he's a doctor. . . ."

Sometime later, Saul sent away for a brown-wrapped infor-

— 65

mation manual written by a doctor and put out by the Cadillac Publishing Company. The booklet promised diagrams, complete scientific information about male and female reproductive systems, plus an accurate description of the mysterious "sex act," including its purposes and consequences. Aunt Gerda intercepted the manual when at last it came in the mail; she handed it over to my father. Saul had almost stopped looking for the book, thinking he had been conned out of $3.95, when my father invited him to go for a ride. As they sped down the highway, my father pulled the catalog from under the seat.

"It's an accurate enough presentation," he grudged, gesturing with the brown-wrapped book. "But I can't understand why you'd send away to some stranger for this information, why you wouldn't come to me. " Before Saul could answer, he went on. "It presents a wordly view. Birth control, for instance, is the devil's pet theory. Reduces sex to a sport. And masturbation—so they call it—is self-abuse, destructive to the will, debilitating to the body, and deadly to the spirit."

Saul studied his shoes in silence throughout the interview. If he disagreed with my father's statements or resented the intrusion, he was unaware of such feelings in the mighty numbness of the moment. He accepted the manual, when at last my father handed it over at the close of their ride. He went quietly to his room and educated himself about sex. He was twenty-one years old.

Saul and Isaac began school in a whorl of uncertainty and over-exposure the year my father entered prison. With the mothers' pictures splashed across front pages throughout the world, family photos in *Life* and *Time*, and Saul hitting my father's pitch squarely to make a home run on Movietone News, the boys were likely to be recognized by classmates and teachers. They went about in daily dread of a confrontation.

Although the subject of polygamy rarely became an overt issue, Saul soon sensed that people in the world weren't as stupid as the family liked to believe, that many of them knew about the family, yet said and did nothing. He felt confused by their silence, yet grateful for it. He maintained a certain distance from his peers, a remote but respectful outsider. His integrity, leadership ability, and native consideration did not totally displace the burden of difference. Some hidden expectation of trouble or rejection gave an edge to his remarks and a swashbuckling style to his performance.

If people knew nothing of our family, Saul tucked his defensiveness away, quiet as a garter snake in his pocket. But if people knew about us (unless they had proved their loyalty), Saul agonized through a spell of hypersensitivity when he took everything wrong, struggling through an emotional obstacle course ranging from embarrassment to distrust to shame—huge barriers to prospective friendship.

Still, the boys did not lack for friends, even had they found no one in the wicked world beyond our group. Cousins by the score visited often and sometimes lived at the compound with us. Big cousins, dark-haired and handsome, who stretched out muscular arms and invited us younger children to prove their strength by hanging two on each arm, our legs swinging and tangling and the cousins red-faced and grinning. Blond cousins who set us high on their shoulders and toted us to the apple orchard where we could grab a skirtful of ripe or green apples and eat them under the willow. Cousins who played basketball and baseball as if their lives depended on beating the pants off Saul and Isaac and our other brothers. Cousins who disappeared behind the barn doors for long moments, whispering, and then burst forth with a great yen for team-tag or pomp-pomp-pull-away, in which we younger children were invited to join. For we were rich, we were abundant beyond measuring, despite the many patched and mended places in the fabric of our lives.

Saul and Isaac and later Jake and Danny proved themselves exceptional athletes. Championships began in third grade with marble shooting and progressed to baseball and basketball in junior high school and football in high school.

Like any American dad, my father attended the games when he was able, cheered for his sons, denigrated referees and umpires, and rejoiced in his sons' victories. But he never let them think for a moment that he was satisfied with their physical coordination alone; he encouraged no dreams of pro ball or college scholarships. He reminded his sons that a healthy, synchronous body was one of God's blessings, a mere stepping-stone to spiritual achievement.

The boys' schoolmates and teachers took pains to demonstrate their high regard. Saul was voted captain of the basketball team and shop foreman. Isaac gave speeches as a class representative and sang solos with their choir.

If the schoolchildren took note that fifteen (or more) towheads lined up at the bus stop each day, every one scrubbed and combed, dressed in starched shirts or pinafores, carrying their homework (completed) and identical lunch sacks, none mentioned it to Saul or Isaac. The older girls in the family carried on whispered explanations in the lavatory, half fact, half fabrication. Danny once got in a fight over a classmate's remark about his father's many wives. ("It was true, so I couldn't deny it," Danny later defended himself. "What else could I do but hit him?") Otherwise, the face of things was calm and accepting.

Despite the unperturbed mood, Saul was keenly aware of the stigma of polygamy. Peter Ames had been fired the day after his boss found out about his second wife. And "Uncle" LeRoy still hadn't been able to get work, not since his picture was published during the polygamist roundup. Any occupational future looked grim for a young man of polygamous stock, regardless of his character and ambition. Saul knew that his success in life would require extraordinary effort and awareness.

Isaac seemed more trusting (whether by nature or naiveté) than Saul. He was not so dogged by fear. His faith was stronger. And he seemed indifferent to relationships beyond his home life, where he was fulfilled and happy as tender big brother and obedient son. The worldly choices that plagued Saul had no relevance for him.

Saul also was tender and loving, both as brother and as son. But he could not be called obedient, at least not according to the blind and humble pattern that my father preferred. Saul longed for an arena where he could show himself in a positive light, a place where he could be appreciated and praised for his unique talents rather than condemned for his questioning mind. The anxiety and insecurity of his life mounted as he became more and more dependent on the high regard of people outside the family. Never did he want to deserve the doubt and distrust he was indoctrinated to feel for others. He was scrupulously honest in all areas, save those regarding the family. And he resented lying, even to preserve our unity and freedom, such as it was.

Persecution hung above him, above us all, like an anvil threatening to fall at any moment. Saul, standing below, could do little but gaze upward, wondering when . . . how . . . where. On the one hand, he was constantly reminded to keep the family secret from friends. On the other hand, he was reminded that we would be persecuted anyway as a test of faith. And in the same meeting, almost in the same breath, my father or one of the council would promise that God would bless and protect us all for living every single commandment, including the Principle, and that this was the key to salvation, both earthly and celestial.

A purpose, perhaps even more central than individual growth and its movement to universal meaning, guided Saul and Isaac and each of my brothers. The dream of becoming a good father generated all manly endeavor in my father's family and in his father's before him: to create, to procreate, to build, to foster, to provide, to guide, to bless, these were the patterns of their lives and the purpose of their being. In his heart each boy carried forth my father's obsession to become a beneficent and loving patriarch at home and in "the world," launching new ships on the seas of eternity, firing up genetic satellites, flinging into time and space the magnetic crystals of intelligence, letting flow the warm seeds of love, so like the benevolent, eternal Father to whom we said our prayers.

Chapter

5

Despite the solidarity of so many dedicated parents, we hadn't enough mortar of love or spackle of secrecy to chink my father's household against the wind of fear. I came to know fear irrevocably in 1953 and again in 1955.

My parents had lived with fear's ominous howl since the family's start, only a few months after the first "polygamist roundup" in 1935, which resulted in the arrest of two Short Creek patriarchs and one woman. My father had already assimilated the degree of sacrifice demanded by "this hard Principle." During the cottage meeting where he first met my mother, he described losing his first wife and children. "It was as though the limbs were being torn from my body," he confessed with tears in his eyes.

My mother's eyes also filled when she spoke of sacrifice and persecution—the cornerstones of our fear. "I suppose we all knew we would each have a cross to bear, that we would go through some personal torment just as your father did for the stand we'd taken." When my mother talked this way, I knew she was thinking of her illness. "Still, we were surprised when the persecutions came, even with all the rumblings of trouble. I guess it began for us about the time Sarah came into the family.

"Not that we minded having Sarah in the family," she hastened to add. "Quite the opposite. Having Sarah around was like having Christmas every day. We thought her the wittiest, most talented girl we'd ever met. Marrying Sarah was like welcoming home a long-lost sister. And whatever we did together—oh, we had fun!"

Aunt Sarah, with the ruddy strength of a farmer's daughter and the devotion of a lifelong Church member, bonded instantly with the twins and stood unwaveringly in Aunt Gerda's wake.

Aunt Sarah also brought trouble. Always one of the more devout members of her Mormon farming community, she trembled with conviction when my father spoke about the Principle. She could scarcely be sure which she loved most—him or the gospel.

Aunt Sarah's father, Brother Berna, a man of few words, did not explain why he stalked out of the house when the young doctor visited with his whole harem and invited his oldest daughter to go picnicking with them. But when Sarah returned, he made it clear to her: no daughter of his would get caught in a web of polygamy. Brother Rulon was no longer welcome in his home.

The constraint came too late. All afternoon my father had courted Sarah, oblivious to the looks and murmurs of his other wives. He carried her across a brook she could easily have jumped and chased her through the moonlight under the guise of hide-and-seek.

"Rulon's going to ask you to marry him," Gerda buzzed in Sarah's ear as the evening ended. Aunt Gerda seemed to take pleasure in announcing my father's moves before he made them, as an eager child at a birthday party will announce what is inside a gift before the guest of honor can open it.

The next time my father visited, Sarah sneaked out of the house to join him and Gerda for a drive through the rolling countryside, darkness cloaking them as they sang favorite hymns and love songs.

"You'll do better to harmonize with the twins," Gerda said bluntly. "Now Rulon and I, our voices fit. But you sing too high. You'll do nicely with the twins."

And Sarah did do nicely with the twins. She came to Salt Lake City for Mormon Church conference but was secretly married in a home my father had rented only blocks from the Salt Lake temple. Then she returned to her native town of Brigham, behaving as though nothing special had happened.

She even accepted a couple of dates with old boyfriends so that her parents wouldn't get suspicious, but by nature Sarah's family repelled lies and deception. Soon the truth came bursting out. Her mother wept. Her father roared and paced the room. Her parents took her to Salt Lake City so that Church authorities could "bring her to her senses."

The appointment with a high-ranking Church official was aborted; no one knew why the apostle was absent that day. Sarah saw it as the hand of God; her parents saw it as the work of Satan. They allowed her to visit her sister-wives for half an hour while they waited in the car. When the thirty minutes were gone, Grandmother Allred followed Sarah to the front door and gave her a reassuring hug.

"Oh, Mother Allred, what shall I do?" Sarah choked.

Grandmother stepped back and looked into her eyes. "Don't worry. The Lord's hand is in this, as in all things. He will open the way."

Then Sarah was whisked back to Brigham. Some weeks later she bicycled off to the grocery store, ostensibly to buy some baking soda. She met my father by the delivery door and left her home-town for good.

Brother Berna followed them to Salt Lake and spread word that if he found his new son-in-law, he'd hang him up by his heels. Some distorted the message into a literal hanging, while others ru-mored that FBI and local police trailed my father.

"You'd better stay off the streets for a month or so," Brother Musser counseled him. The family hastily moved in with the Sherwoods, group members whose big house, divided into apart-ments, accommodated the growing Allred family. A dapper patri-arch with a keen sense of humor, Ted Sherwood thoroughly en-joyed the circle of happy young women who joined him in the evening for cards or bright chatter.

My mother and Aunt Henni attended the local wardhouse, paying half their tithing to the bishop and the other half to Brother Musser, for they had set their hearts on going through the temple before it was too late. Soon after they had completed the rituals and made the secret vows to dedicate their lives to God, thus re-ceiving their temple endowments, the bishop accosted them in the wardhouse foyer.

"You girls must move from that apartment house, the sooner the better. I know you don't realize it, but you're living in a den of polygamists!" My mother and Aunt Henni suppressed giggles that effervesced despite the danger of being discovered, and returned to the Sherwoods with the warning.

The family moved again . . . and again. Pregnant wives were sent to relatives or sympathizers, where they stayed inside from the time they showed, learning the true meaning of "confinement." Meanwhile, Aunt Sarah's mother became desperately ill, but Sarah dared not return to Brigham for fear her father would keep her from going back to her husband and sister-wives. She quietly bore the death of her first child, of diphtheria, with the support and sympathy of her sister-wives. She grew up quickly and gained wisdom beyond her nineteen years.

In 1941 my father procured the big white house and its spacious grounds with a $25 down payment and no notion of where the first payment would come from, since his practice in Salt Lake City was still fledgling. The rambling two-story structure had been built by an early settler in the days when polygamy was sanctioned by the official Mormon Church, before the manifesto was signed and the Enabling Act passed to gain Utah's statehood. Soon after they settled there, the Church authorities formally notified members of my family of their official excommunication from the Church of Jesus Christ of Latter-Day Saints. The reason: living polygamy in defiance of the manifesto and against the dictates of modern Church authorities. Then Aunt Sarah discovered that her mother had died. She felt she had lost mother and father, sisters and brother, child and church to "the Lord's Hard Principle." My father became her father, brother, husband, lover, and advisor. Her sister-wives truly became her sisters, their children her children. The loss of one family made her cling devotedly to the one she now held in unreserved embrace.

Aunt Sarah was taking her turn in the white house kitchen the morning of the raid, making biscuits for the throng of women and children about to descend on the breakfast table. When the knock came, Aunt Sarah flung open the door expecting to see an impatient patient or one of the councilmen in need of my father's counsel.

An officer flashed his badge. Aunt Sarah slammed the door in his face. "FBI! There's no use trying to escape!" the officer shouted from outside. "We've got men everywhere!" Aunt Navida, who listened from the door of her room, started upstairs to warn the others and met my mother coming down, a load of laundry in one hand and my oldest brother, Saul, clinging to the other.

"The FBI are all over the house and grounds, Hannah!" Aunt Navida whispered. "They've surrounded us. Where's Rulon?"

No one seemed to know. Aunt Sarah regained her composure, opened the kitchen door and invited the agents inside. Several local police officers, including a matron, accompanied them. With their pistols and brusque manners, they seemed equipped for an extensive manhunt, and their faces fell when my father entered the living room, cheeks pale and eyes red-rimmed but in full self-control.

He listened to the charges with half an ear, knowing what they said well in advance: he was charged with unlawful cohabitation. As he read the warrant, his wives clustered around, wanting to reach out with reassuring touches but not daring to show their concern before the officers.

"May we have a few moments alone? A family member is sick in bed. If we could go upstairs . . . ," my father said.

The agents followed them and waited outside as they met in Aunt Rachel's room, where she was convalescing after the birth of her fifth child in about as many years. They knelt around her bed, clinging tightly to each other's hands, and prayed for deliverance.

After the prayer my father said, "Now, dear ones, we must decide which of us will go to jail. I must go, of course; the warrant names me as the principal party. But some of you girls must go so they can have 'proof' of these charges."

Somehow they decided that my mother and Aunt Henni would represent the mothers in jail. A matron was waiting in the hall when they emerged from Aunt Rachel's room. She followed my mother into her bedroom and watched her remove her housecoat and don something to wear downtown.

Meanwhile, other arrests were underway: Brother Musser sat by as FBI agents rifled his papers, ignoring his demands that they produce a search warrant or respect his civil rights. In addition to unlawful cohabitation, he was charged with "distributing lewd and obscene literature through the U.S. mails"—his beloved tract, "The Truth." The "lewd and obscene" charge was based simply on the fact that the pamphlet advocated plural marriage. FBI agents also stayed at the white house, combing each room for diaries, journals, letters—anything that might be considered "incriminating evidence" of unlawful cohabitation. At lunchtime Aunt Sarah fixed a plate of sandwiches and a pitcher of hot chocolate to refresh the agents as they sifted through my mother's belongings. The agents, nonplussed by her courtesy, perched on my mother's bed, munching and trying to make light talk with Aunt Sarah, who, in her attempt to balance fear with goodwill, didn't think to ask for a search warrant.

My mother and Aunt Henni were booked on conspiracy charges, my mother for playing the piano at meetings, Aunt Henni for teaching Sunday school. The newspaper photographers clustered around, wanting front-page shots of the twins accused of marriage to the same man.

In the next day's newspaper, beneath photographs of Brother Musser and Brother Barlow, Aunt Henni faced the camera squarely, chin lifted, head high, and eyes smiling as though proud to be jailed for the Principle. Beside her, my mother's head was bowed, her big eyes dilated, and shame written on her features. An acutely painful awareness of being thought a criminal suffused her face.

All that day and into the next, women from the group arrived, until six of them clustered in a single cell. They watched through the barred window as the men were led across the street for arraignment. My mother and Aunt Henni called and waved their handkerchiefs through the bars, trying to get my father's attention.

"Look!" my mother exclaimed. "Those fine men of God in handcuffs!" Later they learned that John Y. Barlow's wrists were pinched until they bled. He was a big, heavy man, and the officers had no handcuffs to fit him but insisted he wear them anyway.

The afternoon passed slowly, and the women missed their children. Bail, set at a minimum of $2,500 each, dismayed these people who sometimes subsisted on pigweed from the yard.

Next morning they combed each other's hair for the arraignment, where they found the whole group thronged before the City and County Building, as if for a picnic celebration. Sandwiches and lemonade and chocolate cake appeared, and everyone hugged and kissed. The other wives, excepting ailing Aunt Rachel, carried overnight bags and announced they would be spending the remainder of the twins' time in jail with them.

As they left the City and County Building, they were approached by a large broad-faced woman whom they recognized as a group sympathizer. "You girls won't spend another night in jail," she proclaimed. "I promise you that." Someone whispered she had mortgaged her property for the bond of the thirty fundamentalists arrested in the roundup.

In a newly warm and bright cell the women laughed over everything and talked of going home. At seven o'clock, a grumpy matron brought keys and papers for their release.

About two weeks after their release, my mother received a letter from a widowed doctor, inviting her to live with him and care for his two sons.

"Refuge, I think he called it," my mother said. "But of course I didn't want to go. I wouldn't want to be anyplace on earth but here with your father and my loved ones. I wrote and told him 'No thank you.' And that was the end of it."

But it was not the end of it for fifteen patriarchs charged with various felony crimes: some with unlawful cohabitation, some with distributing obscene literature through the U.S. mails, and some with violating the Mann Act or the Lindbergh Kidnapping Act by transporting young women across state lines.

All charges against the women soon vanished, but the courts prosecuted the men with enthusiasm. The Church had helped put teeth in the original antipolygamy legislation, which at first stood as a simple misdemeanor punishable by fine or at maximum by a six-month sentence. But Church President Heber J. Grant—who had himself been arrested and fined for living polygamously after the manifesto, so that he stopped living with his plural families—stated: "I shall rejoice when the Government officials put a few of these polygamists in the State Penitentiary." He added: "Any person who has entered plural marriage since the Manifesto is not a credit to any community, and the same may be said of their children."

A Church member who was active in state politics authored an amendment to the original illegal cohabitation act. The amendment made the crime a felony, punishable by five years in prison. A Mormon legislative majority had quickly passed the amendment and the governor had signed it.

The ill-defined separation of church and state in Utah affairs had an effect almost opposite to its influence during the polygamous epoch of the 1800s. Now all the Church's power concerted to stamp out, rather than to protect, polygamy. As the trials progressed, it came out that the Church had hired detectives and ordered member-spies to infiltrate the fundamentalist sector. A Utah judge, disqualified because of Church connections, gave way to a district court judge from Denver.

The defense founded its basic appeal on the First Amendment to the U.S. Constitution, guaranteeing freedom of religious worship. But even the second judge overruled attempts to quash on those grounds.

During the trial Mormon logic surfaced—the way established in the early days to avoid telling the truth without actually lying.

But this time Mormons fenced with Mormons, and with both parties adept at Mormon logic, the truth took strange twists and turns, in approaching facts and issues.

But the central issue remained the question of religious freedom. Could Americans, in pursuing a religious belief, break the law—specifically, section 103-51-2 of the Utah Code, which charged that any person illegally cohabiting with another was guilty of a felony crime?

It was to this issue that the four Utah justices spoke in their final statement, invoking the U.S. Supreme Court decision in *Reynolds* v. *the United States*, a pioneer polygamy case that upheld Utah's Enabling Act prohibiting polygamy forever:

> In our opinion, the statute . . . is . . . constitutional and valid . . . the only question which remains is whether those who make polygamy a part of their religion are excepted from the statute. . . . This would be introducing a new element into criminal law. Laws are made for the government of actions and while they cannot interfere with mere religious belief . . . they may with practices. Suppose one believed that human sacrifices were a necessary part of religious worship, would it be seriously contended that the civil government under which he lived could not interfere to prevent a sacrifice?

And so my father faced up to five years in prison. In the days between the trial and sentencing, Brother Musser promised my father that if he would "complete his quorum" of seven wives, he would be demonstrating his willingness to serve at a higher level and therefore would receive a special blessing. Thus, my father's call to the council was contingent on Aunt Lisa.

Before she was "Aunt" to my father's children, Aunt Lisa had been the mothers' preferred babysitter. With her porcelain skin and thick, dark ringlets, she was also sought after by the young men of the group from the time she showed signs of childbearing ability. Under considerable pressure to choose from among her many suitors while only fourteen years old, she confided to her father that Dr. Allred was the man of her destiny. Her father ("Uncle" Levi we called him), as one of my father's staunchest supporters, delighted in the prospective match but at some distant time, with

Rulon's wives prepared for a family addition and when Lisa finished high school.

But the trials and sentencing changed all that. One evening Lisa sat propping her bare feet in the coal bucket as she scribbled math problems on the kitchen tabletop. My father rushed in to pick up his sister, Uncle Levi's third wife, for an examination.

"We're going to Brother Rulon's office," Uncle Levi announced. "Come with us, Lisa."

Aunt Lisa gasped. "Dressed like this?" She gestured at her housecoat and laughed in her breathy way. "At least let me comb out my pigtails and put on a dress. I was ready for bed!"

Uncle Levi glanced at my father. My father shook his head.

"No time, dear. Come as you are."

They drove to my father's office in downtown Salt Lake City. Lisa clutched her coat and walked in the shadow of the others, hoping passers-by would not notice her coal-dusty, slippered feet and housecoat.

Soon they were inside my father's office. My father ushered his sister into an examining room. Uncle Levi and his daughter sat quietly in the outer office. "Are you ready to get married?" Uncle Levi asked.

Lisa blushed and looked at her blackened ankles. "I'm sure I will be when the time comes. I've already embroidered six dish towels and crochet-edged a set of pillowcases."

Uncle Levi cleared his throat and stroked his square jaw. "Well, you better get those pillowcases out of mothballs, because the time is right now."

Lisa's mouth dropped open. "Now?" She blushed furiously. "I can't get married like this!"

Uncle Levi explained about the special blessing in store for Rulon. "You wouldn't want to let him down, would you?"

Aunt Lisa put her hands to her head. Her pigtails were hard and knotty. "No. But Daddy . . ."

Just then my father came into the room. "Ready?" he whispered.

Uncle Levi nodded. Lisa glanced wildly around. "But what about the others? I thought my sister-wives would be here. . . . And Mother! Daddy, what will Mother say?"

Uncle Levi studied the hardwood floor. "We must keep absolute secrecy. Even after the ceremony you must not tell Mother—

or anyone. Too much pressure's been put on us, and there's no telling who to trust. Some people like to talk, and your mother's one of 'em. Come on, girl, it's now or never."

Lisa stood. Her knees trembled. My father took her elbow and Uncle Levi stood before them, reciting the words. Lisa felt she was in a murky dream, the neon from a nearby hotel flashing red as the sacred promises were made.

As soon as my father had said "I do," he strode toward the examining room door without another word. When he put his hand on the knob, Lisa blurted, "Aren't you even going to kiss me?"

My father ducked his head and came back to peck her on the forehead. Aunt Lisa, barely fifteen, was married for time and all eternity.

On May 12, 1945, my father and fourteen other patriarchs entered "the Bug House," as the group called the state prison. A few hours after their incarceration, Church President Grant, who had worked so hard to see his one-time brethren imprisoned, died happy in the accomplishment of his goal.

My father occupied the cell where former Church President Lorenzo Snow had served time for polygamy in the late 1800s. My father confided that while there, "I was able to have the spirit of the Lord with me almost all the time. It was as if President Snow left me not only his example but his courage."

My father grew closer to the other men, to Uncle Levi and Brother Musser in particular. They formed a community distinct from the criminals who surrounded them, yet they were respected, even liked, for their general good spirits and honesty.

They received frequent visits until prison officials prevented them from seeing their plural wives. Thereafter the prisoners' only contact with their plural families was a quick encounter through the fence when they worked in the garden. There they could hope that a touch on their children's faces would be retained by young minds. Some children were never again to see their fathers. Some of the men learned in prison just how high the cost of celestial glory could run and thereafter gave up the Principle and their plural families after the fashion of Heber J. Grant.

On the August day when the first atom bomb exploded in Japan my father worked in the prison fields, ignorant of the earth-shaking news.

Meanwhile, defense attorneys made an appeal to the U.S. Supreme Court. When word came back that the court had refused to review the case, the patriarchs met and developed another strategy. When their cases came up for parole hearing, they presented a notarized draft promising to refrain from advocating, teaching, or solemnizing plural marriages. In interviews many of the men declared their belief in the Principle but vowed not to practice it. They concluded their remarks by expressing their wish that other laws pertaining to public morality could be enforced with equal zeal. The strategy was successful. My father was released December 15, 1945, having spent seven months in the state penitentiary. Although conditions of his parole kept him from living with his plural families, he doctored Danny through a pneumonia crisis and ushered in the hope of Christmastide.

By eavesdropping and asking "too many questions," I learned early of the arrests and my father's imprisonment, but I was ordered not to tell the other children.

"The law has said that Daddy mustn't live with anyone but Aunt Gerda," my mother told me one day when I was questioning her about the arrests and trials. "All you little ones are living proof that he disobeyed. They could put him in jail again."

"But he already went!"

"I know."

"It isn't fair!"

"I know." Then she grasped me by the shoulders. "Listen, Jeannie. You must not tell anyone about these things. If you tell the wrong people, even some of your own brothers and sisters, they might tell someone else. Then the authorities would find out and take you away from me!"

I gasped. "Away from you?"

She nodded. "Do you understand?"

A great black terror grew within me. I nodded very hard.

My mother gazed at me for a long time, her eyes misty. I followed her down the hall to the bedroom. She knelt beside her bed and put her face in her hands. I knew that she was praying.

One Sunday in July of 1953, we packed picnic lunches and headed for a wooded ravine above the city. I rode with my father, who had agreed to transport the younger children while the mothers drove the older ones and babies in two other cars.

Six or seven of us crowded in the cavernous back seat of the Hudson. Since it was Pioneer Day, the 106th anniversary of Brigham Young's announcement from Emigration Point overlooking the Salt Lake valley that "This is the place," we had planned a meeting with my uncles and their families plus other members of the group.

We began to climb the magnificent Alpine Loop of American Fork Canyon, a blue trough of sky above, a close wall of green at either side, the quakies shimmering gold-green like sunlight dancing. Little gullies of snow clung to the north slope and to the shadowed glens, yet brief bright dots of wildflowers gave an air of festive delicacy to the verdant mountainsides. The air tasted crisp and clean as garden lettuce; joy filled the car and spilled out the windows (as the mothers never would have permitted, had they been nearby). Aunt Navida's Serena and I hung out one window; Aunt Lisa's son, Lee, and daughter, Margot, draped themselves over the other. We shouted at the squirrels, chortled at any vehicles edging past us on the narrow highway, and drank the fresh air like spring water.

Suddenly my father shouted for us to be quiet so he could hear. We immediately shut up, for he never raised his voice except when preaching the gospel or lamenting his luck at pinochle.

News crackled over the radio, I listened to the deep throb of the announcer's voice, recognizing the names of some people and the place called Short Creek.

When we reached the site of our mountain meeting, my mother explained to me that the Arizona State Police, in collaboration with Utah and Federal lawmen, had arrested some members of the other group. When the police arrived, they had found all the men, women, and children assembled on the Short Creek schoolhouse steps, pledging allegiance to the flag and singing "America."

"They won't arrest Daddy, will they?" I asked, when she explained that none of the women or children had been taken. My mother turned away then, her face set in a way that frightened me.

That evening, as the sun cast rays like fishnet through the trees, we were startled by a knock at the back door. One of the councilmen burst into the room.

"They're on their way, Rulon!" Brother Cartright cried, "You've got to get out of here."

My father gazed thoughtfully at the rug and did not move. After a moment he spoke. "I won't run from them. The little ones must be hidden. They're the proof we haven't followed the government's damnable orders."

In a flurry my mother dressed me in a nightgown and sweater. We piled into the Hudson with all the small children except Aunt Gerda's Bennie and Heber. I was one of the oldest in the car and was quite taken with my new authority. "Stop crying," I ordered the toddlers. I was so busy being bossy, I didn't have an inkling of fear.

We slept in the Helms' basement, north of the city. The cold dank wall was drafty on the crown of my head, and the place was shadowed with cobwebs. I had never slept in a strange house before. The toddlers whose mothers had stayed at home seemed to cry all night.

Next morning, my father telephoned that it was safe to come home. The raid was over. But our complacency faded all at once when we got home and saw the newspaper. On the front page of *The Salt Lake Tribune* was a picture of Sister Atkin, weeping as a matron led her along. I knew Sister Atkin from our Sunday meetings before the group split.

"Oh no!" my mother breathed. "They've taken her children away!" She turned to Aunt Henni. "I never thought they'd do such a thing!"

As usual I was listening. "Took them away? Where?"

My mother stared down at me, then glanced at Aunt Henni's grim face.

"Might as well tell her," Aunt Henni shrugged. "She's bound to find out anyway."

"They took her nine children away from her and put them in foster homes," my mother said, her eyes reddening as she spoke. "They put each child in a different family, with people they don't even know, so that they couldn't be taught about the Principle! How can they treat people this way just because of what they believe? As if the Principle was hurting them! It isn't right for them to do this to us! It just isn't fair!" She broke into tears and left the room.

Horror reverberated through me. My knees shook back and forth, and my fingers and arms and stomach trembled.

This time my fear did not go away. For days I didn't leave my mother's side. Everywhere she went, I was close on her heels, compelled to follow her to the basement—which I hated for the black-widow spiders Danny had shown me, tangling sticky disordered webs in the windows of the washroom—and up the stairs again with loads of laundry, me stumbling to get ahead of her so that an FBI agent or stern-faced matron would not nab me from the shadows that loomed behind. When my mother went into the bathroom I waited outside with my back pressed against the door, watching for intruders, until each creak of the house became a warning and I cried for her to let me in. When she lay down for a nap, I would not let her sleep, afraid they would kidnap me without her knowledge and I would be gone forever. Sometimes she crept into the linen closet, saying, "I have to get some sheets. I'll just be a minute." Then she closed the door and through the keyhole I overheard the soft sounds of her weeping.

The days of the "scare" waned, and my little brother, Stephen, was born. Then came my mother's illness, her tears descending on our household like a flood, her depressions a pall on our relief at escaping the roundup. Every other day she accompanied my father and Aunt Henni to the office, where her massages and injections, her treatments on the diathermyl or vibrator machines, her steam baths and spells under the ultraviolet lamp lasted all morning.

My mother seemed to fade like overwashed jeans. She had lost weight, her face was pale, and her fingers shook so that it was hard for her to practice when she forced herself to sit at the piano.

One morning, as I hovered near the bathroom door watching my mother clean the bathtub, she suddenly stood up and shrieked. Then she ran into the hall, scratching furiously at her fingers.

"This eczema! It itches so!" She began to cry, digging at the running sores that had broken out on her hands and spread up her arms. She paced into the kitchen, to the window, down the hall, then whirled and went back, her movements frenetic. She rubbed her arms, then hugged herself and moaned.

"These nerves. They crawl. Why do they crawl?" She turned her tormented face to me. "Look. Look, you can see them crawl."

She held her arms out for me to see. I could see the weeping sores, but I couldn't see them crawl.

"Little worms. Little snakes. Wiggling all day long. How can I stand it?"

Little Stephen began to cry in the bedroom.

"Oh, no! What have I done now?" She burst open the bedroom door. The baby stopped crying and stared, wide-eyed. She huddled beside the crib, clawing at her wrists, whimpering, "Please stop itching." Then she was silent, holding her head between her hands and shaking all over.

I stared, heart and breath suspended. Then I ran as fast as I could down the hall, out the door, and across the yard to get Aunt Sarah. When we returned, my mother still huddled beside the crib, weeping. The baby was fast asleep.

"My nerves . . . ," she murmured, staring at her hands. She wouldn't look up. Aunt Sarah went to the phone and called my father's office. Her voice was soft but firm.

"We've got to do something for Hannah. This isn't fair to her and it isn't fair to the children."

Then she came back to my mother and put an arm around her, drawing her to her feet and leading her to the kitchen.

"Sit down, Hannah. You and I are going to have a good visit. You know, Rulon ought to swallow his pride and get you some help. Even if it means going to another doctor. Both Henni and I have told him so."

And so began my mother's visits to one doctor after another: vitaminologists, neurosurgeons, internists, acupuncturists. But her illness did not diminish, not until some years later when we were safely anonymous and temporarily beyond the sweeping arms of the Church and the law.

The March following the onset of my mother's illness, Stephen's birth, and Grandmother Allred's death, I woke up one Sunday morning to hear the Mormon Tabernacle Choir warbling from the oversize brown radio, "All is well, All is well!"

An early morning priesthood meeting was underway in our living room. I heard the rumble of voices and crept out of bed, tiptoeing down the long hall. I listened and watched from a door crack, where the men could not see me. Two of my father's younger brothers sat together, near-replicas of him: Uncle Andrew almost as tall and fervent, Uncle Lawrence almost as handsome and gentle. Other men filled the room: Brother Trent, with his balding head, black moustache, and shadows along his cheekbones, reminded me of a modern Wyatt Earp. Brother Bigler was an imposing man whose heavy body repelled thoughts of a Principle so demanding to the spirit, yet his devotion was as weighty. Brother Sampere, with his mischievous twinkle and good looks, could pound the pulpit louder than my father. Brother Cartright, with drawling cowboy charm and what my father called "maverick notions," sat in a hardback chair keeping lookout by the window. The last member of the quorum, Brother Duckworth sat with head bent, lips pouting, and knee pumping like a piston.

Singly, each of the men was warm and personable, smiling and hugging their way through the crowd, stopping to pat me on the head or lift me up and kiss a cheek. But as a body—lined up on the blue sofa of the meeting hall or massed, as now, in a single room—this group of men who stood together outside the law radiated undeniable power and influence.

Usually the men spoke of "the Other Side" and "the City of Enoch," or my father brought up group problems. But today Brother Cartright took the floor. Threats of another raid circulated, directed this time at my father's group and my father's family in particular.

My father spent most of the morning in meetings behind closed doors. The mothers moved red-eyed and quiet through dinner preparations. Sunday school felt empty without the men, the hymns sung like dirges, the prayers mournfully long.

The day passed in a haze of worry, until my father got a call from a sympathetic policeman who confirmed that another polygamist roundup was in progress. He explained that all children born since my father's prison term must be taken beyond the borders of the nation, for we were proof of his broken agreement with the state. We had only hours to get away.

After dark we loaded some clothing and a hamper of food into the big green Hudson. When I had bathed and dressed in my nightgown, my mother sent me downstairs to kiss my brothers good-bye.

Aunt Henni led me to the car, weeping silently. My fear mounted, for Aunt Henni was the one who didn't cry—as though my mother had taken all the tears and Aunt Henni all the strength.

Serena and Hugh, both near my age, were already in the car, crying. At the sight of them, my control vanished, and I began to sob.

Then Aunt Sarah came out with four-year-old Laurine in her arms. "Now kids," she said, her voice strong and sure, "you're just going away for a little while. Do you even know where you're going?"

I shook my head. "You're going to Mexico, where the Indians—the Lamanites—live. You'll see all sorts of strange, lovely things. A big orange moon three times the size of this one. And beautiful flowers. And when you've seen everything, you can come home."

Aunt Sarah reached into her apron pocket and took out a small cellophane bag of peppermint drops. She gave each of us two of them. "Here now, one peppermint drop for you and one for the special friend you'll find in Mexico."

"What if we don't find anyone special?" Hugh hiccupped. "Can we eat the other one too?"

"You'll find lots of special people in Mexico. You'll stay with Brother Goldstein and his family; he has lots of little children. And remember, Mexico is the place where Nephi and his brothers first landed when they settled on the new continent. You know, Jeannie—in *The Book of Mormon?* Now I want you to play a game with me. Let's make a list of all the things they had to bring with them on the boat, OK? Laurine, you start."

Our list grew long and our eyes grew heavy. One by one we snuggled against the plush and drifted into sleep.

I woke with a start in the cool predawn. An orange moon glowed like an oversized street lamp, throwing soft light across the bodies that curled kitten-like around me. I sat up very slowly. There was Aunt Henni driving and my mother beside her, holding little Stephen. In my father's other car, several yards behind us, traveled Aunt Lisa, Aunt Rachel, and their children. Although I could scarcely feel the motion of our car, we skimmed the highway at great speed. The land was flat and empty except for cacti, which jutted from the earth like totem poles, and the horizon fenced with mesas.

Next morning we raced the sun down the highway until evening, when we reached El Paso, where we planned to cross into Mexico. Aunt Henni warned us well ahead of time that there would be a checkpoint at the border. We were to keep our mouths shut.

"With the Federal authorities involved, the border patrol might be looking for us," Aunt Henni said. Her voice was grim.

As long as we were moving down the road, I had felt safe. Now I worried that the border guards would arrest the mothers and put us children in foster homes. After a fitful night in a dingy El Paso motel, Aunt Henni decided to push onward and enter Mexico at Laredo.

"Too many polygamists have already crossed at Juarez; it's the way to the colonies. Besides, you remember how terrible those

Mexico roads are, Hannah. We'll do better if we stay in the States as long as possible." She sighed. "I don't think I could endure an ordeal like last time."

I remembered the vague references to Mexico throughout my younger years, and I suddenly understood the origin of my parents' conversations in Spanish when they didn't want me to understand.

"We went there with Navida, Lisa, and Rachel in Forty-seven because your Daddy was on parole and we only got to see him for a few hours on weekends," my mother reminisced. "We brought all the children, of course, except Tyrone, who was a tiny baby in Aunt Gerda's arms back in Salt Lake City. She stayed to work, because the family had to have some kind of income. When Dayer LeBaron wrote to your father and told him to bring his plural families and live on the ranch at Los Parceles, your Daddy jumped at the chance, even though he also had to jump parole. A few weeks later he telegraphed that we should join him, that he was ready to receive his family in Mexico. We packed some clothes and bedding into Brother Pedderson's car. That's Aunt Navida's brother, remember?"

She told me that he had driven them to the border. They had hitched a ride south to barren Los Parceles—the Parcels.

There, in a little adobe set in the middle of nowhere, was Maud LeBaron, who directed them a mile down the road to a big tent, where they found my father. When they entered the tent, which had nothing but a pick and shovel propped against the center pole, he spread his arms out as though it was a mansion and shouted, "Welcome home!" Aunt Henni had wept, saying, "I can't live here."

The campsite crawled with rattlesnakes, spiders, and scorpions. Once one of the women came into the tent and found a rattlesnake coiled on top of her sewing basket. Another time, instead of going right to bed in the darkened tent, Aunt Navida lit a candle to read some scripture. Sitting on her white pillowcase was a huge tarantula.

Aunt Navida gave birth to Tommy while they lived in the tents, and Aunt Lisa had her first baby in a new adobe house the men had built with their own hands. Right after the family moved into the adobe, one of the seven LeBaron sons encouraged Saul to ride their bronco, Diamond. Saul was bucked off, and the horse kicked him in the face, breaking collarbone and jaw and scattering his seed teeth, so that they came in helter-skelter and kept Saul from smiling until he was twenty-four and could pay for orthodontics. My father was away when it happened—preaching the gospel to the Mexicans, my mother said. Saul was unconscious for hours, but when my father returned, he unperturbably promised my mother that Saul would get well and proceeded to administer to him. Saul came to immediately after the blessing.

Some of the family contended that the LeBarons had meant for Saul to be hurt, that Diamond couldn't be ridden by anyone. True, some of the LeBaron men walked about casting dark looks and grumbling threats. But Joel let the children help him in the vegetable garden, patiently teaching them the secrets of his green thumb. Their mother, Maud LeBaron, shared everything she had and lamented that she hadn't more to give. Her two daughters, Esther and Lucinda, prevailed on my mother to give them piano lessons. Esther showed great talent and determination (one day she would become a virtuoso), but Lucinda, despite a gift for music, suffered periods of irrationality. Sometimes she was uncontainable, and her brothers kept her in the bedroom or tied her in the goat pen where she sat in the hot sun. They seemed oblivious to her thirst and discomfort. Aunt Henni said it was probably Ben's idea to tie her in the goat pen.

"The Lord has His own justice. Ben's strait-jacketed in the Arizona state mental hospital himself right now. 'Do unto others as you'd be done by.' " After letting the Golden Rule sink in, Aunt Henni commented, "Your father says insanity runs in the family. Dayer always said the madness came from Maud's side, and Maud said it came from Dayer's. I'd say there's a good argument for Dayer's side, based on his claim to be the one who holds the keys to the priesthood. He says he's the only one on earth who can seal plural marriages or head the Church, and that he got his authority from his mother's father who was somehow related to the Prophet Joseph Smith. As if the priesthood presidency was passed along like the divine right of kings!" Aunt Henni snorted. "Ben is Dayer's oldest. He got his queer notions from his father. The LeBarons didn't like Rulon having so much influence with the Lamanites. I remember once when Ben was haranguing Rulon. 'Don't you know I hold the keys to the priesthood?' Ben would rant, and usually Rulon just ignored him. But this once Rulon retorted, 'Why, you've no more priesthood than that mesquite bush over there.' That shut Ben up." Aunt Henni tilted her chin in a tight smile.

— 88

"The only thing I remember about Ben was the last time the LeBarons came to our meetings in Salt Lake," my mother added. "Ervil—he's Maud's fifth son—was complimenting me on my playing, when Ben came up to him, growling. And I do mean growling. He slugged Ervil and said, 'A man of the priesthood ain't supposed to talk to women!' Ervil shrugged like there wasn't anything he could do and let Ben pull him away. And then Ben turned back and roared, 'I am the Lion of Judea!' Imagine! I had to cover my mouth to keep from laughing."

"It's a good thing you didn't," Aunt Henni said. "No telling what he'd have done. Fanatics like that are what give a bad name to all our people."

I stared out the window at the darkened desert, picturing Ben LeBaron as being like Cain or Esau in the Bible stories book— bearded and hairy chested, with a club and fierce black eyes.

I was relieved to find that we were headed not to where the LeBarons lived but to Monterrey. If only we could get across the border without trouble. When at last we rolled into the border station outside Laredo, my heart thundered in my ears.

But the guard was friendly. He motioned at Serena, Laurine, and me. "Triplets'?" he asked. A nervous shimmer passed through the car as the mothers smiled and laughed, managing somehow to avoid answering.

He confiscated our oranges but at the last second handed back one for each of us. "To keep you until lunch." He smiled, teeth bright against his dark face. "*Vaya con Dios*."

The Mexican highways, paved only occasionally, led past shacks that dotted the countryside, surrounded by animals and people seeking shade from the blistering noonday sun.

"Why do the kids run around naked?" I asked, envying their bareness.

"Because they have nothing to wear," my mother said, a hand trailing against the side of her face. The wistful, bleak expression of her illness appeared like a shadow. "And I thought *we* were poor," she murmured.

"If nothing else, maybe this trip will help us count our blessings," Aunt Henni stated firmly.

There was no middle class in Monterrey, and we would stay in the richer part of town with a friend of my father, a man who was just beginning to live the Principle. Although he was only moderately successful by American standards, in Monterrey he was wealthy. Just as I had never seen such poverty, neither had I known that such wealth existed for ordinary people. Statues and figurines adorned the grounds and exterior of the three-story white stucco house with red trim where we would live for the coming month. Inside, a huge marble staircase led to seven or eight bedrooms, and another broadened into a living area on the ground floor, with fish pond and dining hall, the kitchen backed by servants' quarters. I wandered through the house, pretending to be a movie star, but it wasn't fun; I kept thinking of the hungry children and their glassy eyes.

My mother helped me write notes to my father. At first I didn't want to write; even his memory sent jets of pain into my left arm and through my heart, leaving me with a distracted, half-realized feeling of having lost something without knowing what. Then I pretended I was really talking to him, cradled on his knee, and I began to enjoy our note-writing sessions, me dictating as my mother printed hurriedly on the page to give the impression I had written it myself.

"Why do you write 'I'?" I wanted to know. "Daddy starts with D."

She cleared her throat. "Well, uh, we've each taken one of the vowels for our mail-name. I'm U, Henni is E, and your father is I. We do that so the authorities can't use our letters in court. It worked fine in the old days, but now there are more of us than there are vowels. Sometime soon we'll have to invent a new system, with real names this time."

When we had been in Mexico about a week, I ventured outside and peered over the hedge. Aunt Lisa said that we shouldn't talk to the neighbors at all.

"Why not?" I asked my mother. She was silent for awhile. Finally, she said, "According to scripture, dark skin is a curse for doing evil."

I watched the Mexican children, remembering the *Book of Mormon* story about the rebellious people called Lamanites who were cursed with a dark skin so that the light-skinned people, "the children of God," would not be attracted to them. Would the Lord who heard my prayers put a curse on little children? I thought of the Mexican children, how happy and clean the rich ones seemed. Only the poor children seemed filthy, the way the story had said.

The moon was waxing full again when the city ran out of water. To make matters worse, the babies had dysentery. Diapers piled up in each of the three luxurious bathrooms, so even the sweet gardenias blooming around the stucco mansion couldn't camouflage the stench.

Each day the babies grew weaker, more diarrhetic. In one week my little brother Stephen, now nine months old, became as spindly as the day he was born. His skin sallowed, and his cry was pitifully weak.

We bought water as long as jugs of it were available, and when that was gone, we bought Seven-Up to drink. In Salt Lake, soda pop was a rare treat, but after two days of drinking nothing else, of tasting it in our food and dabbing it on our lips, I hated the sticky sweetness. At last, when we learned that the entire province was out of water and when my baby brother's temperature reached 104, Aunt Henni called my father.

He arrived three days later, weary but smiling, and, we could tell, very glad to see us. He had driven straight through, stopping only to nap for an hour or two on the roadside.

"I'm taking you girls home," he declared as he came through the front entrance, stooping to miss the doorframe.

The mothers ran to him and clustered in the circle of his arms, weeping with relief.

"Is it safe?" they asked him, although no one really cared at that point.

"It will have to be safe, won't it? The Lord will prepare a way for us, dear ones. I'm taking the twins back with me; Rachel and Lisa can follow in due course. I need Henni to help me out in the office—and I want my family together again."

My father examined the babies, did what he could for them, then slept for four hours. When he awoke, the mothers had packed and loaded both cars. We left Monterrey at dusk, and I was so happy that I didn't mind the burning in my stomach that my mother warned was the beginning of dysentery. I stopped worrying about my baby brother and the other children who had been throwing up everything they ate. My father was with us; he could cure any sickness. Aunt Henni followed us, driving the Hudson. I remembered that she said that on their last return from Mexico, my father was sent to prison for thirty days because he broke parole. The jail was so crowded, they put him on Death Row.

"Will they send you to jail when we go home, Daddy?" I asked.

My father laughed, his gold teeth flashing in the dusk. "Not a chance, Princess. The Lord is on our side!" My mother smiled and snuggled against him. The baby slept on her lap. I had the whole back of my father's station wagon and my parents to myself. As we scaled the hills overlooking Monterrey, my father began to sing, smiling over his shoulder at me as his nasal tenor filled the car:

"Vaya con Dios, my darling. Vaya con Dios, my love."

My mother harmonized with him, and I felt tears push into the corners of my eyes. I watched the gigantic orange moon as it sat, seeming suspended on the horizon. At last it slipped skyward, like an overripe dream. For a moment I buried my face in my father's hair, then turned back to the window.

"Good-bye, Mexico," I whispered. "I'm going home."

One day, while swinging on the rope from the hayloft, I saw a battered blue pickup truck storm down the driveway. Somehow I knew it was the LeBarons'; my father had said they were in town. A shiver of curiosity traversed my spine and I walked to the barn door, gaping, as the truck crunched to a stop.

As usual when someone came to visit, the whole family erupted from the house, spilling from doors into the graveled yard. The children stopped about twenty feet away and stared as the two LeBaron men got out of their truck and fiercely slammed their doors. Then they strode to the back end of the truck and sat on the gravel, leaning against the flopped-down tailgate.

Aunt Gerda hurried out the back door of the white house, letting the screen door crack the silence. Aunt Lisa gasped and locked the screen, while Aunt Gerda marched directly toward the men, seeming in control of the situation, as usual. But I noticed that she halted a good ten feet away from them.

"Hello, Ben. Hello, Ervil. How are you boys?"

The two men didn't even glance at her. Aunt Gerda waited, hand on hip. She wasn't used to being ignored.

"Well, what do you want?"

Ben picked up a handful of gravel and put it in his mouth. He began to spit pebbles out, aiming at the house. Ervil did the same, but he put the pebbles in one at a time so that he could spit them a lot farther. Then he began to throw them. Some of the rocks hit the window.

Aunt Gerda retreated. "Call Rulon," she ordered Aunt Lisa.

I couldn't stop staring at the two men. I had never seen a grown man put rocks in his mouth. I moved a little closer to the truck, wanting to see their faces more clearly. Ben saw me and spit all his pebbles into his hand. Drool seeped through his fingers. I shrank against Danny. Then the two men stretched out on the gravel and began doing push-ups. Danny whispered that they were trying to prove how strong they were. "They want us to say they are the heads of the priesthood. But we know Daddy is the one."

Soon my father's car appeared in the lane. Once parked, he jumped out, smiling, and with his hand outstretched halfway across the yard.

"Well! How are you, brethren? Brother Ben. Brother Ervil. What can I do for you?"

The family's tension disappeared like spring snow into the gravel, and the mothers clustered together, whispering and clucking tongues. The two LeBarons stood silently before my father, hands in pockets, watching their feet shuffle pebbles.

My father turned to us. "Go on inside," he called with a wave of his hand.

The others went away, but I hid behind the pump. I heard the LeBarons speaking urgently, angrily, to my father. I hadn't heard anyone speak to my father in that tone since the meeting when Brother Musser declared him head of the council.

"I'm sorry, gentlemen," my father said. "We all have to do what we see is right between ourselves and the Lord. It would be good if we could just accept our differences and stay on friendly terms."

"You'll pay for this," Ben growled. "No man can deny my power. I have the Mantle of Joseph."

He and Ervil jumped in their truck and drove furiously out of the yard, screeching onto the highway.

I stood and ran to my father. "Daddy, Daddy!"

"You should be in the house," he said.

"What did they want, Daddy?"

He sighed. "What they always want. To interfere with the Lord's work. To exercise their nonexistent power."

"Why did they talk so mean, Daddy?"

He shook his head. "Because they have no true priesthood. They struggle with Satan every day, and he will gradually take them over."

"But we don't have to worry, right, Daddy?"

He squinted at me in the bright light. The way his brow furrowed, I thought he must have a headache. Then suddenly he broke into a wide grin and picked me up. "One thing's for certain, darling. *You* don't need to worry about it."

I started kindergarten in May, certain that I would love school. Most of my brothers and sisters had excelled there, competing for the top place in class; I expected to follow in their footsteps.

But I had not yet learned about the state of Zion, how the members of the Church of Jesus Christ were not always so Christian to those who weren't of them. And we fundamentalists were an embarrassment, like poor relatives or uninvited guests at a wedding, a reminder of a past that the Mormon Church preferred to keep buried.

The start of school induced my first realization that beyond our fence, our group, I was considered illegitimate. I had no birth certificate to present to the principal as proof that I had been born. And my mother had no marriage certificate like Aunt Gerda's to back up my presence on earth. No one seemed concerned about these two missing documents but me.

"In God's eyes we are legal, and that's what counts, darling," my mother reassured me.

But I could not be so certain.

On the first day of school I discovered that the teachers knew all about my family. Despite the fact that Bennie and I each were registered by a different mother and that we sat at opposite ends of the semicircle of chairs, the teacher commented nasally, "Two Allreds. How nice. And are you related?"

"Cousins," we answered in unison, as coached.

The teacher raised an eyebrow. "Oh. Is that what you call each other?" Her voice was biting.

Bennie and I glanced at each other, then quickly looked at our shoes.

The next day Marilyn Brownlee snubbed me. The day before we had played together and decided to be best friends. She was a tall girl with lovely red hair and a manner that I later called aristocratic. Marilyn had gone to her good Mormon home with stories about the little Allred girl who was to be her friend forever. But her older brothers and sisters knew too much about us. The oldest Allred boys had been in their classes, and everybody knew how their parents lived. No matter how nice the Allreds *acted*, they told Marilyn, the way the Allreds *lived* wasn't nice.

"So I can't play with you," Marilyn told me haughtily and walked toward another girl on the playground. I stood feeling I'd been slugged in the stomach, staring at the quills of sunlight that bounced off the slide until I could pretend its brilliance made my eyes water. And I waited until we had spread our rugs and settled for our naps before I let tears flow down the sides of my face and puddle in my ears.

My father had always talked about the official Mormon Church as though it was our church—the One True Church on the face of the earth, he said, although it was currently out of order. When "the One Mighty and Strong" came to set the Church in order, we would be welcomed with the other saints to go through the temple gates.

But after he returned from Mexico, my father spoke about the Church in an impassioned and tearful way, as though damming some huge wave of hurt inside him. He said that our group must never think of itself as being apart from the official Church, even though they reviled us and plotted against us. He spoke of the Church scriptures and pointed to our common background.

"These records and doctrines have ushered in the Last Dispensation of Time," he said at one home evening in the white house parlor. "This is the final chapter of the earth as we know it." He spoke words like "apocalypse" and "millennium" and "fullness of time." He often seemed sad and tired, and I wondered if this was "fullness of time." Time was something else for me in those days: a long, untrammeled corridor with high, domed windows, waiting for my exploration.

But my father's eyes deepened sadly, his forehead lined as though he foresaw no future, or perhaps the worst possible future. He spoke of the "Last Days" and of the moon turning red and of the streets of Zion flooding with blood.

"These things will take place within your lifetime," he told us children. "They will happen before your eyes."

My stomach quivered and the room slanted strangely.

He spoke of terrible earthquakes and wars and famine. "The only way you can survive the oppression of corrupt governments and the betrayal of your fellowman is to have the Lord with you. Only those in the holy places will be saved."

Where are the holy places, I wondered, and felt a huge steel fist clenching around me, cutting off my breath.

And then my father spoke again of the martyrdom of Joseph Smith, of how he had been hounded, tarred and feathered, imprisoned, and finally assassinated.

"The faces of the mob were blackened. They blasphemed and threw rocks at the Prophet's cell. Then bullets broke glass and pierced the walls." My father's face was suffused, lips quivering. "There was pounding at the door, and shots. The Prophet leapt to the window and stood there, defying evil. And they shot him from every side. 'Lord, my God!' he cried, and fell to his death."

The room echoed silence as my father put thumb and forefinger to his eyes and rubbed violently. Although he had accepted the deaths of his father and mother and of little Marie with such serenity, the martyrdom of Joseph Smith always turned his eyes sapphire bright with tears.

I remembered that my father had nearly died in the winter of 1953, following the raid on Short Creek and ensuing rumors of another roundup. His ulcers flared and grew worse daily, until they hemorrhaged on Christmas Eve. We somberly crossed the yard to Aunt Sarah's cottage, where we stood around the bed to "kiss him good-bye." No one expected him to live till Christmas morning.

Late that night the council had come and formed a prayer circle. My father said he had felt the bleeding stop as they prayed. The next morning he was pale but smiling as we brought him our small gifts or an offering of nuts and candy from our stockings, which he placed in a box beside him "for later."

And so, as he spoke of the death of Joseph Smith, I thought of him, bleeding "from worry" as my mother said—worry that the authorities would swoop down and disassemble his family with their barrage of laws and social services. And the meaning became increasingly clear to me: God's chosen should expect to suffer, to carry a cross, to pay for each blessing with a measure of misery, to give up family, security, and even life to the Lord. Persecution was pain, and it lay ahead of me somewhere, ready to enfold me at some undisclosed moment.

Yet this threat emerging from my father's words had the effect of sharpening life: the outline of trees was more distinct, the mountains more rugged, the pucker of lemon more sour. It seemed to force the flow of time into a higher pitch, a quicker pace, so that sitting in the parlor at my father's feet became an adventure, an experience as total as my first dip in the cold artesian waters of our swimming hole.

Just before Independence Day, 1955, my father received a call from our sympathetic policeman, Captain York. Within the week, another raid would be launched. With the Church's spies in our group and our houses under surveillance, they'd have no difficulty arresting my father and perhaps the mothers too. The general plan was to disperse the children to foster homes throughout the state, to put us in typical Mormon homes where official doctrines prevailed, to keep us separated, so that the Principle could be erased from our minds and the life-style stamped out forever.

"You know, polygamy will always be illegal in Utah," Captain York had told my father. "The conditions under which statehood was granted stipulated that the Utah State Constitution outlaw the Principle forever. You'll never be at home in Zion."

My father began making long-distance phone calls to friends and relatives who might help us relocate.

My uncle brought his hay truck over, and when my brothers returned from the spinach fields at noon, my mother hurried to meet them.

"We've been warned of another raid. We've got to move—today."

The boys looked at her dazedly. Then they turned toward the house and moved mechanically throughout the afternoon, loading the table, chairs, mattresses, and sofa. On top of these they loaded clothing and dishes and bottled fruit. We would have to leave many things behind—my mother's piano, the mahogany buffet, the bedsteads, and my kitten.

I had assumed that we would all be going together, following each other into Mexico or Canada, where polygamists had taken refuge in the days of the manifesto. When we were finally packed and the loads tied with bristly ropes from the barn, the other mothers and brothers and sisters crowded around our truck to kiss me good-bye.

"What's happening?" I said, trying to smile, but tears jumped into my eyes, and I must have understood even before I was told that each of the families would head in a different direction (except my mother and Aunt Henni, who would go West together). This would minimize the chance of anyone being followed and captured by the police. A sudden swelling filled my chest, as though I had been caught by a gust of wind and thrown into the sky; my heart pounded in my ears, and I couldn't hear what people said. Then my father was kissing me, holding me tight until I felt my ribs would break, and my heart with them.

"Good-bye, my Princess." Something like a sob stifled his voice, and he set me in the truck beside Saul. We followed Aunt Henni in the green Hudson, past the grapevines and pear trees, past the sentries of pine and poplar, past the chain-link fence. As we crossed the threshold onto the highway, the truck lurched, and my lip struck the dashboard. The pain gave relief from the ache in my chest, gave me an excuse to cry. I set my head against Saul's shoulder and wept until we were far down the road and home was out of sight. Our lives were never to be the same again.

Chapter

6

We arrived in Mountain City, Nevada, after midnight, driving beyond the tiny village and some distance down a bumpy road. A dog barked and a coyote howled in answer as we stepped out of the truck, and a shiver of presentiment traced my spine.

For two months we would stay in some long-abandoned miners' quarters. Above us the wheels and chains of the silver mine rusted, and its buildings were besieged by sagebrush. The tin bunkhouse was a huge square oven at noonday and a refrigerator at night. Belladonna grew around the privy, twining its slats, and black-widow spiders spun webs beneath the wooden seat.

In mid-July a letter came from Aunt Sarah, reporting on the other families. My father and she had stayed together one night longer than the rest, bidding good-bye to the white house grounds. The next morning, "Aunt" Bertha, a woman in the group, arrived to keep house for my father so that he could maintain his practice and keep money coming in until the last possible moment. Aunt Sarah regretfully drove away with her four children, heading for Blackfoot, Idaho, where she would stay with my father's sister. Bertha was most willing in her labors for my father. (Later, after many lonely widowed years, she would join his family.) One morning the police presented her with a summons for my father. She ignored the summons and refused to let them search the house without a warrant. As soon as they had gone for the necessary papers, my father sneaked out of the bedroom and hid on the gritty floorboards of the car while Bertha drove him outside the county. He dropped her off at a bus depot and left the state.

Meanwhile Aunt Gerda and Aunt Rachel settled in Idaho. Aunt Gerda found work immediately and instructed Aunt Rachel to stay with the children. Two weeks later Aunt Gerda went out on her lunch break and met Aunt Navida, who was supposed to be in Rock

Springs, Wyoming. Aunt Navida, unable to find housing or employment, had come to Idaho, thinking it a good place to remain anonymous. She settled there with Aunt Lisa, who would care for the children.

Aunt Sarah came to the same Idaho city to find a job. When she found four other Allred families had coincidentally invaded the city, she planned to join us in Nevada.

We were delighted, for we missed Aunt Sarah's good humor and her children. But Aunt Sarah wrote bad news as well, of another split in the group. As soon as my father left Salt Lake, Brother Duckworth had challenged his authority and broken away, taking some of our people with him. One of the defectors was Dean Brady, Saul's former Boy Scout master, the man who had nurtured Saul's respect for himself and his understanding of nature.

Saul, deeply upset by the split, went walking down the dusty dirt road in the mornings before it was too hot, talking with my mother. The fissure unearthed other, older questions, ones my father had reprimanded him for asking. Why, he asked my mother, did everyone else have a testimony that *The Book of Mormon* was divinely inspired and that Joseph Smith was a true prophet of God, while he had no such knowledge? How, he wanted to know, could he be sure that my father was right in his priesthood calling? Where, he asked her, could he find such assurance?

My mother quoted the same Bible passage that had inspired young Joseph Smith to pray in a secret grove, the site of his first vision. "If any of you lack wisdom, let him ask of God. . . ."

One morning Saul disappeared before daybreak. Later we saw him descend the east hill above the silver mine. In quiet tones he told my mother he had asked for a sign, some indication that he should trust in Joseph Smith and in our father.

"Nothing happened, Mama," he said, his face pinched, his eyes dark and burning.

In the days afterward Saul spent a lot of time whittling or walking alone. His sense of humor, a wry wit reminiscent of my father's lightheartedness, disappeared for a time. No one, not even my mother, would look into the dark fiery whirlpools of his eyes for very long.

Just before Aunt Sarah was to arrive, Saul and Isaac got work as ranchhands twenty miles away, working from sunup to sundown and sleeping in the bunkhouse with seasoned ranchworkers—coarse, weatherbitten men with salty tongues and stories that exploited the sixteen-year-olds' naiveté.

About this time, I began to dream nightly about wolves. They came at me through the sagebrush and stood off, watching as I scrambled up the high wooden step of our tin shack. Their teeth dripped, their mouths foamed, and their eyes mocked me. They never snarled or howled but moved steadily upon me in the terrible silence of my dreams.

In September we moved sixty miles to a larger Nevada town, rimmed with sagebrush and blotched with bright casinos. There, Isaac and Saul could receive a passable high school education, and those of us who were able could get work. The only work my father had found that would protect his identity was as caretaker of a large estate in Idaho. Aunt Gerda's son, Tyrone, barely eight, told the phone company what their father did for a living, and it was printed this way in the next directory: R. C. Allred—Grasscutter.

Unlike Mountain City, where people had been uniformly poor and uniformly ignorant, our new town had its social strata: a trailer village, cheap saloons, and red-light houses on the wrong side of the tracks and "respectable" folks in modest homes on the right side, where we lived. Above us, on the bluffs at either side of the Indian Reservation, lived casino owners, doctors, and lawyers in their sprawling mansions.

The mothers worked out stories for us to tell the townsfolk— Aunt Henni's children implying that their parents were divorced, Aunt Sarah and children saying they were "separated," and my mother stating that her husband was a traveling salesman.

"Just let them think what they want to," Aunt Henni said.

"And we *are* separated—most of the time," Aunt Sarah reasoned.

"My husband certainly does travel," declared my mother. "And he's been known to sell a bushel of peaches now and then."

More Mormon logic. Even now I cannot gauge whether the people of the town actually believed us when we explained our family circumstances. Such an influx of Allreds must have inspired notice, for our town was like most small communities in its capacity for gossip.

Entering school was an ordeal, for the mothers had to work out different paternal names for the school record: "J. Allred" for

Aunt Sarah's brood; "R. Clark Allred" for Aunt Henni's; and "Rulon Allred" for my mother's children. With our fair skin we shared a tendency to blush, so lying brought on an infusion that my classmates noticed right off. After a time I couldn't decide which made me more uncomfortable, the lying or the blushing.

My mother sent out word to local music teachers that she was available to assist them with their piano students. Isaac and Saul each found part-time work in service stations. Amanda got an after-school job at the local Dairy Queen, Jake established himself in a paper route, and Danny sold *The Daily Free Press* downtown.

Aunt Henni waitressed in a casino coffee shop, leaving at four-thirty in the morning, driving the Hudson when it would start but more often trudging through the dark streets, passing drunks as they stumbled back to the reservation, trembling as the wind stirred dead leaves behind her.

When she came home in the afternoon, she sat at the dining table, propped her swollen feet on a chair, and emptied her apron pocket. My mother and I stood by to watch her count her tips, for this was our food and utilities; Aunt Henni's salary barely covered the rent.

Sometimes Aunt Henni let me stack the dimes, nickels, quarters, and half-dollars for her, and she taught me to count change. But more often, she was exhausted to the point of irritation. Why were we so messy, making our poor mother do our work for us? Why couldn't we be quieter? Didn't we know how hard grown-ups worked? And with all she had to worry about—she didn't know how we would ever make ends meet—hadn't she earned some peace?

Aunt Henni tried to provide a firm hand in our household, but my father's absence was keenly felt. My brothers stayed out too late. Moreover, they balked at turning their earnings over to Aunt Henni.

"Look here," Aunt Henni exploded, having walked to and from work because of the empty gas tank. "Amanda and Isaac always put gas in the car. Why can't you kids? What makes you so good you don't have to contribute to the family welfare?"

My mother went about her housework, head bowed, eyes red. I knew she anguished over Aunt Henni's having to provide for us. "I'm grateful for all she does," I had heard her say, more than once, "but I hate to impose."

When we went off alone into her bedroom to read or talk, my mother looked at us searchingly. "What gets into you kids?" she asked. Neither she nor Aunt Henni could understand why we weren't naturally good, as they had always been.

One by one we presented our side of the situation. "It isn't fair to make us give up everything we work for," one of the boys said. "People have to have rewards."

"She doesn't like taking care of us, Mama," I added.

My mother sighed. "I wish your father were here. He would know what to do."

But when my father came, she said nothing to trouble him. During the first year he visited only once every three or four months. He parked outside town and waited until dark, then rolled slowly into town, so as not to arouse the lone patrolman, and parked near a casino. He walked in the shadows of trees, then came through the back door, shushing us until the door was closed and the living room drapes drawn. In those seconds he seemed almost a stranger to me, skulking in the dark like a burglar. Could this be the same father who stood before a thousand people and thundered scripture? But when the lights were switched on, he was standing erect, holding out his arms so that when we went to him, he seemed to engulf all nine of us at once. And our little house was filled with light for another quarter year.

After the first year he established a routine, visiting us once a month. In the beginning we anticipated his weekend visits with the same relish as Christmas or Easter. Thursday was terribly slow and Friday crawled. My mother rescheduled her Friday piano lessons and scurried to give the furniture an extra shine and wax the floor. When Aunt Henni came home from work, she bathed instead of plopping into a chair, exhausted. The boys cut ball practice, and Amanda changed her dress. When we sat down for supper, the house was vivid with excitement. The boys told jokes, and we chattered and sang as we cleared away the dishes. And then we sat, waiting.

Sometime between eight and midnight he came, sneaking up the basement steps, whistling under his breath. I sat at the kitchen table so that I could see him first, shouting out, "Daddy's here!" as though I had sighted land.

Always he brought something for us: cheese or margarine, honey or powdered milk, a bushel of fruit or a bag of potatoes—most of it donated by friends or family members. With the car unloaded, he sat at the kitchen table eating the supper my mother kept warm, and we clustered around him, darting questions answered between mouthfuls, hearing his news of the other families.

I watched him change from one visit to the next. At first fear made his mouth tighten, his posture unsteady. Sporadic employment bowed his shoulders, and he spent much of his time trying to relocate the families:

"We can't have everyone in Idaho. The law is bound to catch on to us. Bill Goldstein has offered me temporary work in Albuquerque, and I'll need one of you girls to go with me to keep house."

My mother glanced at Aunt Henni, whose eyes widened.

"I'm not going without Hannah. She needs me." Her chin lifted.

My mother's head bowed, and she said, almost simultaneously, "I can't go without Henni. I need her too much." Both women were crying. The opportunity to separate, to live independent lives, vanished from the twins' reach.

Aunt Sarah sighed. "It doesn't take a genius to figure out who is left. When shall I be ready to go, Rulon?"

My father worked in Albuquerque as a mechanic's apprentice, dark greasy work that strained his eyes, stained his hands, and agitated his ulcers. Soon the stomach sores ruptured, and Aunt Sarah hovered over him as he retched blood.

"Rulon, we've got to do something." Over his protests she called her children to kneel beside his bed and pray, then raced for the corner phone booth where she called Utah, Nevada, and Idaho. "Pray for Rulon!" she blurted. By the time she returned to the tiny apartment the bleeding had stopped.

My father gave up mechanics and moved Aunt Sarah to Oregon and Aunt Rachel to Montana. He seemed relieved by these changes but voiced a new concern: Aunt Navida seemed to avoid spending time with him when he visited, and he had heard a rumor that she paid half her tithing to her brother in the other group.

An opportunity to regain our Salt Lake property revived his spirits and the hope of returning someday. "One day there'll be an end to all this," he promised on one visit. "Before long we'll all be together again on the old homestead."

During his monthly visits, he tried to compensate for his long absence. Saturdays he took us fishing or we visited ghost towns, petrified forests, and Indian diggings. No matter what questions we asked, he seemed to know the answer. Yet he was almost a stranger to me; his world became less and less my world.

For Saul, the worlds were dividing sharply, indelibly. He was reading everything he could get his hands on: philosophy, psychology, sociology, political and educational theory. He dated

Protestant and Catholic girls. Some of his friends drank when they were not in training for football or basketball. And he was developing his own opinions, as staunchly and righteously defended as my father's.

On Sundays, we held small meetings in the living room with the drapes drawn, without the piano to accompany our singing of hymns for fear the neighbors would hear.

One Sunday, my father began to speak about honoring one's father and mother. I saw him glance at Saul and Jake. Isaac and Amanda sat by, listening carefully, but we all knew my father's sermon was not for them.

"Except ye be as little children ye cannot enter the Kingdom of Heaven," my father recited.

I gazed at Saul, noticing that his Adam's apple had grown larger and seemed to throb with the blaze of his eyes. He had to shave every day now. I glanced down at my long, gangly legs, thinking of the months since my father had picked me up when I ran to greet him, since he had held me on his lap or cradled me in his arms. I would not be a little child much longer. And Saul's time for being a child had passed.

One Friday he and Isaac came home with news that made the mothers gasp.

"We've both been nominated for student-body president," Isaac announced.

"We'll be running against each other," Saul added.

"How wonderful!" my mother exclaimed. "Both Allred boys nominated to the highest office in the school!"

"And to think we've only been here a year and a half!" Aunt Henni added.

"Who do you think has won?" someone asked my father as he was about to leave for Idaho. The election results would be announced next day, and the weekend had been rife with tension. My father scratched his head.

Aunt Henni jumped in. "I'm sure it's Isaac. With Saul's teeth crooked and all, the girls like Isaac just a little better. Don't you think, Rulon?"

My father hunched his shoulders in a shrug. "You're probably right."

My mother bowed her head. My face grew hot, and I was remotely aware that I had clenched my fists and left the hallway without kissing my father good-bye.

Over our Sunday night supper of peaches and peanut butter toast served with cocoa, I studied my two oldest brothers, comparing them.

Saul's sense of humor had long since returned, and he made one wisecrack after another until we were choking on our food and my mother begged him to stop. Isaac joined in the laughter, his manner serene and sincere as ever. Saul's features maintained a radical clarity that, combined with his fiery eyes and slow, shy smile, spoke of action, leadership, and artistry. Isaac's gentle, solid face shone with compassion and openness.

Each of them saw me gazing and smiled in turn. I couldn't perceive either of them as being more handsome or desirable than the other. Saul loved to hunt rabbits and fish with his best friend, Jack Turner, but he had all the dates he wanted, and plenty of girls let him know that they longed to go out with him. Isaac had a steady girl; he and Teresa spent every spare moment together and had already spoken of marriage in general and their aptitude for the Principle in particular. Teresa said that she could never bring herself to share Isaac with another woman, but Isaac was serene in his faith. Everyone assumed he would follow in my father's footsteps.

Saul was the unpredictable one, driven by his probing questions, always puzzling why this idea did not fit with this doctrine, until my father declared again that "there is no doubt in the presence of faith."

I remembered Saul and Isaac wrestling on the living room rug, grunting and giggling, smiles and grimaces interwoven. On the playground Saul was our champion and leader. In the meeting hall Isaac was our example. Whatever rivalry existed between them, it had to be good-natured and loving, for they were as close as my mother and Aunt Henni in their way. I knew that I would never want to choose between them as my father had done.

The next day Saul came home from basketball practice ahead of Isaac. He said nothing and walked to the kitchen for a glass of water. Isaac came in a moment later, kissing my mother as she came through the hall. "I guess Saul told you," he said, his voice gentle.

My mother's eyes widened. "The election announcement! It was today!"

Isaac nodded and looked over my mother's head at Aunt Henni.

I watched them, my eyes darting from one face to another. "Who won?" I blurted.

"Why, Saul did. You mean he hasn't told you?"

My mother shrieked and ran to the kitchen.

"Not really," Aunt Henni murmured. And then, her chin lifted, she said, "It must be because all the girls know you're going with Teresa. And Saul isn't going with anyone. All the girls must have voted for him." Her voice became surer, more resonant as she spoke. Isaac shook his head and turned away. I frowned and followed my mother into the kitchen.

One day I was sitting on the front step, aimlessly pushing a roller skate around with my toe when Danny dashed around the corner with a double-size stack of *The Free Press* under his arm and asked me to help him sell them.

I jumped up. At last one of my brothers had asked me to do something. "Should I change into my Easter dress?"

"Naw, I don't want you to look nice."

We started off. "Why not?"

"We don't want them to think you're rich."

The busy section of the gambling village was a few blocks away, and as we walked, we discussed the changes in our lives since we left Utah. I felt grown-up and important, striding alongside Danny.

I gazed up at him and saw early adulthood settling like a thin mask on his round, handsome features. There was a worldly squint to his eyes, independence in the jut of his jaw, and a swagger in his shoulders that would never disappear.

He stopped at the entrance of the first casino, a sprawling, brightly lit place with a cafe at one end. "Now, you ain't supposed to go into the gambling places."

"Mama says you shouldn't say 'ain't'."

"I'll say what I want," Danny muttered. He handed me a dozen papers. "Go into the cafe first, and walk up to the men—not the ladies, but the *men*—and say 'Paper, sir?' as nice as you can. If they ask for change, tell 'em you don't have any. Then, when no one's looking, go into the casino and walk up to the people playing the slots. After that hit the card tables and roulette wheels. It's dark in there, so nobody'll notice you. Then bring me the money. I'll be right here, selling papers on the street."

Danny scooped a little dirt from the corner of the sidewalk and rubbed it in his hands like he was up to bat. Then he patted my face with his dusty hands.

"Don't! You'll get me dirty!"

"That's the point. We want 'em to feel sorry for you. If anybody asks, tell 'em you're selling papers because your Dad is dead."

I gasped. "That's a lie, Danny."

He shrugged. "We have to lie about the family anyway. May as well tell 'em he's dead as tell 'em he's a traveling salesman."

I whirled through the mirror-plated revolving doors, my heart pounding. The smell of hamburgers frying lay on the air, but underneath, the sharp sting of liquor mixed with a hard, tongue-nettling smell of money: coins clattered into slot machines, and sweaty, crumpled piles of bills lay on felt tables. People milled all about me.

I wanted to whirl back through the revolving door and tell Danny to take me home, but then I thought of the useless feeling I had at home. And I thought maybe Aunt Henni would approve and possibly tell my father I was helping the family. I veered into the casino.

An Oriental man in a loose shirt printed with red seagulls and yellow palm trees stood near the entrance, looking lost.

"Paper, sir?" I asked, lowering my eyes.

The little man knelt down, making himself shorter than I. "How old are you, little one?" He had a soft, gently accented voice.

"I'm seven. Would you like to buy a paper, sir?"

"I'll buy a paper from you, little one, if you will do a favor and take a picture of me beside this bear." He pointed at a twelve-foot glass-encased stuffed polar bear, the casino's trademark. He held a large, fancy camera out to me and knelt beside it, as though to emphasize his smallness. I wondered why he had no one to take the picture—a mother or brother or sister or wife. I clicked the camera. Then he had me take another shot of him with the singing showgirls in the background.

He gave me a ten-dollar bill but refused the paper. "I do not live here," he explained.

My mouth fell open. "Can I keep it, sir? I don't have any change."

"Yes, you may keep it, little one." He sighed and patted my head. "Now listen, leave this place. It is a house of evil—not a good place for you."

I nodded, then ran from the casino, through the swirling mirrors, waving the note at Danny as I raced to the corner. He smiled wisely as he put the bill in his wallet.

"I knew it would work." Then he turned to me. "We can quit now. You made more in five minutes than I'd make selling this whole stack. Let's go get a treat."

We stopped for lemon ice cream cones at Warren Drug.

When we reached the house, I held out my hand. "Do I get some money?"

"It's my money," he said. "I got the papers, remember? Without them, there'd be nothing to sell."

"Well, they didn't buy the papers. They just gave me the money."

"Just the same," Danny said. "It's my money. Here." He handed me a quarter.

It was the most money I'd ever had. I was satisfied.

Almost every day after school Danny stopped by to take me selling papers.

One evening we stayed out until ten o'clock because the selling was so good. As we walked past the Kodiak Lounge, we heard shouting and scuffling and sobbing. The bartender threw a naked man into the alley. Danny and I watched him lying there, vomiting and swearing and feeling the ground for his clothing.

When we told my mother about the naked man, she wouldn't let me go selling, and she made Danny come home before dark. But she had no money for school clothes and baseball uniforms, and we all had to go to the dentist that year, so after awhile she relented to our pleas and vows to stay on the right side of the tracks and to steer clear of the Kodiak Lounge. We were a partnership again, selling until sunset and topping off the day with lemon ice cream or two-for-a-nickel doughnuts. Sometimes we begged my mother to let us see a movie before coming home, and we sat in the Hunter Theater, our empty stomachs rumbling until Danny bought popcorn. Occasionally he left me alone and went to sit with his friends.

"What's the loge?" I asked him one night as we walked home.

He cleared his throat. "It's—uh, it's a place where you can talk during the movie."

Then he confided he had a girlfriend. "But don't tell Mama. You know why I like her?"

"Why?"

"Because she hardly ever talks. I like a girl who keeps her mouth shut."

It was difficult, but I kept my mouth shut the rest of the way home.

Since I had exhibited uncanny skill at zeroing in on the big tippers, I soon demanded half our profits, hoping to take some credit in whatever was turned over for the family budget. But Danny refused and never took me selling papers with him again.

That year I began to be beset by fears and a pervasive sense of guilt. The large rawboned man in the duplex next door beat his wife and tiny baby. We could hear their screams through the wall. My mother wept as she listened, but she said, "We can't contact the law. We can't afford to call attention to ourselves."

I clenched my teeth, a black terror raging through me. And I began to have trouble sleeping at night. I stared into the dark closet and imagined the wolves of my dreams hiding there.

My father had said that we should fear only the Lord, that any other fear was of the Devil. I wondered what I had done to invite the Devil into my heart. Was it because I was lazy and sloppy, as Aunt Henni said? Was it because I was greedy, wanting half of everything when I went selling with Danny? How had I sinned?

It had to be the lying. Even though I hadn't been baptized, I knew I had broken one of the Ten Commandments. The lies began with the ones we were told to tell, then grew like a big black bush inside me, blotting out the light. I had added to the things we rehearsed as a family. "My father is a traveling salesman," I would begin. But it sounded hollow. And there were the lies I had told earlier that I now had to cover somehow. "That is, he used to be. Before that he was a doctor, and then he was a mechanic, working on diesel engines. And then he quit because he didn't like grease under his fingernails—he has to keep his hands clean in case he has to stitch up a cut—and now he travels and he . . . sells . . . things. . . ."

The lies spawned questions. "Why isn't he a doctor anymore?" they would ask. "Did he let somebody die? That happened to Dr. Redondo and they took his license away."

I would make up more lies to answer them. After awhile, I was terrified to have my schoolmates meet my family, certain that someone would tell the wrong—or rather, the right—tale. My only consolation was that my own string of lies ultimately had more truth in it than the story my family had adopted.

I knelt in bed and asked forgiveness for my sins. But somehow I knew even as I prayed that tomorrow or next week, someone would ask about my family and I would lie again.

I tried to think about good things—the creek and the garden back home, the times we stood around the bonfire, singing. I remembered the miracles—how I got what I wanted for my birthday, how my father had not died when his ulcers hemorrhaged on Christmas Eve. My thoughts enfolded me like a soft silver blanket, and eventually I drifted into sleep. But sometime during the night I dreamed about the Gulf of Mexico, of being sucked deeper and deeper into its bottomless darkness, and woke myself and my mother with my cries.

When I was barely eight years old—the Mormon age of accountability—my mother mentioned during my father's weekend visit that it was time I was baptized.

He looked up as if startled, his eyes intent and fully focused on me for the first time in months. Then he looked at my mother. "Come north with me. It's a beautiful place, and Sarah has fixed the cottage real cozy. She'd love to have you for a week or two."

When we reached Wolf's Crossing, we stopped the car and waited until dark. Then we drove on a few miles and waited until Aunt Sarah let us know the coast was clear—the owners of the estate absent from their lovely summer home on the hill above the cottage.

Unlike most remembrances that become smaller in the maturing eye, Aunt Sarah seemed larger than I remembered, and harried. Suddenly I noticed a cradle and a baby waving its fists and yelling. Everything had changed! My father had changed, I had changed, the other families had changed. This angry, red-headed stranger that my father cooed and prattled over was the final evidence. Nothing would ever be the same again.

We children lined up to be briefed on the rules of Wolf's Crossing. First, we were not to shout or call attention to ourselves. Second, we were not, under any circumstances, to go near the big house. We could roam the forests and play along the shores of the lake as long as we stayed below the cottage. And third, we must call my father "Uncle Jim."

My father went by the name of Jim Allred at Wolf's Crossing, so as not to be associated with the R. C. Allreds in Ronan, where Aunt Rachel lived with her growing family—an even dozen since the twins, Milton and Myron, were born.

The Saturday after our arrival we walked down to Flathead Lake. The day was cloudy and the family somber as they clustered along the beach, my mother clutching her sweater about her as my father and I waded into the chilly, whitecapped water. I shivered and my teeth began to chatter. I had a strong impulse to turn around, to go back to my mother.

My father had spoken briefly to me about baptism that morning. "A person who has been baptized can no longer blame his failings on Mother and Daddy. He is accountable."

Accountable. A word neutral and flat as an airless balloon. Did being accountable mean that I would no longer need to ask him questions? Did it mean that I would be punished for the lies I had told? If so, which lies would I be punished for—the family lies or my own, or both? Would all the lies be washed away, as I had been promised that all sins are washed clean by baptism, and would I no longer feel compelled to tell them?

The clouds seemed to thicken with my spirit, and I pushed more slowly through the water, my loose-fitting white trousers clinging in the front and billowing out behind. We waded out beyond the pier into chest-deep water. My father stopped and peered at the sky.

I was vaguely disappointed that the sun had not shown itself, and irritated that I was wearing trousers instead of a dress for my entrance into God's kingdom. "I don't know why I didn't think to make you something appropriate," my mother had apologized as we left the cottage.

My father placed an arm around my shoulders and took my right hand with his. "Are you ready?"

I paused and the fears of my sleepless nights throttled my brain. Would my baptism push them away or bring them closer? Would my father hold me under long enough to stifle them? Would he hold me under too long? I felt bent beneath his remote gaze, felt he held me too surely, too tightly. I wouldn't be able to struggle or save myself.

I trembled. Certainly he would not let me drown. But something in me would die as Marie had—the child who believed in going home would drown and drift heavenward. Only a grown-up would surface and stand in the lake. There would be no more simple mistakes or white lies; there would be only sins. I would be washed of my childhood—my heartfelt world of hope and miracles, of things quickly broken and mended—into the world of adults, with evil all about.

But I was not grown! I felt an impatient tremor in my father's fingers, heard him hiss as he studied the clouds. My body quaked. It was too late to turn back.

"I'm ready," I gasped.

Afterward, I felt cleaner and more refreshed than after an ordinary dunking. My father had not kept me under for more than a second, and none of my parts had bobbed to the surface. Then I saw my mother clutching herself and shivering on the shoreline. I smiled, waving, and started toward her. The sun broke into two shards on either side of a cloud.

Chapter

7

In January of 1959 my father invited Aunt Gerda and Aunt Henni home to the foreclosed white house. They readily moved their possessions and their children—Aunt Gerda to maintain my father's household and Aunt Henni to maintain my father's office.

My mother faltered for a week or two after Aunt Henni's departure, then regained her footing. She smiled more, laughed freely, talked willingly of her thoughts and feelings, struck up friendships with neighbors and members of the local Mormon church, and soon was playing the piano all over town. She unfurled before our eyes, like a wilted bud suddenly given new life.

With Aunt Gerda and Aunt Henni at the white house and his naturopathy practice growing, my father's dream was almost within reach, and he spoke of it often during his weekend visits, sighing his fatigue.

"The state is making it as difficult as possible for me," he reported. "They've tried everything under the sun to close me down. Next year I'll have to take state exams so I can prescribe drugs and perform minor surgery. I wonder what they think I've been doing all these years. The Healing Arts Committee is trying to take my license away—because of my record as a convicted felon." He sucked his teeth. "They don't care that the U.S. Supreme Court would have overturned our sentences if we hadn't already served them. No. They're just worried about their own hides. The pressure's on from the medical men. They just can't stand the competition of osteopaths and naturopaths and chiropractors. Means they might lose a few patients and a few dollars here and there." His biting edge of sarcasm pointed up his fatigue and frustration. "If I can just keep it alive till this wave passes over us . . ." He shook his head again, and my mother came to him, rubbing his neck and massaging his scalp.

"If I didn't have all this traveling to do," he added. "I'll be grateful when that rat race is over. I haven't nearly enough time for my priesthood duties as it is. And we know the Lord's work comes first."

He told of the growth of our fundamentalist group from one to two thousand in the years we had been away.

My mother nodded. "You'll just have to cut something else out." But her face looked pinched and worried, as though she thought she might be the something else cut.

"Right," my father said. "That's why I've decided to move Rachel and Lisa to Wells." He named the gambling village sixty miles away.

"Oh no!" My mother clapped a hand over her words. "But Rulon . . . do you think it's wise? Wells is such a small place, and you know how Nevada is, with inter-town sports and all—people would find us out in no time."

My father didn't respond for a moment. Then, rubbing his forehead, he spoke. "I just don't know what else to do."

My mother didn't mention the relatives in Wells again, but I could tell that she worried. Since Aunt Henni's move all vestiges of my mother's illness had been banished, and she turned whole-heartedly to her piano and her coterie of students. Occasionally she was asked to play a solo at church or to accompany a noted singer in a casino. When she returned, the smell of smoke or banquet clinging to her coat, her figure straight, her eyes wide, and her skin pink, I was reminded of a rose in fullest bloom. I knew she did not want the independence and excitement of her new life ruined.

My father always encouraged us to plan carefully so that in his absence we would be provided with the necessities of life. We prepared for famine by keeping an extra sack of flour and rows of bottled peaches in the cellar. We adjusted to poverty by accepting boxes of secondhand clothing from people who had more than we did. When we had no money for rent, everyone fasted and prayed, and somehow the funds materialized.

The one need we could not plan ahead for was the one service my father could freely perform—medical care. Accidents and illnesses always seemed to strike when he was away. Without money for medical bills, we never considered going to the hospital or calling another doctor, and insurance had never been part of our lifestyle. Paradoxically, my father's valued skills—those healing powers that helped so many others—aroused our Nevada community against us.

I'm not sure why he failed to plot a strategy to follow in the times when the mothers' lard-and-turpentine plasters or salt-and-vinegar poultices didn't cure us. Perhaps the failing was ego or myopia, for he was human as any of us. Perhaps he trusted no other doctor with the health of his family, for he bore a trenchant skepticism toward surgeons or medical doctors too anxious to cut away organs and dish out drugs instead of stimulating the body's natural processes of healing. And then, like any shaman, he was reluctant to share his province of secret knowledge with others. But most likely, the nearness of his dream of having us together within his beneficent aura again made him work doggedly toward reunion, ignoring the darts of probability poised in our direction.

One summer afternoon I awoke suddenly from a nap, my heart drubbing in my ears. I went to the screen door. Danny and Jake were standing by Saul's blue Ford, home much too early from their hunting and fishing trip. I ran outside.

Danny's nose was running and his eyes were bloodshot from crying. "Saul's been shot."

I felt the words before Danny's thick, anguished voice reached my ears, as though a distant memory had been aroused.

"He isn't dead," Jake added quickly. "He's in the hospital."

"Is he . . . will he live?"

"Nobody knows," Danny said.

"He'll be all right," Jake broke in.

"But it's bad. Went through right here, where his heart is."

I wondered what Saul had done to deserve this. Could this be his punishment for asking for a manifestation from God? My father had warned him about that. But surely God didn't punish people for asking questions. Did He? I felt suddenly cold.

"He's in the hospital?"

Jake nodded. "He didn't want to go there. He wanted me to take him home."

"He said Mom could take care of him," Danny snorted. "Crazy. Every time his heart beat, more blood gushed out."

Jake nodded. "He'd have bled to death. We had to take him to the hospital."

"What will Daddy say?" I asked. He had never told my brothers not to hunt, but anyone could tell how he felt. I didn't want any more distance between them. It was hard enough, loving them all and feeling the earth split so that I had to stretch to reach in both directions.

Jake and Danny shrugged simultaneously. "What can he say?" Jake asked. "We did what we had to do."

Danny told me how Saul had been walking back to the car and stopped to tie his bootlace, propping the gun against his shoulder. Then he stood up, the gun bouncing against his chest so that it went off.

"Damn bootlace," Danny said, snuffling.

"The safety on that thing never was any good," Jake muttered. "Always had a hair trigger."

My father came as quickly as he could, arriving in the evening to see Saul as soon as he was out of surgery. Even though he didn't dare remove the dressing, knowing the doctors would object, he promised Saul that he would live. "The Lord has an important work for you to do," he promised. "It isn't your time yet, son."

My father's statements had taken on a more authoritative air. People in our group were calling him a prophet, asking his advice on every little thing. I don't know whether Saul believed what he said, but I did. I couldn't bring myself to believe otherwise.

Saul's life had been saved by a hairbreadth, the surgeons claimed. We lingered together, expressing our gratitude that the Lord had spared him.

He came home too soon, against the doctor's orders, thinking of the bills and believing that my mother would be able to care for him as well as any nurse. But at home there were no shots for pain, no instruments to keep the punctured lung cleared of blood pumping regularly into the cavity, making him howl like a car-struck dog. He coughed up blood and groaned and worried about the hospital bill.

"How will I ever finish college, Mama?" he asked as she gently forced him back into bed.

She shook her head. "You must lie down, Saul. When you pace the floor, it makes you bleed harder. The doctor said we must keep you in bed."

"But the bills, Mama? I've got to get back to work so I can pay the bills." And he would fall into fits of delirium until the pressure and pain made him sit upright again.

My mother called my father at his office in Salt Lake. "He's in so much pain, Rulon. I just don't know what to do for him."

My father told her not to worry. "That pain is keeping him

alive, Hannah. It wakes him up and makes him move. And that will help him mend. Suffering can be restorative, darling. I wish you wouldn't forget that."

But Saul's distress peaked hourly, until he begged my mother to call the doctor. In a few minutes they were on their way to the hospital to have blood drained from Saul's lungs. The experience left him shaken and pale, and each time he prepared to go back, his skin became clammy, presaging the pain.

After each visit the doctor warned, "He ought to be here, where he can receive constant attention. I don't think you realize how close he came to losing his life, Mrs. Allred." And he would explain, again, that the bullet had missed a major artery by this fraction, his heart by that fraction.

My mother bit her lip and shook her head, not knowing what to say. She wore her embarrassment home. "They must think I don't care about him," she said after one hospital ordeal. "They must think we're a mighty strange family. . . ." And she wept quietly into her hands until Saul stopped moaning and fell asleep.

Saul recovered slowly and went back to work long before he was well, determined to work through the autumn and enroll in winter-quarter classes at the University of Utah. When he left for Salt Lake, Aunt Henni returned, bringing a few of her things and marvelous news.

Brilliance washed over her face as she told us, "The Lord's promise to your father and me has been fulfilled. We have been blessed with a child."

She was expecting in the early spring and would have to "hide out," as my mother had done when she was expecting me. She resumed her old bedroom in our Nevada duplex, planning to stay for the winter.

"I'll have to keep indoors all the time," Aunt Henni sighed to my mother. "We can't have anyone from the casino catch sight of me, or you know what they'd think!"

In January, the beginning of a new year and a new decade, Aunt Rachel went into labor with her thirteenth baby. My father told us about the ordeal during his next visit.

"I don't know why Rachel put off letting anyone know that her time had come, but when Leora rushed over to Lisa's and pounded on the front door, it was almost too late. Lisa knew right off there wasn't time to send for me, so she hurried about, getting everything sterile—Rachel hadn't found time to prepare—and Lisa delivered the child herself." His worried tone vanished and he grinned. "She's just beautiful—a gorgeous little girl, with the longest, blackest hair you ever saw."

"Black hair?" We were all amazed. Little Jennifer would be the first—and last—brunette in our family of towheads.

After preening, my father frowned again. "The neighbors found out, somehow. They've been snooping around, asking questions about Lisa and Rachel. Maybe someone saw Leora go for Lisa. Or maybe it's just too obvious, even without this birth."

"Oh, Rulon," my mother broke in, "how can it be ignored in a town the size of Wells!"

My father nodded glumly. "And I suspect some of the kids have been blabbering again. You know how some of them just can't keep quiet."

Although the population of Wells, Nevada, was largely comprised of truck drivers, dealers, change clerks, and prostitutes, the entire town suddenly adopted a self-righteously meddlesome attitude toward the Allreds in Wells. Why, they queried, hadn't Aunt Rachel gone to a hospital, as normal people do, to have her baby? Where, they wanted to know, was her phantasmic husband? Where did he get his money? If he worked, why were the children so poorly clad? Why didn't their mother apply for welfare assiatance if he wasn't supporting them properly? And what, they challenged, was the relationship between these two families who moved into their town in one weekend, whose children seemed always to have known each other, and who looked so suspiciously alike?

One morning a policeman appeared at Aunt Lisa's front door.

"We know all about you, Mrs. Jacobs," he sneered. "I hope you know the way you're living is immoral and illegal."

On Aunt Lisa's porcelain cheeks two bright spots appeared. "It might be illegal, but it isn't immoral! Why don't you go bother some of those women in the red-light houses across town?" she blurted. "Now that's immoral!"

"We can't bother them, Mrs. Jacobs. Prostitution is legal in Nevada."

"Well, think of me as one of them, then!" Aunt Lisa shouted, and slammed the door in his face.

The policeman gazed at the door for awhile. Aunt Lisa watched through the window as he scratched his head and walked back to his car.

But the rumors circulated through the ranch houses and coffee shops until they reached our town via ranchers and truck drivers and highway patrolmen.

"You folks any relation to the Allreds over in Wells?" someone asked my mother.

"There are Allreds in Wells!" my mother exclaimed, a trace of question in her voice. "Someday we'll have to get together and trace our genealogy."

During these unsettled times, I added immeasurable complications to our situation. One afternoon in February I fell off a huge snowball that two of my classmates, Linda and Michael, and I had rolled from thick, new-fallen snow on the school playground. I put my arms out to protect my face and heard the thud and snap as I landed.

"You bully," Linda was screaming at Michael. "What did you push her for?"

I looked down at my arms spreading in a triangle before my face. They curved and wavered like something liquid. My knees were tucked under me and I wondered why I hadn't moved. I stood up, and a skyful of falling stars passed before my eyes. My left forearm sagged in the middle as I tried to raise it. I lifted the droop with my right hand. The left hand hung loose like something dangling from a string.

"My arm is broken," I heard myself say in a hollow voice. I smiled frozenly at Linda, who laughed when someone threw up in class. I didn't want her to laugh at me unless I was laughing too.

"Let's go to the nurse's office." She put her arm around my shoulders. "See, her light is on."

I looked around the playground. "Look, just take me to my house."

"You have to see the nurse. C'mon." Linda's voice was firm.

"My aunt will know what to do. She's a nur—" I bit my lip and longed to clap a hand over my mouth.

Linda stared curiously at me. I closed my eyes, wishing to lie down. One of the red shadows in my head whispered that Linda's father was a judge. Another told me that judges work with policemen.

But my mind could not reach my feet somehow, and I felt Linda guiding me up the front steps, telling me when to step up.

The school nurse took one look at me and set me on the cot. She put a pillow under my broken arm. I watched her talk on the telephone. She was Italian, I knew from her name—Mrs. Guardino. She hung up the phone and gave me a sharp look. "Your mother doesn't want me to take you to the hospital. She wants me to take you home. What do you think about that?"

I looked at her, blinking, trying to focus my eyes elsewhere, feeling that I would lose track and tell the truth if I looked into her eyes long enough. I felt I should say something, but my mind would not form words.

"Who is your doctor?"

I raised my shoulder in a shrug. With words I could have covered the lie, as I had always done before, but I couldn't speak, so I closed my eyes. It felt good, shutting out the light. I let the darkness cover me.

Dimly I knew that Mrs. Guardino's cool hand was on my forehead. I wanted to tell her that I would walk home, wanted to ask if my mother knew she was coming, but she propelled me to the car and told me to lie down on the back seat. I looked at the grim set of her mouth and closed my eyes again.

When we reached my house, fear rallied me.

"Thank you," I said as she opened the car door for me.

But she didn't leave. She led me up the walk to the front door. The foyer was like the inside of a box, all doors leading to other rooms shut tightly.

"Thank you," I said again. Mrs. Guardino didn't move.

"My mother is giving piano lessons. She doesn't like to be interrupted."

She moved toward the door that led to the back bedroom, to pregnant Aunt Henni.

"My brother will take me to the hospital," I blurted. "As soon as he gets home from basketball practice." I knew she would remember my brothers from the town ball games.

Mrs. Guardino wavered, then turned to the front door.

"You're sure . . . ?"

I nodded.

"If you need help, be sure to call me."

I nodded and managed a smile. She closed the door slowly. Then I heard the car door slam, the motor roar, and I breathed my relief heavily, leaning against the wall as the first genuine pain jagged through my arm.

My father arrived after dark, seeming in a vast hurry and very irritated. Almost immediately, he went out again to get plaster for my cast.

I lay back, anticipating my father's attention. No school for a day or two, everyone could sign my cast, and my father would stay to take care of me. Perhaps we would have time to talk.

Then he returned, bustling, bumping into furniture as though the room was too small for him. He took a roll out of a brown box.

"Daddy couldn't get plaster without going to the hospital, and that would mean questions he couldn't answer," he said.

I nodded, wondering why I hadn't thought of that myself.

"What is it, Daddy?" I asked as he unrolled cotton.

"It's a sticky bandage—like an Ace bandage. It will do just as well."

I looked at my bowed arm, my dangling wrist, the bones protruding against the skin. "But Daddy, will it hold my bones in place? It's so soft! What if I fall down again?"

He looked sharply at me. "I don't know about a little girl who thinks she knows more than her daddy. Now . . ." he said, reaching for my arm.

"What are you going to do?" I shrank away holding my good arm out, my body twisting in fear. Shame blazed through me.

"I'm going to set your arm," he said impatiently. "Come now, I haven't much time."

"Will it hurt?"

He shook his head slightly, fumbling in his grip.

"Have you ever had a broken arm?"

He nodded. "When I was about your age, a little younger. My father set it for me, and he wasn't even a doctor. It healed fine, and I wasn't silly about it, either."

"But will it hurt?"

"Nothing you can't take."

I let him take my dangling hand. His long cool fingers lifted my arm. I felt beads of sweat spring onto my forehead.

He jerked, and my broken bones ground together. I felt my eyes rolling back into my head, into a red-speckled sea going black.

Next morning my hand was swollen and blue. My father had already left with Aunt Henni, whose baby was due any day.

My mother came into the bedroom. "Your daddy says we mustn't let anyone know you're home or the school will get suspicious. And of course they'd wonder about that thing on your arm, too. It will take about six weeks to heal; then you can go back to school.

Six weeks! My mind reeled and I tasted bile. I was furious with my father. I thought of my mother, confined for six weeks with rheumatic fever. Six weeks without sunlight. My life stretched like a long dark culvert beneath the highway.

One morning when the six weeks were almost up, Mrs. Guardino knocked at the door. My mother went to the door in her faded housedress, her hair uncombed.

Mrs. Guardino pushed past my mother and put a stack of books on my lap.

"You've missed a lot of school," she said brusquely.

I nodded.

"How are you?" She searched my face.

"Fine."

"Your arm." She examined each of my fingers. "Move them." I did. "It seems to be healing properly," she muttered. Then she looked at me long and piercingly. "Who set it?"

I faltered and glanced at my mother who stood with a fist against her mouth, her eyes dark with worry. "My doctor."

"No doctor would use this—this stuff! This arm needed a cast! Broken in two places, maybe more. Who set your arm?"

My mother spoke. I was amazed by the dignity and careful control of her voice as she said, "A doctor did set her arm. You see, Mrs. Guardino, my husband is a doctor, but he hasn't been licensed in Nevada. It isn't that he's incompetent—he's a fine doctor. He delivered all my children and has always cared for us in sickness. But the law won't allow him to practice. He's a . . . a . . . ." She took a deep breath. I wanted to run and put a hand over her mouth, terrified that she was about to tell about the family. "He's a naturopath," she blurted.

Mrs. Guardino's face was immobile. She said nothing, looking at the floor and then at my mother and back again in the silence, as if waiting for her to reveal something more.

My mother spoke again, meekly, pleadingly. "If the authorities were to find out, it would cause trouble for our family."

"A naturopath is nothing more than a certified quack," Mrs. Guardino snapped. But she seemed disappointed.

My mother's back stiffened. "You know we raise fine children—good students and athletes. Please . . . we don't want any trouble." My heart ached with her humility, and I suddenly wanted to throw Mrs. Guardino out the door, like the bartenders in town did with mean drunks.

"I'm sure," the nurse said brusquely. She looked sharply at me. "I must be going." She left as abruptly as she had entered.

My father was due to visit that weekend, and when he didn't show up, we sat up half the night worrying. He telephoned that Aunt Henni had given birth to a healthy baby girl, Deborah. His jubilant voice broke through the receiver, electrifying our household. Even our report about Mrs. Guardino's visit didn't break the elation that buzzed through the telephone wire.

"Well, they've been harassing me here, too," he said. "The AMA is trying to get a monopoly on the health of this nation. But I'm getting the schooling that'll give me the right to prescribe drugs and perform minor surgery. Henni's helping me study for exams right now. Pretty soon they'll run out of bones to pick with me."

Before he hung up he gave me permission to go to school on Monday. Instead of anticipation I felt anxious and wished for snow. As I settled on the living room sofa to complete the last of my homework, I saw a police car pull up in front of our house.

I spilled my books onto the floor and ran to the kitchen. "Mama!" I could hardly speak. I felt I was to blame for what happened next.

She smiled, not looking up. "What is it, darling?"

"A policeman. At the front door."

She blanched and stood frozen, staring at me. I gave a dry, hoarse cry that seemed to push a button inside her. She moved frenetically, swooping the ends of her hair into the bun she hadn't yet combed for the day, retying her wraparound, wadding clothing from a chair by the door and tossing it out of sight. She took a deep breath and opened the door, and in that second, I realized—though she might not yet know it herself—that she could deal with anything that life placed before her.

She smiled. "Hello." Her voice quavered only a little.

My knees began to shake and I sat down, listening.

"Good morning, Mrs. Allred." It was the county sheriff, a man who could almost be counted a family friend. Aunt Henni had served him coffee every morning when she waitressed at the casino cafe. My mother had played the piano at his daughter's wedding. He always made it a point to stop my brothers, red lights flashing, to congratulate them on their performance in the evening's basketball game. He had even driven me home from the library on one occasion when the sun had nearly set.

"It's very uncomfortable for me to pay you this visit," he confessed, studying his shoes, "but we've had some complaints from over in Wells." I saw his feet shift and he rubbed his moustache vigorously, as though trying to ward off a sneeze.

"Complaints?" My mother's hand had flown to her throat.

He nodded and coughed. "Uh . . . it seems one of the girls over there has been telling the neighbors that her father has several wives—and that you're one of them." He cleared his throat. "You know, Mrs. Allred, a lot of us knew about you folks from the beginning, but no one wanted to make trouble. You've been fine citizens, and your kids are a real asset to the community. The way I felt about it—and I told the county attorney this myself—the Allred kids set a real good example for the other young folks in this town—not smoking or drinking, and clean-talking, too. Why, I'd have trusted my own girl with your Saul if he'd seen fit to date her. Way I felt, we needed you folks." He scratched his head. "That's why I hate to make trouble for you now, but when we get a complaint, we have to deal with it, you understand. All of Wells is crying for something to be done, and I expect it will be—soon. Some of those kids aren't too well dressed, and they're hungry. Folks get upset over things like that. Anyway, I thought you should know."

My mother nodded and leaned against the door. "Thank you. I'll speak to . . . uh . . . Something will be done right away. I'm sorry you had to . . . bother with us."

She peered through the drapes until the black-and-white car disappeared over the hill. Then she sank her face into her hands. I couldn't hear her weeping but saw a flush creep up her neck and into her face. After a moment she lifted her head and I saw the same misery in her eyes that I remembered from her newspaper portrait when the family was arrested in 1945.

She went to the phone, and soon I could hear the distant crackle of my father's voice. "The law's been here, Rulon," she said and began to weep. She told him everything in a wet, snuffling rush, then calmed immediately as his baritone registered reassurance.

That evening Saul arrived unexpectedly from Salt Lake. He had gone to Wells with our cousin Harry to tell Aunt Rachel and Aunt Lisa that they must pack. He planned to return after dark and move them out of the state. Police were already watching both houses; in a matter of hours someone would be arrested.

"What about us, Saul? Do you think they'll do anything here?" My mother's hand was over her heart, her face pallid.

Saul shook his head. "The chief of police and the county sheriff consider themselves family friends. Even if they were pushed into action, I think we'd get plenty of warning."

He tousled my hair. "Keep your fingers crossed for us. We're going to need all the luck we can get."

"Be careful." My mother and I followed him to the door.

We watched him drive away between two slumping shoulders of sagebrush. Toward morning he returned, and at breakfast we heard his account of "the fiasco," as he called it.

"For people who live in poverty, they sure have their share of belongings!" he began. "Of course, it's mostly junk. Mama, what would Aunt Lisa do with a box full of empty milk cartons? And old tuna fish cans?"

"Now, Saul. She makes all her own gifts." She grinned. "And you know Lisa's motto: 'If I don't have it, you don't need it.' "

"Well, it took us two hours to load Aunt Lisa's things alone. And then Aunt Rachel's. When we got there, we found a police car was parked in front of the house. So we drove around awhile, hoping the patrolman would get bored and leave. But he didn't. Finally we drove down an alley and into the backyard. We had to move everything in the dark, in absolute silence. You can imagine what that was like, with all those kids running around."

Saul sighed. "After about twenty minutes, my nerves were like Mexican jumping beans. And everytime I looked out the window, there was that cop, smoking one cigarette after another, not taking his eyes off the house. I arranged with Cousin Harry to drive Aunt Rachel and her brood in the truck. And Aunt Lisa insisted on driving her own car. But she picked up a whole convoy of police cars even before she hit Main Street. So she came back to her house and sent one of her kids over asking what to do.

"I've seen this trick performed a hundred times in movies, and it's the main principle of duck hunting, so you wouldn't expect modern policemen to fall for it. But I didn't know what else to do but to set up a decoy. I arranged for Harry and Aunt Lisa to wait until I had time to get out of town before they headed for Salt Lake. Then I pulled my car around front and deliberately went into Aunt Rachel's. I put on one of Daddy's panama hats, then sneaked into the house, knowing that cop was watching every move I made. Then I took a couple of boxes of trash and carried them out to the car.

A few minutes later, I pulled away from the house, leaving my lights off until I hit Main Street, so that I looked really suspicious." Saul grinned rakishly. "That hooked him, all right. By the time I hit the outskirts, I had three police cars behind me. I kept them at bay for about three miles, then swerved onto a dirt road we used to take hunting.

"I was afraid they'd find me, but by then I had my lights out again and I didn't hit the brakes, so they had no clue. They just headed down the highway, all three sirens screaming." Saul chuckled and then laughed outright. "While all three of Wells's finest were chasing me around in the tules, Aunt Rachel and Aunt Lisa were well on their way to Salt Lake." He grinned and stretched. "If we're gonna get some serious fishing done, we'd better get cracking, Jake. Let's go." His pleasure in outwitting the police, right down to his gestures, reminded me unmistakably of my father.

The next day, my father called, ordering my mother to pack a small bag and meet him in Idaho for a family conference. My mother's face was bewildered as she kissed us good-bye and boarded the bus. "I wonder if we'll be moving soon," she murmured as she left.

When she returned Sunday evening, driven by Aunt Henni, we admired the new baby, Deborah, but Aunt Henni was long-faced and my mother was red-eyed.

"What's wrong, Mama?" I asked as we got ready for bed.

She blew out a long breath. "There isn't too much I can tell you, honey. Except that Aunt Navida is leaving the family."

"Leaving the family? You mean for good?"

"No one knows."

"But why?" I thought of Tommy and Serena, my playmates back at the white house, and tears welled.

My mother shook her head. "Her brother has had his influence, I'm sure. He'd like her to be in the other group. Which means she has to defy our priesthood council. And she feels she hasn't had her fair share of time with your father. But we've all felt that way at times."

"What does Daddy say?"

My mother shrugged. "He said a lot of things. He chastised her for supporting the other group and talked about his calling. But there's not much he can do. It's really up to her, and she thinks your father pushed his way into his position, that he begged Brother Musser to give him his calling. We know that's not so, but Navida's in a bind. I feel so sorry for the children." She began to cry. "Your daddy loves her and wants her to stay with us. We all do."

"Can't something be done?"

"Not unless Navida does it. When he married them, Brother Musser promised her that if she'd stand by your daddy, he would carry her into heaven as his backload. But if Navida doesn't want your daddy to carry her, there isn't much anyone can do."

The mystery of Aunt Navida's "divorce" from my father gnawed at me. It gnawed at my father too, making the holes in his stomach bleed and holding him to a diet of cottage cheese and milk.

A question rose from my heart: if the Principle is true and the way God wants us to live, why are we having so much trouble? The people in Wells had been upset about Aunt Rachel's children. The school nurse had been afraid I wasn't being properly cared for. I had begun to question whether my arm had been set properly (it still hurt and I couldn't control the movement of my fingers yet) and whether I was getting what I needed to grow up right. And then Aunt Navida spoke against my father, saying he was wrong, that he didn't have a calling in the priesthood. And she had left him, saying she didn't get enough attention from him—a feeling about my mother and me I had hidden inside. She wouldn't say those things about her husband, the father of her children, unless she had reason, would she?

My father always claimed we were the noblest spirits on earth, said God chose us to lead a superior way of life to raise a righteous seed unto the Lord. But I didn't feel righteous or superior; I felt small and frightened. I wondered how all this confusion and trouble could come to people supposedly better than other people. Something was terribly wrong, I knew that. But I didn't know what or where or whose fault it was.

Somehow, I lulled myself into believing that our Nevada neighbors had forgotten or ignored the rumors about us. But one Monday, when I had soundly defeated Linda at tetherball during afternoon recess, she stuck out her tongue, then taunted, yelling and pointing, "Jeannie's dad has seven wives! Jeannie's dad has seven wives!"

Her chant rang through my head and made my cheeks burn. Other children stood watching, staring at me. I felt a circle form and I moved away, afraid they would join in or maybe throw rocks at me. The bell rang and I ran into the building, my eyes stinging. Linda's voice followed me like an enormous horsefly. As I entered the classroom, full realization hit me. I understood the fear of the past weeks, my guilt over breaking my arm. The town knew all about us. Soon the police would come again, asking questions. Rumors of arrests would circulate. And we would move again.

I sat erect in my seat and the flush left my face. I felt my head clear, and when Linda pointed, giggling behind her hand, I stared coldly back at her. You can't hurt me, I told her mentally. In a few weeks I'll be gone from here, and I'll never have to look at you again.

Chapter

8

My premonition about moving proved accurate. My father announced on his next visit that he and my mother were expecting another child. We would return to Salt Lake, staying with Aunt Henni in the gray house apartment until we found a place of our own. Entranced by the news, I focused my dreams on the summer and a new life.

Saul and Jake and Danny—not so delighted by the move as I—resolved, against my father's wishes, to keep our Nevada house for the summer while we headed for Salt Lake to search for a new home.

The white house hadn't changed in any perceivable way, yet I sensed a difference. Aunt Gerda, her three boys, and my father rattled through the large rooms where plaster quietly cracked like aging skin.

My father, perpetually irritable and always in a hurry, came in from milking, stomped barn dust from his good shoes, put on his suit coat, and rushed off to work at his new office in Murray. Each evening he stayed at Aunt Gerda's, not visiting the gray house for fear of spies or investigators. His days were distended with visits from people inside and outside the group who came to talk about the gospel or personal troubles. He went to bed late and arose early to study scripture before his day began. When he talked, his voice held a note of complaint, but he never spoke directly to me or even acknowledged my presence at the white house. We survived as individuals. The great white circle that once drew us together had disappeared.

I felt at once stifled and abandoned; overstimulated yet shut off; surfeited, yet lacking sufficient nutriments for my psychological growth. I needed my family, but I needed people from the world as well. The many changes at the white house threatened both my memories of wholeness and my hopes for the future.

I worried about the upcoming school year. If we stayed in the area, I would attend junior high school with the children of my kindergarten class, and I longed for anonymity, for a chance to be gauged on my own merits. I felt I could only be acceptable to the world if no one judged me by my parents' way of life.

My parents' way of life. When did I start thinking of the Principle that way? When did it stop being our way and become their responsibility, their choice, their fault?

At the end of summer, we moved across town to a cottage with a big backyard and lilac bushes hugging the red brick, a house all to ourselves, with no one above or below or attached to us, a house with ash trees out front and my own room. For the first time in my thirteen years I didn't sleep with my mother or double up with my little brother. Moderately well-to-do people lived around us— nice people with barbered yards and clean children, who gave no special significance to the name Allred and who relegated polygamy to a remote corner of Church history. My brothers joined us from Nevada, and from the day we moved in I felt at home there.

At my new school I found a friend. We shared our names and our birthdays; we were both called Jeannie and had been born within a week of each other. We shared secrets, too: I told Jeanne everything I dared without coming right out and stating that my father was a polygamist. I opened my heart and poured out my feelings about people, life, death, and dreams. We compared our bodies and our relationships with our brothers and discussed the peculiar character of the human male. At last I knew what it meant to have a best friend.

Jeanne's mother regularly fed us homemade banana bread and peanut brittle (Christmas treats in our household) and indulged our overnight visits and long walks. But she asked too many questions about my father. Why, in all her visits to my house, had Jeanne never met him? What did he do for a living? Traveling—what an awful way to survive! Didn't my mother get lonesome during the weeks he was away? Another sensitive point was my burgeoning figure. Mrs. Stanton assessed my almost-overnight growth with surprise and distrust, as though she suspected I was padding my chest.

The boys at school didn't seem to think I padded my chest, and my brothers teased that I couldn't get my feet wet in the shower.

I blushed frequently, and Jeanne and I took to wearing our brothers' largest shirts—she to look like me as I minimized the embarrassing phenomena of my body.

I envied Jeanne her ten-year-old's figure and her father being home, and she envied my sudden womanhood and the attention I got from boys. We giggled, confessing our wish that we could exchange bodies for awhile.

My mother loved Jeanne. At first she called her "that nice girl," and then "honey." She described her as "refined" and "mannerly." When we stayed overnight at my house, my mother always baked because Jeanne praised her hot bread with butter and Montana honey as being the best treat she'd ever had.

Mrs. Stanton tolerated our friendship because Jeanne loved me and because I encouraged Jeanne to raise her average grades. Knowing that Mrs. Stanton regarded me askance didn't prevent me from admiring her. Everything from the decor of her large Tudor-style house to her perfume struck me as elegant. As with Aunt Henni, her life spoke of order and arrangement, a stark contrast to the confusion of mine. But that year my own life became fraught with a beauty visible only to me. Happier than I had been since we first left the white house, I discovered that light collected in my body, reawakening my senses and casting radiance on the world. I found generosity in the wrinkled face of the English teacher the others called "Battle-ax." I found courage in the ramblings of our math teacher as he recounted his World War II experiences. I saw my own fragile dreams reflected behind the shy or surly or mischievous masks of my classmates. Even newsprint marched its characters in dignity as I read the events of the world that opened its arms to receive me. The discovery that I loved everyone seemed a great and terrifying miracle. So this was God's world—a vaster space than my lost home, yet so sunny and beautiful!

Another brother was born that year. In my mind his christening blessed the red-brick house as well. Aunt Henni bore pans of water and stained linen from my mother's room, stopping to speak confidentially about the birth as though acknowledging my new womanhood. Her talk made me warmly anxious, like an initiate to a club who knows nothing about the rites of membership. But I was glad to note that only joy, not wistfulness, resided in Aunt Henni's face this time.

I held my baby brother, Jon, for a time and gazed at my mother in awe as she nursed him. Later I went to my bedroom and stood before the full-length mirror that Saul gave me for my new bed-room and imagined myself with child. "So this is what it means to be a woman," I breathed, suffused with light and warmth. Then the feeling overwhelmed me, and I went outside, where cold dark spaces hung like wet sheets between the houses, and made a dozen adolescent angels in the snow.

My father stayed with my mother that night, the only night he slept in the red-brick house. He left before daybreak so that the neighbors would not see him.

On the weekend, when Jeanne stayed overnight, my father did not come at all. "Where's your dad this weekend?" Jeanne asked.

"He's on another business trip," I sighed, hating the weight of the lie.

"You've met everyone in my family," she reminded me. "When can I meet him?"

"I don't know!" I said, rankled. "I never know when I'll see him myself."

"I love my dad so much," Jeanne confided. "My mom yells at me sometimes, but he never does. When I have a cold, he always comes up to my room and talks to me and rubs Vicks on my back."

My eyes stung with the remembered odor of eucalyptus, and an image of tenderness between Jeanne and her father that domi-nated my mind for a moment aroused sadness fraught with grati-tude that at least this much was shown to me—how a father could behave with his daughter, how my father would treat me if he had the time.

One Saturday morning my father slipped through the back door and appeared suddenly in the kitchen, although it was daylight and the neighbors were in their yards, making the first spring forays against winter. Jeanne had stayed the night, and I brought her out to introduce them.

"Hello," he said abruptly.

"Mr. Allred," Jeanne breathed. "I've wanted to meet you for so long!"

My father turned to my mother and made a sharp, cutting mo-tion with his hand. My mother signaled me, and I propelled Jeanne back to my bedroom.

"He's older than I thought," she whispered. "But he seems very nice."

I nodded. "He is." Then my mother called to me. "Jeanne will have to go home now. Your daddy wants to talk to us."

Jeanne went home, perplexity in her soft brown eyes, and my brothers and I sat down in the living room across from my father and mother.

"The time has come for us to move your mother," my father announced. "We will find a duplex for her and Aunt Henni to share."

"No!" The word burst out involuntarily. I was amazed at myself. How much I wanted to keep this house, where our lives would be our own, where we could make our own choices.

My father explained that Aunt Henni wanted us to move back to our old district, close to his office, so that she could frequently see her little Deborah, whom my mother now tended just as she had cared for Isaac and Amanda years before.

I knew that my father doted on Deborah—a beautiful, blue-eyed toddler with shining ringlets—and I feared he had forgotten about me and my mother.

"I want to go to school where people don't know about us," I persisted.

Pain registered in my father's face. He opened his mouth to say something, then abruptly closed it. He passed a hand over his eyes. "We'll have to see."

Jeanne was shocked when I called to tell her we were moving. I explained with the old half-truth about our family obligation to my mother's twin. Jeanne approved and exclaimed that a duplex on her block was for sale.

"Of course he'll buy it," she insisted when I shared my doubts about my father's susceptibility to our plan. "He loves you. He wants you to be happy, doesn't he?"

Monday evening when we met for family home evening at Aunt Henni's gray house apartment, I timidly approached my father.

"There's a house in the neighborhood—a duplex, and not expensive. If you bought it, I could go to the same school and keep the friends I have now."

My father stared at his hands for a long moment. Aunt Henni left the room. When my father looked up, his eyes were beady, squinting. I caught my breath and said a silent prayer.

"We've already found a house. It's a few blocks from here, close to my office. Mother Henni found it, and she likes it."

"She likes it!" The words were flung like rocks, someone else's voice coming from my mouth. "What about me? What about

Mama? What about Saul and Jake and Danny? I don't want to move here where everybody knows about us and the kids call us 'plyggies.' "

"I'd rather live nearer the university," Saul broke in. "I'd just as soon Mama stayed in the same area. It would save me some gas money. And Jeannie could keep her friends. It's an important time of life for her—for both of us."

My father leaned forward in his chair. "What about my gas money?" He bit each word. "Do you children ever think of anyone besides yourselves? Do you think you're the only members of this family?" He shook his head. "Such selfishness! Where on earth does it come from? Now, Amanda, for instance, has never complained, not once, about turning over half her earnings. Yet others"—he pinpointed Saul with his eyes—"so caught up in their own selfish dreams they can't be bothered to help out. . . ."

"We're not the only selfish ones!" I blurted. "Someone else is always there before us. And what someone else wants is always more important!"

My father's eyes flickered. "Go in the other room while we finish this discussion."

I fled and locked myself in the bathroom. In the next room my father's voice droned on, dictating, preaching, planning. He had forgotten all about me. "No," I whispered to the water stains on the ceiling, "he doesn't love me after all."

The next morning Jeanne's brown eyes sparkled in greeting.

"Well—is he going to buy it?"

I shook my head, lowering it so that she wouldn't notice my red eyes. "He wants a place closer to . . . his office."

"But why? He travels so much, he's hardly ever there!"

I sighed heavily. "Look, Jeanne, we have to talk. Not now. After school."

All day I rehearsed what I would say to her. Various stories formed, then flew apart like clouds in a windstorm. I couldn't lie to Jeanne anymore. She, of all people in the world, knew who I really was. If my background made her turn against me, then I was nothing anyway, and in any case I could trust Jeanne not to get my family in trouble.

We met at the grammar school and sat on the lawn. "All those things I made you think—about my father being a traveling salesman and that we're just being nice to Aunt Henni by including her in our family—I didn't exactly lie, but I . . . See, Aunt Henni really is in my family." I waited for it to sink in.

"Well, of course she is. She's your mother's twin." Jeanne's eyes pleaded with me to cheer up. She patted my arm.

I shook my head and squeezed my eyes to keep the tears back. In a moment I opened them and took a deep breath. "Jeanne, have you ever heard of the Principle of Plural Marriage?"

She frowned and shook her head slowly.

"It's also called polygamy. The Church used to practice it."

"Wait—my mother said her great-grandfather—he's one of the Pratts—lived plural marriage in the olden days. But I don't really know anything about it. . . ."

"My father lives it. He has several wives. Don't ask how many. Don't ask who. Aunt Henni is one of them. I have lots of brothers and sisters—more than you can imagine. And I love them. And my father will get sent to prison again if you tell anybody, so don't."

Jeanne stared at me, her eyes round and disbelieving. Then she coughed and gasped, as though she had been hit in the stomach. In a moment the shine came back to her eyes. "So your mother and her twin are in the same family. They won't ever be apart."

I nodded. "Sometimes it's wonderful. Sometimes it causes problems. That's the real reason why we have to move." I told her about it. What a relief to talk to someone!

"And he's a doctor, not a traveling salesman."

"A doctor!" Jeanne breathed. As the afternoon waned, she asked all the questions anyone would ask, about what we believed and how the family worked. ("What number wife is your mother? How does your dad decide which one he's going to stay with? What do you call the other wives?" etc.) Then, questions and explanations exhausted, we sat on the lawn, watching the sun drift, hazy pink above the Lakeside Mountains.

"I'm going to miss this place . . . and you, Jeanne."

She threw her arms around me and we held each other. When we separated my shoulder was damp.

"Do you think any less of me, knowing all that?"

She grabbed my shoulders and looked into my eyes. "How could you think that? I love you. You're the best friend I've ever had. Don't you know that?"

I hugged her tightly, then sighed and stood. We walked to our halfway point in the twilight.

A couple of weeks before we moved, Mrs. Stanton took Jeanne and me downtown to do some shopping. We wandered through the best stores fondling scarves and jewelry, daydreaming over leather gloves and velvet jackets, gazing at figured sheets and wallpaper. Mrs. Stanton bought a blouse for Jeanne and a small leather purse for me. I was quietly grateful, feeling that no words could explain what the Stantons had added to my life.

On the way home we stopped at a seafood restaurant. Greenery fell around us and a waterfall trickled near our table with colored lights playing over it. I was all agape.

"Are you ready to order?" Mrs. Stanton asked me, smiling. Her skepticism had vanished, perhaps in her relief that I was moving. But she had said she would miss me, too.

I stared at the menu. How could I order something that cost half of my mother's weekly grocery allowance? "I . . . I don't know what to choose."

Mrs. Stanton seemed to be enjoying my confusion and awe. "Shall I order for you, dear? Halibut au gratin for three."

I relaxed and began to savor everything, the appetizers, the shrimp cocktail, relishing its hot sauce and completely forgetting that shellfish ranked with pork in the Old Testament and my father's estimation—an evil akin to drinking whiskey. "This reminds me of Mexico," I told Jeanne.

"You've been to Mexico?" Mrs. Stanton seemed surprised. The pitying look she had worn all day left her eyes for a moment. "When, dear?"

Through the meal I told them of our Mexico visit, avoiding any allusion to our way of life. But Mrs. Stanton knew and understood why we had gone.

"Still, it isn't the same as a vacation—not when you're forced to go," she murmured.

I nodded and ducked my head.

"My great-grandfather hid from the law for the same reason." Mrs. Stanton said as we finished our cheesecake. "But he was a fine man. And I wouldn't be here without polygamy."

"Neither would I!" I blurted, and we all laughed.

The white house was sold that year. Some of the money went for the mothers' new homes. My father invested the rest and whatever else he could muster in some Northwest acreage—lake-studded, pine-sentried land we called "the ranch," though no real ranching went on there. Initially my father wanted to move us all there, to cluster his families together under only the eyes of God and wilderness, where we could forget about the law. But the mothers dissented. How would he keep his practice going, they queried. Who would pay monthly mortgages if all were stranded in the middle of nowhere, unable to get work? Besides, they liked living in the city. They had learned to like earning their own money, making their own way.

In the end only my father's younger families, with the mothers who could not work, were moved to the ranch.

Aunt Lisa was the first to live there, and Aunt Rachel soon followed with her brood—those still at home, for her three oldest girls were married with babies of their own. We visited only once, for a group conference, the beautiful land with lakes and ponds, evergreens and wildflowers, and bees—everywhere bees for making honey.

"We've transplanted the beehive state," the residents joked.

"I wouldn't mind living here," I told my mother. "It feels safe." Anything would be better than that new duplex. "We're so far from a city—people wouldn't bother us. Even if they knew about us, they wouldn't care, and they're too far away to hurt us. We could have our own school and our own stores. . . ."

My mother shook her head vehemently. "It's too remote for me. After all, Salt Lake is Zion. And it's my home. I don't want to leave again."

I didn't realize it then, but my dream of fostering a self-sustaining community on the ranch was also my father's dream and the true purpose of the land's purchase, a goal he spent many hours and thousands of dollars trying to fulfill. He encouraged others to invest their money in homes and businesses that would support them on the ranch. He sent group members on missions to "settle the north," just as Brigham Young had done. He collected from his patients and spent the better part of his earnings to set up a general store. With his encouragement, the men started a construction company and a clothing store. Some people invested a lifetime of savings in my father's faith.

We moved into the new house in July. Aunt Henni had chosen the south apartment, the one protected from the cold north winds that blew every winter, the one with good sunlight and white floors. My mother protested in her mild, ineffectual way.

"How come you get to choose which side you want?" she asked Aunt Henni. "You got to choose the duplex."

"I'm having it, and that's all," Aunt Henni said, lifting her chin and turning on her heel. She had moved her things into the south side before my mother had even begun to pack.

My mother did not like her side of the duplex. Each time she returned from Aunt Henni's, she surveyed the kitchen and sighed, "I wish these floors weren't so dark." Or "If only there was a bit of south sun. Henni's not even home during the day to enjoy all that light."

She even complained to my father, wonder of wonders. The two never spoke an unkind word to each other let alone quarreled, so we were shocked when she said to him, "I didn't want to move here, and neither did my children. Henni got to choose the duplex, so why couldn't I at least choose the apartment I wanted?"

My father stomped around the kitchen like a nervous stallion about to be bridled. "It is amazing to me that people have so little concern for others. I need Henni in the office. I must have her help. Can't you see that?"

My mother nodded, but she was quietly insistent. "You know I don't like to make trouble, but it isn't fair, Rulon."

He complained about my brothers' reluctance to "magnify their priesthood." He listed his debts and obligations. He spoke of his troubles with the Healing Arts Committee, his fear of state interference in his practice, and his problems with group members.

My mother listened quietly without retracting her stand. Finally he sighed and put his arms around her. "Keep this apartment, please. I'll buy new carpeting, if it'll make you happy."

She relented. Soon she returned to her true character, studying the brighter side of things. "The wood of my cabinets is much nicer than Henni's," she confided. "And I'm glad I don't have to contend with those neighbors."

Meanwhile, the friction between Saul and my father increased. There was the old argument about money, for my father wanted Saul and the other boys to pay all my mother's expenses beyond the mortgage payment.

"I'll never be able to finish college if I have to do that," Saul countered. Saul knew that my father sank much of his money into his ranch dream. It was not a dream they shared, since Saul felt the group was already too alienated from the rest of the world.

But my father had no patience with Saul's position. "That university has only taught you the ways of the Devil, not the ways of the Lord."

Saul swallowed and stared at my mother's new carpet. My father waited for him to speak, but Saul said nothing, the muscle in his cheek pulsing.

"When I was a young man, I practically supported my father's family," my father stated. "He was sick with rheumatism and he had heart trouble. For awhile I was the only steady source of income for our family of eleven. And you boys think it's an imposition to pay board and room to your mother!" He did not mention that he had married and left home soon after he turned eighteen.

Still Saul said nothing. He was probably remembering the trouble between him and my father over the draft. While supporting my mother, Saul ran out of money and quit school for a quarter to work full time. Almost immediately, he received notice to appear at the induction center. Saul composed a letter, explaining that his father lived plural marriage and that he, Saul, had been required to support his mother financially. But my father had refused to sign the document.

"It incriminates all of us, son. Can't you see how this letter, sent to the federal government, would jeopardize my freedom, and your mother's as well? You know, they're trying to push a bill through the Utah Senate that would penalize plural wives as severely as the patriarchs themselves!"

Saul had nodded. "But they would keep it confidential, Daddy. It's illegal to reveal confidential information, even among government agencies."

My father shook his head. "Nonetheless, it incriminates you as well because it isn't true. You haven't been the sole support of your mother, so your excuse is invalid. Your problem, son, is that you don't budget your earnings."

Saul's voice had cracked, his fists clenching, unclenching. "This is all beside the point. How will you feel if I'm drafted? There's a war brewing in Southeast Asia."

My father clasped his hands and leaned forward. "We will have to leave it in the hands of the Lord; His will be done."

We had prayed fervently that Saul would not be drafted, and as it turned out, he was classified 4-A, thanks to his old bullet wound. We had breathed our thanks then, hoping the trouble was over. But Saul felt my father had failed him when he needed him most.

Now Saul met my father's eyes. "Can't we compromise, Daddy?"

My father's mouth tightened. "Compromise! You sound like your mother. Can't you see that there is no compromising? I am overextended myself. If you boys can't find a way to pay your board and room, then you don't need to live here."

"I can live more cheaply by myself," Saul muttered.

"So be it." My father left the room and sat at the kitchen table, shuffling cards for solitaire. One week later Saul moved into an apartment near the university.

Jake and Danny also had gone against my father's advice, returning to Nevada so Jake could court his girlfriend and Danny could finish high school. My father harped that the boys were deserting their responsibilities to the family and their priesthood duties as well. When we met for family home evening, taking turns at each of the mothers' homes, he often made rebellion the subject of discussion. Although he never named my brothers, I was sure that everyone in the room knew of whom he spoke. But gradually I realized that his frustrations extended beyond those that my brothers provoked.

I guessed at his problems from what I overheard when he or Aunt Henni spoke with my mother. Sometimes, he reported, Aunt Rachel's family barely survived. The ten of them had lived on a large sack of carrots for a two-week period until my father could bring them flour and honey, dried milk and potatoes. In addition to my brothers and me, others had "selfish desires." Since Aunt Navida had left the group, she no longer paid her tithes to my father's priesthood order and had made no attempt to help other members of the family for a long time. And Aunt Gerda bought new carpeting or new furniture or draperies every so often, saying, "If I give my money to Rulon, he'll just spend it on someone else." She stated openly that she worked hard, and if others wanted what she had, they should be willing to work for it as she did.

Some of the mothers rationalized that if we lived together, a united effort would flow naturally. Then Aunt Gerda wouldn't stand by and watch Aunt Rachel's children starve. But I remembered Aunt Rachel's bare rooms at the white house, the orange crates for furniture, the tiny allowance for what remained of her children after Aunt Gerda took them over. Like the Principle, the United Order was subject to human foibles and pettiness.

My mother confided her feelings to me. "Look at Rachel. She doesn't have Gerda's drive or energy. She has twelve living children to Gerda's three, and most of them are still at home. And she's not trained for any sort of work! She was so young when she married—and didn't even finish high school!—while Gerda worked for nearly ten years before she married. You tell me how Rachel would earn a living? Housecleaning or baby-sitting? Why, she can hardly keep up with what she has now!" Whenever my father broached the topic of my brothers' selfishness, I could almost feel my mother thinking of Aunt Gerda, although I never heard her say so.

But when one of us children complained about our financial state, my mother would shake her head and cluck her tongue. "Daddy's right. We should be living the United Order. Then there wouldn't be all this confusion and contention."

My brothers and I took this to mean that as long as the principal members of the family—those who had actually chosen to live plural marriage—resisted the United Order, there was no reason we should be bothered with it either. We ignored the fact that some members made quiet contributions to the family fund. Aunt Henni's Amanda and Isaac, for instance, had turned over half their earnings until they married and left home. And Aunt Henni usually gave up her small salary for working in my father's office to whoever needed it.

Danny returned to Salt Lake to work that summer, saving toward fall room and board. He was bent on completing his last year at the Nevada high school where he had been selected for the varsity football, basketball, and baseball teams.

One night Danny didn't come home from work. I was awake half the night listening for him, knowing that something was wrong. My father had paid a rare visit to his basement room earlier in the day, and experience taught that my father spoke privately to my mother's children only when he was displeased.

When I arose the next morning, Danny's car wasn't in the driveway, and my mother's brow was furrowed.

"He never did come home last night. Your daddy and he had words."

"What words?"

"Daddy wants him to stay here and pay room and board to the family. But Danny wants to go back to Nevada where he can play ball. And I don't blame him. He shouldn't have to give up his goals so that someone else can have new drapes every other year."

I sighed, and a dark pit seemed to open in front of my eyes. "If Daddy would talk nicely to us . . ." I began. I couldn't finish.

My mother nodded sympathetically.

Danny already resented the fact that my father bought a car and paid expenses for Aunt Sarah's Sterling, while Danny crowded work between sports and studies.

After my father had come for Aunt Henni, Danny returned. I followed him downstairs. "What happened?"

"Nothing."

"Come on. I know Daddy talked to you. What did he say?"

"He said if I was more like Isaac or Sterling, he'd be glad to help me. He said if I'd mind him and stay in Salt Lake and turn over everything I make, he'd help me get what I need. I told him 'never mind,' that every person needs to learn to handle his own money. Then he told me to pay him board and room or get out."

"Oh, Danny! What will you do? Where will you live?"

He shrugged. "Sleep in my car. Catch fish to eat. When school starts, I'll live with Jake in Nevada."

I began to cry. "This is terrible. It isn't fair, not at all." I couldn't stand the thought of my brother being driven from home by my own father. "Please stay, Danny. I'll ask him to let you stay."

"No!" He turned sharply to me. "Don't you dare talk to him. It's my problem."

"Well, pay him the money then. Why won't you just give him your money?"

"Because I'm not sure he's right. You know the Church says he's wrong to do that—to go against the manifesto."

"I know all that, Danny."

"Besides, I need the money—so I can go to Nevada."

"Oh, Danny, I wish you wouldn't go. It's hard enough losing Jeanne and my friends without losing my brothers too."

He hugged me briefly. "I have to go. I can't explain it. I just have to."

That same summer Jake determined to marry Adele, a small French Basque girl, a rancher's daughter, whom he had introduced to my parents the year before.

"What is her religion, son?" my father had asked, disregarding Adele, who huddled beside Jake, already seeming part of him.

Jake seemed surprised, as though he had suddenly been awakened from a deep sleep. "Uh . . . she's Presbyterian." He craned his neck and smiled lovingly at the small dark features overwhelmed by luminous brown eyes.

My mother's face paled, and she disappeared into her bedroom. I knew she would be weeping. My father stayed on, speaking to the two of them, insisting that Jake convert Adele to the gospel.

"If she can find it in her heart to embrace Mormonism—and hopefully, the Principle—then we will gladly give our consent," he announced.

Like a small, soft cottontail ducking buckshot, Adele flinched at his words. I wondered about her home, her parents. What would they say when they learned that Jake's father was trying to get her to become a Mormon and perhaps one of many wives? I thought I saw anger and discouragement riffle over Jake's placid expression, but he agreed to invite the missionaries to visit Adele.

But Adele wasn't moved to baptism. One late summer morning Jake drove in from Nevada and summoned my father from work.

"We've decided to get married, Daddy," he said matter-of-factly. "We'd like to have your blessing, but we'll go ahead without it. I'll be old enough in October."

My father's mouth tightened. "The girl hasn't converted to the gospel. You'll have trouble with her all your life."

"It's no trouble, Daddy. I love her." Jake's voice trembled, his cheek and mouth working spasmodically.

I watched from the hallway, frightened at what my father would say next. I put my hands over my mouth, praying silently for no more difficulty between my father and my mother's children.

My father reached for a deck of cards and shuffled them. He laid them out for solitaire, his favored pastime at my mother's house. "You are making a grave error," he said at last. "I loved a young woman too, and I married her. But she opposed the Principle and she rejected my position as head of the house. It cost me my wife and my children."

Jake cleared his throat. "This is different, Daddy. I'm not you."

"It isn't the girl we object to," my father continued. "She's a fine, sweet girl. But you're trading your eternal blessings for her. You know that he who rejects the knowledge you've been given will be damned. People all over the world would give their limbs to have what you've been given as a gift of growing up in this household. And you reject it for this girl."

"Not reject it, Daddy. If we feel it's the right thing, we'll go that way. We just don't feel it now."

My father shook his head. "What a risk you're taking!" He gathered up the cards and shuffled again.

"She's worth it, Daddy. Do we have your blessing?"

My father shook his head again. "It's like trading a million dollars in silver certificates for a shiny new penny."

Jake jumped up and stood over my father. "She's not a shiny new penny!" he shouted. Tears rained on his contorted face. "I love her! I want to marry her! And I will marry her—with or without your permission!"

I held my breath. My father, head bent, said nothing, only played his cards furiously. Jake snuffled, crouched over my father like a bear. Time was frozen.

Later, when Jake had headed back to Nevada and my father had returned to his office, I learned from my mother that my father had given Jake his consent to marry Adele in the Presbyterian chapel in Nevada.

My father's trouble with my brothers worked silently as a bellows on my resentment. In defiance I attended my former school, riding buses across the valley to preserve my precious anonymity. I spent hours phoning friends, tying up the line we shared with Aunt Henni, until my father had a separate phone installed in her side of the duplex.

Danny finished high school and returned home to work that summer toward college tuition, but he didn't assuage the loneliness and anger that metastasized within me. Our worlds seemed far apart; we did not sit on his bed discussing life and family as we had the summer before.

A week or so after school was over, my father invited me and my mother to go for a drive with him, saying he had to check on a patient. It vaguely crossed my mind that this was a good time to ask him about staying with Aunt Gerda part of the time next year, just on the evenings when school activities were held. But something was wrong inside me. I didn't know what, couldn't find it, couldn't describe it, couldn't talk about it with anyone.

Suddenly I realized that my father was talking to me. "Now, Dorothy Jeanne, if you can't change your ways, helping out and being more obedient, then we'll have to send you to someone who can keep you under control—at the ranch, for instance, where you won't be tempted by these friends of yours."

"I don't know why I should have to change friends," I muttered, irritated by the interruption of my thoughts.

"Because they aren't the right friends for you. They aren't of our people. And they exert a bad influence. And so you will go to the school near your home, and you will make friends among our people. Enough gallivanting around the city. Enough rebellious behavior. You will stay home and help Mother. And I want to see you at every one of your meetings, including the young people's fireside on Sunday nights."

"You don't even know Jeanne!" I burst out. "You're never around to talk to her and find out how fine she is. And I don't know why I should help out at home. No one helps me."

"Such selfishness! Where does it come from? You're just like your brothers!" My father craned his neck around, darting a glance now and then at the road, but mainly watching me as he veered down the highway.

"I've never had a chance to be selfish! None of Mama's kids have! Oh, maybe she lets us have our way, but as far as you're concerned, what someone else wants is always more important. What Hannah's children want doesn't count. We're nothing to you—nothing!"

My father threw on the brakes. The car skidded and jerked.

A sudden snap of my neck, a burning of my cheek. I dropped my head, then looked up. Had he hit me? Really hit me?

He had hit me. Slapped my face. His words rang in my head, burned in my heart. "You hussy!"

My mother sat in front, her head bowed. She said nothing to defend me. But she held herself rigidly, as stunned as if he had struck her instead of me. Tears dripped through my fingers as my father drove us home, recounting my duties: a new school, more time at home helping my mother, my religious meetings.

When my father stopped the car in my mother's driveway, I ran to the house. Then I heard him backing out of the driveway. He had not come to me, kissed me, said he was sorry, told me he loved me. He had so much love for near-strangers but none for me.

Hussy, was I? All right. I could accept that. The boys at school had another word for it. So that was why they called, wrote notes, invited me to parties.

I paced the room, feeling electrified. I could feel my teeth and hair and nails growing. My skin tingled and the hair on my arms stood on end. I sat on the bed and tried to think. My thoughts, refusing to coalesce, blurred colors into blackness. And this strong physicality. He had hit me. Never had he spanked me once as a child. Why? Why? Why? Again I paced, feeling like a tigress. I pulled a brown paper bag from my closet and began to stuff my clothes into it.

There was a knock on my door. My heart stopped. Had he returned?

It was Danny.

"What are you doing?" He sat on my bed.

"I'm leaving."

"Why?"

"Daddy . . ." I could not tell it. My words became a flood of angry tears.

Danny put an arm around me. "I know. Mama told me about it." His arm tightened. "You can't leave. Where would you go?"

"I don't know. To Jeanne's."

"You can't go to Jeanne's. You can't expect her parents to take care of you."

"Just for awhile. I can't stay here." My voice broke again.

"You have to stay here. There's no place else to go. Now just calm down and listen to me. In a while you'll feel better." His arm cinched my shoulder blades together. Anger rose again in me until I felt comforted and suffocated all at once, a reminder of the times when I was seven and eight and nine, when Danny hog-tied me and made me promise I would do what he wanted. I dimly realized that this time the tying down was for my sake, not Danny's, and I loved him for it.

"All right." I nodded. "You're right. There's nowhere for me to go."

Danny left then, going downstairs to bed. I knelt on my own bed, half-strangled with feelings, memories. Sitting on my father's lap during meetings. Each time I wiggled, his arms tightened, holding me closer, tighter. "Hold still. Don't move," he had whispered. "I won't let you go until you do what I say." Had he said that? Or was it Danny? "You have to do whatever I tell you to do. Because you're female, a girl."

I stared into the blackness beyond my window. "I won't leave now," I muttered. "But someday there'll be a place for me, a place to be free. And I'll leave. I won't live in this house. I'll leave."

Chapter

9

When my father stayed with us, the phone rang incessantly, and someone always called at the door. I eavesdropped as I did my homework at the kitchen table or when the sounds of weeping or anger crept under my bedroom door. Men and women came to him, sometimes bringing their children, sometimes alone and bereft of any friendship but his. Sometimes they were the voices of my childhood, but more often came an influx of strange voices, newcomers to the group.

At six o'clock Brother Minson knocked reluctantly and hovered near the door to suggest he wouldn't stay long (though he always did, and never turned down my father's invitation to supper). Then, when we were seated, he got his problem out:

"There's a Ford for six hundred dollars at a car lot, but Brother Brandon's selling the identical model for six-fifty. He won't budge on his price—I've tried. Now, I know you've counseled us to do business with our own people—but Brother Rulon! Fifty dollars is a lot of money!"

"Dear Brother Minson, I know fifty dollars is a lot of money. But I'm sure that by working together we can solve this amongst ourselves." And somehow he convinced Minson of his duty or Brandon of his so that the deal was consummated and brotherhood reaffirmed.

Later Brother Scruggs, a crimson-faced man with huge calloused hands, perched like a nervous bull on my mother's spindly-legged sofa. I watched from the doorway to see if it would break as he lunged back and forth trying to run down his problem.

"There's this piece of land down south, Brother Rulon. Near Capitol Reef, where that first group of saints fought it out with the Lamanites. Somebody told me those savages descended from the Gadianton Robbers and that was why the early settlers struck out down there. Evil souls rule the whole place. Now . . . I don't know, but I do know the scripture warns they'll fight eternally against the children of God, and I've heard they can take over a saint and turn 'im against his children or his brethren—even his wives—in a single night." Brother Scruggs threw himself at another angle toward my father, and my mother's sofa nearly toppled.

"But, my soul, it's a gorgeous piece of land. Sure looks like God's country. I'm scared, but I'll do whatever you say. You said we should settle the south. Should I put my money in it? Or turn the whole kit 'n' caboodle over to the priesthood?"

Tiny Sister Rexford called at least once a week to murmur, "I can't seem to regain my health, Brother Rulon. Is it something I'm doing wrong? Is the Lord punishing me for my faults and failings?"

And when he had reassured her that she would recover through faith and treatment, another of the brethren came to ask my father to decide what most men must decide for themselves:

"Now, what's the word of the Lord about taking another one into my family, Brother Rulon? Louisa says she's more than ready and willing. I'll admit my Berta's had her heartaches, but she'll get over it. Have your prayers for us been answered? Can we go ahead?"

On and on they came, patients and groups members, new and old, each begging magical solutions to problems impossible and problems imperceptible, from which my father—a sort of spiritual Houdini—always found an escape hatch.

"My wives bicker all the time. The second wife simply refuses to stick to a budget. Her father spoiled her. What am I going to do with them?" My father's solution: put both women in one house and let them battle it out between them. "Don't you interfere, my dear brother, or they'll never have an end of it."

And another: "My oldest son is wayward. I know he is being led astray by the world. How can I call him back?" My father, from his eagle's perspective, could see what he'd never been able to see with his own son, Saul. "Free agency is our most precious blessing. Let him exercise it. And when he returns, greet him with a heart full of forgiveness and open arms."

On and on the voices murmured, mumbled, muttered, sobbed. "Forgive me, tell me, show me, heal me."

Far into the evening droned his comforting lull, his gentle prod, his reassuring chant. I lay on my bed wondering why he hadn't talked to me so kindly. Why hadn't he taken time to explain to me, to listen to me? Why did he have money for them and not for us? I too had problems—aches and pains of body and spirit. I too had sinned.

He no longer spoke to me at all, although he sometimes came to my room and kissed my forehead or pecked my cheek. He didn't hug me tightly and murmur endearments as he did with others in the family but held himself in remote rigidity, a tall oak keeping me at bay with myself. So I was surprised one evening that he sat across from me at the kitchen table and spoke.

"Brother Cartright has left us."

I glanced up from my homework, startled. There was no one else in the room. He must be talking to me. "Brother Cartright?"

"Yes. He has gone to Mexico to join the The Church of the Lamb of God. It's one of the LeBarons' schemes to lead people astray. They claim to have the keys of the priesthood through their lineage to Benjamin Johnson. But of course the priesthood isn't a birthright. It's bestowed by the Lord Himself and no one else. I received my priesthood through a patriarch ordained by the Church presidency, Joseph White Musser."

My forehead furrowed. Why was he telling me all this? I had heard it before, the tracing of priesthood authority to its purest origin back to the Apostles Peter, James, and John, a favorite pastime of Mormon men. What was he trying to prove to me?

"Brother Cartright is being led into hell. No good will come of his leaving," he said. When I said nothing, he sat and noisily slapped cards on the kitchen table for solitaire.

Not for many years, after several such unfathomable communications from my father, did I understand why he told me certain things. The incidents he described eventually formed a pattern—a pattern that led, step by step, to his death.

Soon after John Cartright's apostasy to join the LeBarons' Church of the First Born, my father encouraged the young people of our group to join the official Mormon Church, without sacrificing our fealty to the Principle, of course.

"We must never forget where our true affiliation lies," he reiterated. "The Church of Jesus Christ of Latter-Day Saints may be out of order, but it's the only true church on the face of the earth. We have no right to go forth and create our own churches as these brethren in Mexico have done. That path leads directly to hell."

Some of the people of our group objected, especially those raised in fundamentalism or those who had never belonged to the official Church, like Aunt Lisa.

"If your youngsters get involved with the Church, they won't live the fullness of the gospel. The Church will brainwash our children until they believe we're wrong and they're right."

My father gazed thoughtfully over her head. "Our children must exercise their free agency. If they have a testimony of the fullness, it will be strengthened by the Church. If not, at least they will be participating in the gospel to the extent of their abilities."

My growing confusion and alienation from my family made group meetings a torture of conflicting feelings. When I could no longer bear to join my family at my Uncle Andrew's garage, I went to the Latter-Day Saints ward near our duplex, for life without religion was unthinkable to me. At first I basked in my teachers' attention, sitting in the front row and showing off my fine education in the gospel. But then my teachers got personal. Why didn't my folks come to church on Sunday? Was there some problem?

For a time my class was taught by a burly man who struck me as being unusually free-thinking for a Mormon of Zion. I liked Brother South. One Sunday morning, he opened the class with talk instead of his lesson book.

"Today I feel inspired to talk about something that usually isn't discussed in the Church. I want to talk about the Principle of Plural Marriage."

My eyes widened. I had never heard a regular Mormon refer to the Principle, except for the children who called us "plyggies." Grown-ups treated the Principle as a terrible secret, a skeleton in Church closets. Even Mrs. Stanton was embarrassed and oblique in her remarks about it. And this man dared orate about it in Church Sunday school!

"In the early Church, a man couldn't preside unless he married more than one wife."

The boys who had tilted their chairs against the back wall snickered.

"You young fellows might laugh, but it wasn't what you think. And it wasn't an easy life."

He told of the pressure put on the Church and its leaders until the manifesto was signed in 1890, then indicated that some devout Mormons had regarded the manifesto as a political tract rather than a revelation.

"These people still exist," he said, glancing at me. I twisted my handkerchief into a knot. "They feel called to live the Principle, and they've suffered for it. One of the saddest facets of Church history. After being driven from state to state, cheated, looted, and martyred, the Church turned right around and persecuted its own."

I felt his eyes probing me, watching for a response. He knew. I knew that he knew. His message was for me, to explain to my classmates about me, perhaps even to explain to me about me.

Then I realized that they also knew. Everyone in the room was looking at me.

Brother South cleared his throat. "I'm not really supposed to talk to you young folks about this. But it's high time somebody was honest about Church history. We can't go on pretending that the Principle was never lived—too many of us are descendants of it. And we can't cover up our mistakes and injustices forever."

The buzzer sounded. After the closing prayer, Brother South took my hand and held it firmly.

"I feel fortunate to have you in my class, young lady. I admire your knowledge and your strength."

Before the lesson we had overlooked our differences. I could giggle with the girls and flirt with the boys with no mention of the gap between our life-styles. But now they knew, and I knew that they knew and that grown-ups knew as well. Now as I walked outside, talkers in little groups glanced at me, and I was electrified with a certainty that they were talking about my family. After that I couldn't bear to go back to church.

One winter Sunday, when my mother had gone to the group meeting, assuming I would attend the afternoon sacrament session at the ward, a boy named Brian and his friend, Peter, came to visit me. We had met at the school where my father insisted I enroll, a school where I lived in terror of being remembered by former neighbors or long-ago kindergarten companions. Brian was both renegade and leader, a bright, good-looking comic who kept to the periphery of our "popular" crowd—those who held student offices, attended most parties, and paired off in couples. I had been attracted to him the moment we met, enthralled by a first-time sense of déjà vu.

We called a neighborhood member of our crowd, a girl named Joan. She agreed to skip church with us. We sat in my mother's living room and talked, listening to an album by a newly discovered group from England called the Beatles.

"I think they're funny-looking," Joan said, "with their long hair and big noses."

Involuntarily I covered my own nose. My father called our family nose "aristocratic," and my mother claimed it was "prominent." Either way, my nose was twice the button nose of Joan, the cheerleader.

"Why don't you try out for cheerleader next year?" she asked me. "We can practice together."

"I'd love to," I gushed. Then I looked down at my wrist where a large lump protruded, enclosing the finger tendons so that my hand wouldn't move on winter mornings. My father called it a "Bible cyst." Whatever it was, it was keeping me from the female equivalent of my brothers' athletic prowess. "I can't do flips with this wrist," I explained. "The doctor must have really messed it up when he set it." Then, stricken by my disloyalty, I added, "Or maybe there just wasn't anything he could do with it."

Brian took my hand. "I'll kiss it better."

"Uh-oh," Peter said. "We'd better get out of here. Want a drink of water, Joan?"

They started toward the kitchen. I remembered suddenly that my father might come home from his weekend visit to the ranch. "If my father comes in the back way, say 'Hello, Mr. Allred' really loud so that I can turn the music down, OK?" I didn't want them having any long conversations with my father. They might figure something out.

"Right!" said Peter. "We don't want him walking in at the wrong time, do we now?" He grinned and stuck an imaginary cigar in his teeth as he Groucho-Marxed out of the room.

"I Wanna Hold Your Hand!" the Beatles yelled.

Brian was holding my hand. "How did you hurt it?" he asked.

"A boy pushed me. We were on top of a big snowball and I fell to the ice."

"Where is he? I'll kill him."

I laughed. "Oh, Brian."

"Really. No one should hurt you."

"Brian! It's no big deal. It's all healed, see?"

"But you can't do anything with it."

"No. But the other one's strong."

"Hah!" he snorted. "I'll bet you couldn't Indian-wrestle a grasshopper."

"Hello, Mr. Allred!" Peter called from the kitchen.

I jumped up and turned the stereo down. Peter tittered. "False alarm!"

I sat beside Brian and rested my elbow on the coffee table. "I can wrestle you down!" I proclaimed. I used to wrestle with Danny, and he always pinned me. But Brian wasn't that much bigger than I—taller, but thin.

It began with an arm-wrestle, but soon we were really wrestling on the couch, until he collapsed suddenly and I fell on top of him.

"Hello, Mr. Allred!" I heard Joan call from the kitchen.

I struggled to get up but Brian held me to him. "She's just teasing," he said. "Stay here. This is nice."

I blushed and squirmed. "Staring nose-to-nose makes me cross-eyed."

"I like your nose. I like everything about you." His eyes invited me to swim in them. Gently he touched his mouth to mine. My mind was suddenly windswept.

"Nice," I breathed. Then I looked up, sensing his presence above us, feeling his stunned expression even before I saw it: my father.

"She Loves You, Yeh, Yeh, Yeh," the Beatles roared.

My face and body went hot and cold, then hot again.

"Daddy!" I was on my feet, wanting to bow, kneel, kiss the hem of his trousers, do anything to gain his forgiveness. But I did nothing. I had proved his words. I was, as he had said, a hussy.

"Daddy, this is Brian." For once, my fear that our family secret would escape took second place to a greater terror.

"Hello, Mr. Allred." To my surprise, Brian held out his hand. And, greater surprise, my father took it.

"Glad to meet you, young man."

My father nodded at the stereo. "This isn't the sort of music young people should listen to on Sunday." He picked up one of a collection of *Book of Mormon* records he had purchased for each of his families and put it on the stereo. Then he left the house.

My budding relationship with Brian did not survive the chill of being discovered by my father, however. When I glimpsed Brian in the hall at school or danced with him in the gym, I was possessed with the sense that I was being watched from on high by a cold blue eye and that I was being bound by invisible ropes. A kind of claustrophobia came over me then, of being hemmed and stifled—not so much by Brian as by the reminder of my father that he somehow provoked. Perhaps it was the similarity of their piercing blue eyes. Or perhaps it was an unquiet, buried memory of my father's face when he discovered us together. Soon I began to flirt with other boys in Brian's presence, ignoring the hurt and bewilderment on his face.

Saul moved home again, stating that we younger children needed "a father figure." He took a grave interest in my life, screening my phone calls, checking on me as I baby-sat neighbor children, making sure I was chaperoned at parties. One night he took me for a drive.

"You know I'm not a really strict person like Daddy. I've kissed a few girls in my lifetime, and I'll probably kiss a few more. But I want you to be careful about who you get involved with, Jeannie. I'm not saying, like Dad does, that you should 'save your kisses for the boy you marry,' but you've got to be careful not to cast your pearls before swine."

I nodded. But I was utterly unable to determine who were swine.

At Christmastime, while waiting for Saul in a discount store, a sense of worldwide injustice struck me full force. I was tired of having less than I needed. I had grown out of the clothing contributed by my father's wealthy patients. And there was no money to buy new clothes, for my father still insisted that Saul and Danny pay for our necessities; and my brothers balked, explaining that college kept them broke. And now it was Christmas; I had no money to buy gifts for my friends and my family. In one pocket I stuffed a bottle of cologne. In the other I put a tie tack. I felt that the owner of the store had so much, he could not possibly miss one thing here or there. After a few moments, Saul finished in sporting goods, and we started out. But as we reached the door, two men in trench coats stopped us.

The disbelief in Saul's eyes cut through me. Blood boiled into my face. We stumbled to the back room where the men emptied my purse and pockets. I longed for my heart to stop or my brain to lose its light. I wanted the earth to quake and swallow me whole. I could not look at Saul.

Vaguely I could hear the two policemen talking to Saul. Then I heard him telephoning my mother.

"Uh . . . we've had some trouble with Jeannie. She tried to take some things from the store. It's all right, Mom. No, she doesn't have to go to jail. Don't cry, Mom. We'll be home in a little while."

I can't remember what happened after I got into the car with Saul—one of two or three blank spaces in my memory, places so dark and incomprehensible that I cannot summon an account of what was said or where we went, or how I made it through the turbulent darkness into the next day.

Throughout the holidays, I worried that the "youth counselor" would ask questions about my family. Instead, a retired police officer verbally slapped my hands, and no questions were asked about my absent father or our way of life.

Some frightened animal within huddled, hoping that my father would discover me in the dark cave of my sins, that he would nurse me back to the light. One evening during supper, he spoke.

"I was in prison twice, with the worst sort of people in the world," he said to no one in particular. "It is no place to be. The men are vile, with the worst sort of thoughts and language, and no respect for life. It is no place to be."

He bit into a roll and said nothing more. He didn't look at me, not once, for the rest of the evening.

I dated many kinds of boys the year I turned sixteen. At first Saul tried to contain me.

"I'm a little disappointed in you, Jeannie," he said over dinner one evening. "I was hoping you'd stay home tonight."

I smiled sweetly. "I'd love to, but I've had this date all week. I can't break it now."

A few minutes later I heard Saul muttering to my mother ". . . ridiculous how often she goes out . . . not even sixteen yet."

"I was dating when I was thirteen, Saul. What can I say to her?"

"You were different," Saul's voice rose. "You double-dated with Aunt Henni. And times were different, boys were different. It's a fast world now."

I imagined my mother shaking her head as she said, "I don't know what to do with her."

It was true. When she complained about my dress, the state of my bedroom, the hours I kept, I met her objections with snarling fury. I ranted and stomped, threatened to leave home or to throw myself off a cliff. I berated her and gave her black looks. And in emergencies I wept.

Saul spoke to me about respecting my mother. I gazed sullenly and thought, Respect her? She doesn't even respect herself. My mother must have felt my anger and perhaps been afraid of it, for she no longer insisted that I clean my room or even come home on time.

But Saul had not given up. "You can go out tonight, Jeannie, but be home early. OK?"

"OK," I said brightly. I wanted very much to stay close to Saul. He often took time to talk to me about the goals I should be setting for myself. "You're too bright to just settle down and get married and have umpteen children. I'd like to see you go to college, Jeannie, and really make something of yourself."

That night I came home before midnight, but Saul was seething. "I told you to be home early," he shouted. "It's midnight! You're not even sixteen yet! I've been waiting for two hours, worrying, but do you care? All you ever think about is yourself! You never give a thought to other people."

I looked at him coolly. He sounded like my father, but he wasn't my father. "You're not my father," I said.

"What?" He looked at me blankly for a moment, then comprehension came into his eyes. "You're right," he said evenly. "I'm not your father." He turned and stomped downstairs, leaving me with a dark nausea, the knowledge that I'd wounded dear Saul and ripped a hole in one of my life's few comforters.

Aunt Rachel died of a heart attack the year I was sixteen. I sobbed all through the funeral, but I could not articulate to anyone, including myself, the sorrow I felt. Some of her children were too young to understand what had happened. Aunt Lisa had taken them into her home, and already the little ones were calling her "Mama."

I gazed at her fluorescent-lit coffin and then forward to the pulpit where my father spoke, his voice sure and controlled. I looked back at the coffin and remembered Aunt Rachel in an upstairs bedroom of the white house, her soft moan floating down the stairs, while in the living room, the mothers clustered around a quilt and I hid beneath the frame, staring at the circle of smooth kneecaps: half shining nylon stockings, half white temple garments, rolled and gartered. They spoke and I listened. Someone said it was a shame that Rachel went through so much with every baby, and another said it was a shame she couldn't control herself, and someone else said maybe her pain was her punishment.

I looked at the blue-veined hands, feeling the pulse of life in them, and thought of sex and self-control and of my dreams and yearnings between the white sheets, with lilacs heavy in my nostrils and moonlight falling across my naked, blooming body. I thought of what my father had called me. Suddenly I was sweating and scared. I wished that Aunt Rachel were alive to tell me things: about being married, about living to feed the needs of others, about loving the earth, and about having babies.

My father's ulcers erupted continuously after Aunt Rachel's death, and he missed work frequently. As financial difficulties mounted, so did his stomach trouble, and he began to cast about for help, for someone to alleviate his vast burden. That was when he met Joseph Stearn.

Stearn came on like a financier after the style of J. P. Morgan. He flaunted stocks and bonds and talked of big land deals. My father fairly bowed and groveled, burdened by a brightening hope that the poverty that had always dogged him and his people would now come to an end.

I met Stearn at my mother's house one spring Thursday. My father held the door like a page, took Stearn's overcoat (which he doffed like a royal robe), and hastened to introduce us. I was startled by this paragon touted by my father as "the answer to our prayers." He held my hand too long and looked greedily at my body, then forwardly into my eyes. He had the same seamy face and red-rimmed eyes of the old lechers at the diner where I had recently begun waitressing, had the same loose mouth as the used-car salesmen who came in for lunch. He seemed my father's antithesis, or nearly that—or perhaps some side of my father that he would not indulge.

"It's too hot in here," Stearn announced, throwing himself onto the sofa. "Turn the heat down," he directed my mother.

My mother's mouth gaped.

"Turn the heat down," my father repeated, nodding.

Stearn oozed another long look over me, then waved us out. "Your father and I have business to discuss."

My mother's lips made a thin line. "The old goat!" she whispered as we entered the hallway.

I looked up in amazement; my mother never called people names. She went to her room, her face set and worried.

An hour later, when Stearn was ready to leave, my father called us from our bedrooms to say good-bye.

"I don't know how we'll ever repay Brother Stearn," my father said. "He's done so much for our people."

"Just give me one of your beautiful daughters," Stearn said, winking.

Sometime later my mother informed me that Stearn's remarks were not simple niceties. He'd had his eye on two of my half-sisters, hoping to take them as second and third wives. I was not wounded in being excluded from Stearn's interest, except in knowing that even to such jaded eyes as his I clearly was not a candidate for plural marriage.

Months passed and many warnings came from Stearn's relations and former friends before my father accepted the whole truth about Joseph Stearn, that he was a confidence man—from his nonexistent assets to his tainted interest in a plural marriage.

Perhaps the humiliation of realizing his poor judgment, along with the shocking murder of Brother Cartright in Mexico, induced my father's most severe ulcer attack since the years of the raids. He lay wasting on my mother's bed. For days on end he did not go to work. Patients called incessantly, then abruptly stopped calling. Group members were cautioned not to disturb him.

One day Aunt Henni came from the bedroom and sank, sobbing, onto a kitchen chair.

"He won't see a doctor. He won't even consider going to the hospital. All this time he throws up blood; it drains from his bowels. Hannah, he's going to bleed to death!"

When Danny returned from his classes at the university, my mother stopped him on the stairs. "Before you go to work, we've got to do something about Daddy."

"What do you want to do?"

My mother bit her lip and her voice rose in a question. "Take him to the hospital?"

Danny turned and stalked to my mother's bedroom. "Be ready to open my car door," he shot at me over his shoulder.

"He won't like it one bit." I said.

Danny shrugged. "C'mon, Daddy," he stated. "We're taking you to the hospital."

He lifted my father, sheets and all, in his work-strong, sunbronzed arms.

"No!" my father protested, his voice thin and shrill. "Let the Lord work His will."

"You're going to the hospital, Daddy." There was a look of triumph in Danny's face. My father squeezed his eyes shut, and his face grimaced in pain or humiliation.

My mother stuck a pillow in the back seat of Danny's '57 Chevrolet and Danny set my father on it.

"Get your purse, Mom," he ordered.

My throat clenched to hold back tears.

"He was so light," Danny marveled. "Like a little kid."

"What will happen? Will he . . . will he be all right?"

"They'll probably operate. Should have done it years ago."

My mother appeared. "Stay here, Jeannie. Keep an eye on the little ones."

I nodded, relieved. I had served witness enough to my father's humbling.

I visited him after they cut away half his stomach and stapled him up. He lay limper than before, but soft light shone from his thin face and pale blue eyes.

I stood for awhile at the foot of his bed, watching the others as they hovered over him. My hands were damp and my knees shuddered. Something moved me forward, and a hardness in my heart burst like a sand-footed dam. I was washed with tenderness.

"Daddy, I love you," I whispered with a flood of feeling as it came my turn to stand beside him.

He squeezed my hand tightly and mouthed, "I love you, dear daughter."

Suddenly I felt trapped. I stepped back, smoothing my blue wool dress, straightening pearls and hair, wanting desperately to leave the hospital, to run from this place where sickness gave way to life and proud strength submitted to love.

The hospital visit was perhaps the last occasion for me to wear a long skirt in many years to come. As my skirts became shorter and my makeup more artful, I dreamed more vividly, day and night. My daydreams carried me to the attic of our Montana ranch house. There I was safe from city people whose space invaded mine. There I was at peace with nature. When I went out of the house of my dream, I walked alone in long dresses, strolling through cool forests that made lace of bluest sky. In my daydreams I sat in my attic room at a desk, writing, on and on. And when I was finished and the yellow sunlight cooled, I would stand and dress for dinner. Each day I would have a new dress—old-fashioned and girlish, with puffed sleeves and long skirts of gingham check, the type of clothing I presumed my father wanted me to wear—and I was neat and pretty, my face free of makeup and my hair long. I never had boyfriends who wanted to kiss me or touch me. Somehow the letters or whatever it was I wrote all day made up for that. When I descended the stairs for dinner, I imagined that the family would be milling around—Aunt Navida and Aunt Rachel included—and that everything was serene and orderly, with wonderful smells drifting to the rafters. And in my daydream, I would go to my father who would be sitting beside a kerosene lamp, reading. He would look up, his face glowing as it had when I was small, and he would smile and kiss me and we would talk.

But at night my dreams were full of shadows, of dark caverns in mountainsides, of alleyways and abandoned buildings, of people with dark faces and greedy smiles. Sometimes their mouths would elongate, their teeth would sharpen and drip, and they would howl at a lilac-scented moon.

And so I was ripe for what happened the spring before I turned seventeen, steeped in self-disapproval and dark thoughts leavened with stubborn pride. I had been rejected and was now rejecting: first my father, then my mother, then my brothers, then my friends.

It would have taken a keen sensibility to pierce the facade I had created for myself. During my junior year of high school, I held a job, earned high grades, was active in student clubs, won a student-body office, and participated in school plays, marching troupes, and the annual musical. My friends and teachers saw me as the epitome of a well-adjusted teenager: active, friendly, hardworking, dependable. But inside hid an alienated individual, every avenue of her life dead-ending, every achievement empty. I resented those I loved, and those I loved seemed to dislike me. The schism between my interior and exterior life became Procrustes' bed.

Peculiarly, the one place I felt truly comfortable was at work in the small diner near my father's office. My boss—an alcoholic who began his day at six o'clock in the morning with a bottle of Seagram's 7, got amorous around nine thirty, and passed out before ten—left most decisions to me. On weekend mornings I cooked, cleaned, and waitressed for a group of regulars—men who dropped in for the morning coffee their Mormon wives refused to brew at home, high school dropouts who spent their days playing pinball, construction workers who hung out during bad weather.

They teased and I flirted. They came at lunch or coffee break, bringing daisies and early vegetables from their gardens, or their latest jokes and problems from home. I felt necessary and real there, where I could bring a hungry man a good breakfast and a cheerful greeting, where no more was expected than what I willingly gave.

In the smoky diner I hoped to learn enough about the mysterious, exclusive world of men to ease my way into relationships where I could be authentic. Some customers asked for dates, and I usually had the sense to decline. But one young man caught my attention and held it. Smooth-talking and good-looking, his sleek hair, the ripple of his muscles, the glint of his eyes had a sinuousness about them that nearly hypnotized my senses. When he came into the cafe, my hand would begin to shake, and I would spill hot coffee on myself. When he asked me out, I knew the score: either I said yes or there would be no second chance.

I dressed carefully in a blouse of exotic blue print touched with bronze like the eye of a peacock feather. I teased and smoothed my hair, newly washed to bring out the gold highlights, to perfection.

He sat on his side of the car, and I sat on mine throughout the movie. I wondered if he, like me, was all promise and no delivery. But waves of electricity flowed from him, prickling my skin. I wanted him to tell me about himself, but he said nothing. I imagined sliding closer, touching his hand to feel the inevitable spark, but I dared not move. During intermission, he brought a six-pack of beer from the trunk and thrust a can at me.

"Have one," he ordered.

I wrinkled my nose—the too-long, too-wide nose that kept me from being beautiful, the nose intended for rhinoplasty as soon as I was eighteen and had saved two thousand dollars.

"I don't think so."

"Try it." His voice was oily, smooth. "It'll make you feel good."

It was against the Word of Wisdom, of course, but I had been drinking coffee once in awhile at the cafe, and it hadn't hurt me perceptibly. I had broken so many commandments—at least half of them by now. Besides, drinking was a vice, not a sin. And although Salt Lake Mormons recoiled from liquor as though it were blood, I believed the Word of Wisdom was aimed at intemperates like my poor alcoholic boss.

The first beer went down slowly. We drove down the main street of town and gazed at other couples in their cars. He would glance at the car next to us and then at me, then back at the car beside us. If the driver made some sign or comment about me he smirked. I was on display with the furred dice hanging from his mirror or the winking cat in his back window. He didn't talk as he sipped a single beer but urged me to drink another when the first was gone.

He's boring, I thought to myself. But he was good-looking, I had to admit that, so I gazed at him and sipped, and wondered if he thought or talked or if he always sat like a statue, cold and staring. I wondered what it would take to make him laugh out loud— or cry.

The earlier vibration of excitement had disappeared. I wanted to kiss him just once to see if it was real, then never go out with him again. Physical magnetism was nice, but it wasn't enough. I needed someone to talk with.

Besides, rumors surrounded him. Since accepting his invitation I learned that the boys who hung around the cafe sustained a legend about him. How to read the narrowed eyes and pinched expressions when people spoke of him? Was it fear or respect? What was it that made him so formidable? Someone said he'd once been in a fight at school and gouged his opponent's eyes out. Another said he'd been the leader of a south-side gang, that he'd been in and out of reform school since he was twelve. Others said that he simply had gone to live with his grandfather in Idaho, that his reputation was a lot of stories that someone—probably he—had made up.

By the time I finished the second beer, my skin felt warm, then cool, my tongue tingled, my mind itched sleepily. I lay back against the seat. At each corner my head rolled, waking me, but I fell asleep again as quickly. Once I opened my eyes and stared out at familiar surroundings—a brick retaining wall, tall walnut trees, the dip and plunge of the hillside. And then I glimpsed the white house looming dark and empty in the moonlight. I thought I must be dreaming. "I grew up around here," I tried to say. But my words fell garbled in the silence, and I couldn't see his face for the veil of trees that hid the moon. A peacock cried, and I realized we were in Cheaseman's yard, in the grove above the driveway, a stone's throw from the gray house where I was born. I managed to roll down the window, listening for the birds, drinking a deep draught of the soft, verdant air.

"Home," I whispered, and closed my eyes.

I must have fallen asleep, into dreaming so deeply that I was beyond consciousness, for when I awakened, it was with a violent start, a terror of something horribly amiss. I was stretched flat across the car seat and he knelt above me, unbuckling his belt.

"No!" I struggled to sit up. With a hand flat against my chest, he pushed me back and pinned me down so that my head was crushed between his shoulder and the steering wheel.

"Don't . . ." My voice weltered into a sob. I tried to push him away. "Please don't." My arms felt leaden, as though the full cans of beer had been transplanted beneath my skin. My whole being was heavy, devoid of light.

"Come on, baby," he said. I could feel his leer, the canine redness of his mouth on mine.

I twisted my neck and struggled to get my knee up. He pinned my arms over my head with one hand and fumbled my skirt with the other. "Don't. Don't you see, I grew up around here," I whimpered. "This is my home. . . ."

"Don't worry, baby," he urged. "You'll like it."

"No!" I screamed, pulling free to push at him with leaden arms, with legs I could no longer feel. And then it was too late and pain blurred words and severed feeling, cutting deeply into my soul, a cleaver through the center of my being. I was betrayed, had betrayed myself. My spirit strangled. Somewhere the Cheaseman's peacock strutted, screaming "Help! Help!"—a sound that also came from my heart. But it was no use trying to ward off serpents now. I wept silently behind my hand for our two proud souls, winged, unable to fly.

On the way to my mother's house I talked of reporting him to the school counselors or the police—not something I really intended to do, for fear an investigation would unearth trouble for my family. But I wanted him to tell me what had happened, wanted a sign that my feeling was true, that he had violated me. For some reason I didn't think of rape. It was as though I didn't know the word existed.

He laughed shortly. "Hah. I'm not worried."

"Why not?" I couldn't imagine anyone being oblivious to the threat of arrest.

He sneered. "I'll just get a dozen of those guys at the cafe where you work to testify that they've had you too, and I'll be as free as a bird."

I gasped. "That's a lie!"

He shrugged. "That's how it goes, baby."

I began to cry again. "What . . . what if I'm pregnant?"

He shrugged again. "Your problem, baby. Not mine." He stretched against the steering wheel. "You try to hang it on me and I'll just deny, deny, deny."

I struggled to keep control. I could not let him see how beaten I felt, how cut to the nerve of my being.

"I'll get back at you," I warned. "Someday I'll make you pay for this."

He laughed again. "No, baby. You'll do the paying. For the rest of your life, you'll be paying. Even when you're with your old man, it'll be me you're thinkin' of, not him."

I covered my ears and closed my eyes until the car stopped in front of the duplex. I reached for the handle and he grabbed my arm.

"Ain't you even gonna kiss me good night?"

I shuddered and froze. "Let me go. You're done with me. Just let me go."

He released my arm. "You can go. But I'm not done with you, not by a long shot, baby."

After he had sped off, spitting gravel, I stood on the damp lawn, toes digging into the mud, as if my nerves were a thousand bee stings and this soft earth the only poultice for my pain.

At the sight of my father's car in the drive I felt upended, drowning in the vortex of a whirlpool, undercurrent pulling me headfirst through some black unending tunnel toward a terrifying birth.

The windows of my mother's house, opaque but for the faint glimmer of the hall light left on for me, reflected cold starlight. I envisioned Grandmother Allred, her stern face collapsed in a grief she'd never shown in life.

Perhaps no one told me the story, or perhaps I'd heard it and given it no significance, having no point of reference, no intimate knowledge of rape. Later, when I heard it, I wondered again at my weakness and at the void where my spiritual legacy should have shone as it shone for her that dark night when she arrived alone in Logan, disembarking from a train, bent on meeting Grandfather Harvey to continue their journey to Mexico and the Principle of Plural Marriage.

Connections had been fumbled, and she was forced to visit a relative's home at the outskirts of town. She hailed a cab, and the horses trotted complacently down a country road. At first she ignored the innuendos of the taxi driver, then reprimanded him. "Shame on you," she said. When the driver halted his team and reached for her she was ready, her voice sharp as a hat pin.

"In the name of Jesus Christ I command you to stop!"

He stopped. He bowed his head and wept. He begged her forgiveness and pleaded with her not to tell anyone. He confessed that he suffered from perversion, from a burning desire, and lamented the day when polygamy was outlawed.

She regarded him in disgusted silence. He drove her to her aunt and uncle's home, where she promptly turned him in. Authorities soon learned that he had molested seven young ladies of the town, none courageous enough to reveal her shame and terror.

No peacocks cried in Logan that night. No serpents pierced Grandmother's magic circle.

I opened the door slowly and stood in the living room, staring. My parents were in bed, wrapped in the soft white flannel of their love.

Should I go to Daddy, I wondered. Tell him what had happened, ask what I should do?

But how could I tell him, knowing what he thought of me. He would only tell me that I had asked for it—which I had—and remind me of what I was. The people in the group called him prophet. His prophecy about Aunt Henni's baby had been fulfilled, along with many others. And he had predicted what I would be as surely, as accurately as any prophet.

Perhaps, then, I had been made for some mysterious, dark purpose that only my father and God Himself understood. Or perhaps I had willed it to happen. I had been so attracted to this . . . this wolf. Maybe some black corner of myself had begged for this, had given up too easily, willed arms and legs to heaviness, wanting to taste evil, to challenge all I had been taught.

"Honey, is that you?" my mother called.

My throat was too dry for speaking. I swallowed. "Yes, it's me." My voice was dull and heavy as my brain.

"I'm glad you're home," she called gently, sweetly. My father said nothing.

Home? I thought bitterly. My home is gone. I have no home. I'll never be home again.

Chapter

10

"What're you doing here?" Brian looked up from the refrigerator case where he was stacking eggs. "You look like you just lost your best friend."

"I *feel* like I just lost my best friend." My voice trembled and my hands were cold. I was glad that the grocery store where Brian worked was almost deserted.

Brian took another carton from the wire box and placed it carefully. "And who's that?" he said coolly. What if he tells me to go away, I thought desperately.

I stared unwaveringly until he met my eyes. "You."

He shook his head. "Nobody loses me. Sometimes I get thrown away—but lost, never."

I grimaced. "I've been so stupid."

He shrugged. "Even girls have to try their wings."

The conversation seemed to flow from some remote memory, parts written for us by someone else. I felt disoriented, speechless. His eyes were skeptical and cool.

"What you doing tonight?" he asked after a vast silence.

"I have a date—but I'll break it. If you want me to."

"I want you to."

He walked me to my car. "Don't pick up any stray dogs on the way home. The store is having a Christmas party—dinner and dancing, sort of formal—about seven. Be ready. I hate waiting."

I sighed. So Brian still cared for me despite three misspent years since we first found each other. Experience had been so important back then, a voice within driving me beyond my own limits, prodding, "You must taste of everything or you will be unfulfilled."

And now I was surfeited, choking on experience.

— 167

In the months since the rape I had bathed twice a day and prayed morning, noon, and night, but nothing made me feel clean. I was dirt-black inside, and gradually the world too became a lusterless clay sphere dotted with fools and con men. Sometimes, looking into the mirror or out over a gray winter twilight, I reflected that I had been "cast into outer darkness"—the punishment reserved for apostates.

My three older brothers had married, leaving me in the awesome position as oldest in my mother's maverick family.

Saul married a Mormon girl he had met while teaching art in Oregon. She seemed perfect for him, displaying a fine balance of musical ability and athletic inclination. She radiated wholesomeness but was free-spirited enough to allow Saul his divergent thoughts and conclusions.

Danny had "bested" Saul—according to the common cultural standard—by marrying a Salt Lake girl in the Mormon temple (something Saul openly refused until he had gained a sure testimony of the truth of Mormonism). The two were married within months of Saul and his bride.

Jake and Adele now had two beautiful blond children, a girl and a boy. Whenever they visited, I was deeply touched by these little miracles that now lit up our lives like some reawakened hope. My father kissed and cuddled them, nuzzling their necks, tossing them in the air and bouncing them on his knee as he recited "Richardy Robberty" and "A Frog Went A-Courtin'," just as he had all his children and nieces and nephews. And now his grandchildren. Grandchildren. I was an aunt.

Although my childhood concept of marriage had often seemed threatening and a little dull, I had accepted it as necessary to have babies. Four babies, I had thought, even then. Now I longed to regain grace with the male figures in my life, to regain grace with my womanhood.

Simultaneously, I resented my Mormon woman's role. Since Eve was the first to yield to temptation, she must obey her husband, our doctrines insisted. How curious, I reflected, that she was endowed with power to tempt Adam in the first place. Wasn't his destiny to partake of the Fruit and to listen to the Snake? Some Mormon leaders taught the fall of Adam as an indirect blessing, for in being cast out, in realizing the imperfection of the two selves, man and woman came together to make another. Through division they united to create a better whole. So why was Eve the bad one, the weak one? True, Church writings were contradictory; one Mormon Article of Faith states that "man shall be punished for his own sins and not for Adam's transgression." But this native goodness or neutrality didn't seem to include women.

Some early Church leaders had justified plural marriage and certain other inequities, explaining that women labored under "the curse of Eve." Because she had been overly curious, ambitious, and fundamentally jealous of Adam's relationship with God, Eve and all her sisters were denied the priesthood. As unreliable sources of wisdom (having yielded to temptation), the frailer sex would have to cooperate to bring out the best in a man, thereby conquering jealousy. As compensation for this inferior state, bereft of spiritual power, woman received the blessing of children, an experience that would enhance spiritual growth. Still, she was not to be trusted. In our religion, there was original sin for Eve but not for Adam.

Like Eve—yes, even like my mother—I had been overpowered and introduced to my weaknesses, both physical and spiritual. I had been knocked to the ground, my integrity betrayed. Despised for being weak enough to be drawn into temptation, despised for being weak enough to be treated as despised, I must then accept myself as weak and despicable.

Had I known in my youth of a woman's control over sexuality in plural marriage, my relationships with men might have flourished in better health. Later in life I learned that the province given women through the blessing of children involved considerable power. In the Principle of Plural Marriage the sexual activities of all partners are governed by the Law of Chastity, which states that sex is purely for procreation, not for lust. To obey the Law, a man must not approach any of his wives except on special command from the Lord, or when she initiates sexual contact, for she and only she can know when she is ready to bear the burden of a child. Anytime conception is impossible—during menses, pregnancy, lactation, and after menopause—the devout polygamist considers it wrong to engage in sex.

Here, had I known it, was a woman's power, albeit temporary and tragically linked to aging. Still, it was the only power available to me within the confines of the Principle. A fertile woman had power over coming together, power over childbearing, power over the children themselves in their upbringing. A woman could turn a child's heart toward his father or against him. She could subtly undermine her husband's wishes or cooperate to see them fulfilled. Children become the plural wife's ransom against a husband's abuse or neglect, the treasure of tomorrow in today's hold, giving ballast against lost priesthood and physical frailty.

But I didn't know these things when I needed most to know them, since sex was not discussed in my family. My father shied from the topic, shied even from his children from the time they became sexual beings until they were safely married. My mother didn't understand her power, nor that she wielded it unconsciously. There was no one to hold the universe aloft, no one to see me through my rites of passage.

I clung to the belief that men owned all the power in this sexual feudalism and that they lacked the necessary noblesse oblige to make the system work well. I concluded that if I, the oppressed party, was to survive at all, I must outmanipulate, keep the upper hand, go to war. My relationships with men became a chess match; I closed my eyes to the psychological bloodshed of the battle.

While alone with my boyfriends, I inquired after their personal lives. I listened and cared. They didn't know that my tenderness was a commodity, one of my few wiles, the only way I knew to relate to men. I toyed with their passions, letting them kiss and touch, until they held me wildly and groaned, before I refused them.

But if they were reluctant, I would coax them on, forcing them toward a moment of shivering, psychological nakedness, and then I would say, "Oh, you're just a boy," and draw away. I was not kind. Yet I felt myself to be the victim. I didn't imagine that I was really hurting others. It was only a game, to see who would win or lose. And certainly I must play to win, must keep score and take note of each victory, although all the time I felt that I, too, was inevitably losing.

Yet I had maintained a self-deception that I was high priestess of the game, a sorceress and holder of supremely bitter knowledge about this dance of lust that so terrified, magnetized, and spellbound the human race.

That evening when Brian picked me up, I introduced him to my mother and my brothers who were home with their wives for the holidays. They took to his dry wit immediately, but we did not linger.

The Christmas party, like any other company party in Utah, cliqued drinkers versus nondrinkers, smokers versus nonsmokers.

Brian and I, with our quasi-Mormon attitudes, fitted poorly with either group, but somehow I didn't feel the usual aching need to belong and didn't feel lonely as we ate in candlelight at one end of the banquet table, away from the others. I didn't mind that no one cut in as we danced to soft music from a small combo compressed into one corner of the recreation room. For a long time I felt only Brian's arm around my waist, his hand holding mine, his aura seeming to encompass me, surrounding me with love and protection. I was being healed. I was falling in love.

The realization jerked my head up and sent starlight dreams scattering.

"What's happening?" I craned my neck to see his face. He was at least six feet tall, broad-shouldered and long-legged.

"You tell me," he said, his eyes misty in the half-light.

"I'm not ready for this."

Brian steered me across the dance floor, toward the coatroom. "Let's get out of here. We've got some talking to do."

He drove and I talked, telling him to be on guard because I always ruined things before they even got off the ground.

"I don't know what's wrong with me. I'm afraid of men. I love them in a way, hate them in another—even you. Am I crazy?"

Brian shrugged. "Who knows? I always figured women hold all the cards."

"The women! In this valley especially it's you men who run the show. Except when I purposely ruined things between us. And even that was for a man holding strings. When my father found us like that, I didn't dare see you again. Besides, it was getting too serious too soon."

Brian nodded. "I waited."

I laughed. "Sure you did. Stayed home and watched TV for three years."

"No, I didn't stay home. I ran away last summer to San Francisco, and I only came back to finish school."

"What's wrong at home?"

Brian's jaw locked and he didn't take his eyes off the road. "My mother married when she was really young, and she had four kids right off. Then her husband died. As part of her grieving she took up with my father. I was born two years later. None of my brothers and sisters remember the wedding. Just the divorce."

"Divorce!" The word brought an image of light slipping into a black hole. Aunt Susan, the hole in my father's heart. "I don't believe in divorce. If people get married, especially if they have kids, they should stick by each other."

Brian sat silent.

"Go on. . . . I'm sorry. Go on," I apologized.

"My mother married again and they had a couple more. My brothers and sisters have a place in the family. I don't. I'm the mistake they couldn't cover up. My favorite fairy tale, Hansel and Gretel, was like this dream I always had, my family leaving me. I would run after the car, screaming. Either they didn't hear me or they wouldn't stop. I would keep running until I fell. And then the car would disappear."

"Oh, Brian." I knew the terror of being closed out. My recurrent nightmare of wolves and locked doors clotted my thoughts and swelled my heart with sympathy.

"Ever since my mother threw my father out for two-timing her, she's resented me. She and my aunt would watch me play. 'He'll be just like his dad,' my aunt used to say."

My head buzzed. My father's pronouncement of me had come true. Perhaps Brian's aunt's words were just as powerful. "And will you be . . . just like your dad?"

Brian shook his head fiercely. "When I think about him, my chest gets so tight I can't breathe. When I was two or three, he was still around, and my mother worked nights. Once he wanted me to kiss him good night and I said no, not until I asked her. He'd spank me, and if I still wouldn't kiss him, he'd spank me again. That went on all night, I guess. My sisters remember."

I touched his shoulder, wanted to cry.

Brian took a breath. "He's a bastard." He grinned wryly. "And so am I—probably."

"Brian, you don't know the whole story. Maybe he and your mom . . . He must have had a reason!"

"Reason? What reason? He was an animal."

"Stop feeling sorry for yourself!" I spoke sharply, schoolteacherish. Pity was the emotion I would not, dared not allow myself.

Brian's face hardened into silence.

"Look," I said, "I've had run-ins with some animals myself. And as for your being a bastard—*if* it's true—by this society's standards, I'm illegitimate too. There's something I have to say, but I don't know where to begin. . . ."

"Your father has two wives," he stated flatly.

My eyes widened. "How did you know?"

"Not hard to figure out. Your father coming and going from both places. When you grow up without a norm, you stop expecting one."

I nodded. "But it's not two wives—it's seven!" I waited for the impact, but Brian only shrugged.

"My father had thirty-five, near as we can figure. Of course, it's doubtful they were all *married* to him."

"My parents weren't married by the law of the land. But they were married in the eyes of God. In that sense I'm legitimate."

Brian nodded. "That's a lot more than I've got going for me. I wasn't wanted. I don't belong."

"You're feeling sorry for yourself again."

"No. I'm feeling pretty lucky tonight." He grinned smugly at me and stretched his arms against the steering wheel.

"You *are* crazy. After the way I treated you? Even knowing that I'm the daughter of a polygamist—and a black sheep at that? You know what you're asking for?"

"I have a pretty good idea." Again the clown grin.

"Didn't you hear me? Even my father doesn't like me. He knows what I am."

"You're just confused. I can see that. I don't know what your father's problem is."

"Brian . . . some of the things I've done . . . I've gone with one guy after another . . . let them do things. . . . I tried to convince myself that I cared for them. But I was lying to myself—and that's the worst kind of lying."

"I don't think I want to hear any more about it," he said abruptly. "I guess I'd like to take a roll in the hay with you as much as they. But not without making it right first."

I suddenly felt frightened. "I . . . I don't think we should be saying these things to each other. Here I am, telling you all my secrets. Most of them," I added, thinking of the rape. I had vowed never to reveal that humiliation.

"I've told you mine—all about my family. I've never done that before."

"I'm flattered."

"Don't be," he said quickly. "It's not a gift so much as a responsibility."

"Above all, I want us to be friends," he added quickly. "Friendship is life's truest flower."

I grinned. "What are you . . . a poet?"

"Yes."

In the next weeks Brian wrote poems during school and gave them to me when we skipped class for coffee. We spent every possible moment together, attending gatherings arm in arm, spending his paycheck the first half of the week and my check for waitressing the second half.

"All right," he said, "if we're going to get serious, we ought to face each other's families. You show me yours and I'll show you mine."

Brian's mother lived in a pink brick house that she had designed herself. She was an imposing woman, heavy yet dignified, square-jowled and big-eyed, with frown lines etched in the corners of her mouth. Her silver-white hair radiated, giving her an aura of authority reminiscent of my father's. Toward me she was polite and remote and skeptical.

"Glad to meet you," she murmured. But I could tell by the glint of her protuberant blue eyes that she wasn't glad to meet me at all.

"She doesn't like me," I whispered when Brian had closed the sliding doors behind her.

"That's because she knows."

"Knows what?" I sat upright.

"That this is for real. I've never brought a girl home to meet her before."

After our necking session on his mother's turquoise sofa Brian announced, "Your turn."

I hesitated. "You've already met most of my family—my mother and brothers, and of course you remember my father."

Brian snorted. "That's barely scratchin' the surface."

I agreed, yet knew I couldn't bear the intimacy and scrutiny of a family home evening.

"How about a group meeting? You could hear my father speak and I could point out the others."

We sat at the rear of the meeting hall, Brian in a sport jacket and jeans, me in the one long-sleeved dress that reached my knees.

"Where'd all the babies come from?" Brian whispered beneath the din of scraping chairs and chatter.

"As if you didn't know." I grinned. I didn't add that most of the infants were left at home for this nighttime meeting.

The hall was dismal gray and poorly heated for a February evening in Utah. People huddled in the cold. The only warmth centered on the blue sofa where the council members sat under a long fluorescent lamp at the head of the room. Another, stronger overhead light shone on the battered dark-wood lectern set on a long table. My father saw me, nodded and smiled. Relief and pleasure buzzed through my veins. The heat and light of the priesthood no longer seemed so remote.

The old family smell—for the first time identifiable to me as a mix of rising yeast and antiseptic—burned acrid in my nostrils. In Brian's presence I saw the group with new clarity, their straight necks and stooped shoulders, their thin arms and thin white shirts, the devotion in their faces, whether florid or bland. Despite the varying size and coloring, the group had the look of family—no surprise, considering the intermarriage among the five or six major families, until the barrier to bloodlines had to be traced with each new union to insure against inbreeding. They were a family of proud orphans, of impoverished nobility.

"Dear brothers and sisters, friends and loved ones. I am blessed to welcome you to this gathering. How grateful I am to be counted among these souls dedicated to the Lord," my father opened. Then he turned the time over to another member of the council. Brian nudged me and lifted his brows at this apparent abdication of power. He was even more surprised when we sang a widely known Mormon hymn, "Come, Come Ye Saints."

My Uncle Andrew called on Aunt Gerda's Tyrone and one of his own handsome blond sons to bless the sacrament. They crooked left arms behind their backs, right arms raised head-high. Automatically I bowed my head for the prayer. The words, repeated every Sunday for most of my life, now rang like the bells of a foreign cathedral. "That they will take upon them the name of Thy Son. And remember Him . . ."

I tried to concentrate on repentance, but with Brian beside me I had nothing to regret. I peeked at him. He was peeking at me. We grinned.

We eyed the plate of homemade bread as it was passed from priesthood-bearer to partaker and back until our turn came.

After a second prayer I saw with horror that a quart Mason jar made its way toward us. Ordinarily the group shared a single glass, invoking memory of the chalice Jesus had passed at the Last Supper. It was another fundamental foothold against the modernized church with its single-swallow paper cups, and I had always enjoyed the communal feeling of drinking from a common cup. But a fruit jar? What would Brian think? Now, as it came closer, I saw bread crumbs floating in the water. I longed to slip away.

"Do I have to drink too?" Brian whispered.

My father was watching us. "Of course!" I hissed.

During the testimony portion of the meeting things got worse. It was a night for the lunatic fringe to speak. One man spouted John Birch politics until my uncle asked him to sit down. Another man divined that UFO sightings were directly related to latter-day events and clear evidence that the City of Enoch had returned to lift us from the burning earth.

Such incendiary speeches lighted even the stable councilmen to bear witness that apocalypse was at hand, the last days only a push button away. Brian squirmed on his folding chair.

"Let's go!" I whispered as soon as the closing prayer was offered. I tugged at his arm and struggled into my coat all at once like a fierce, silent whirlwind.

Brian nodded and grinned. Then we were outside, the metal lock clicked behind us, the bright stars winking as we breathed frozen air tinged with carbon monoxide and manure.

As we drove through quiet streets, it seemed we were the only two people in the world.

"Most of my problems stem from other people," Brian said. "If it wasn't for other people, I wouldn't have problems."

I nodded. I thought him amazingly profound. "We should live alone, on a desert island," I said.

"That'd be fine, long as we had a radio," he said.

"What will you do when we graduate?" he asked as we cruised the dark mountains above the valley.

"Go to college." I spoke surely. Of all the things in my life, only the dream that Saul fostered of "making something of myself" seemed to have survived.

Brian said nothing, but I thought his profile, etched in the dashlight, had hardened.

"What's wrong?"

"I don't know. I was hoping you had something else in mind."

"Like what?"

"Like . . . getting married."

I felt he had thrown a wet sheet over my head. "Brian, we're so young. How would we live? What would we do?"

He shrugged. "I've always worked. I can always get a job doing something. I could drive a truck with my brother."

"You're kidding! After all the time I spent without my father, do you think I would marry a truck driver? I watched my mother cry herself to sleep too many nights!"

"I see." His voice was cold.

I bowed my head. Brian turned the car toward my mother's house, and we traveled in silence. It wasn't that the idea of marriage repulsed me as it once had. But since the rape a frozen morass had formed within me. Unconsciously I had rearranged my childhood dreams to exclude men. As for the deep longing for children, perhaps I would have to content myself with pouring out the love stored in my lifetime onto my nieces and nephews.

Even with Brian the natural dream of children seemed impossible. In our present relationship he was mostly kind, but there was no telling what he would do once married. I could be expected to sacrifice myself repeatedly to his power, whether physically or spiritually.

No, I thought, marriage at this point would be a kind of sin— a denial of self, a renouncemnt of the little scrap of soul left to me. And so when Brian suggested marriage, I sat in frozen silence, unmoving and unmoved until he took me home.

I have since read that selfish pride is usually rooted in insecurity. If that is true, then the powerlessness I felt when I thought of marriage was probably responsible for my aloofness toward Brian. I was not aware of how much it pained him, of how much he counted on me and on the promise of the feelings that passed between us. I was someone who had so little life I could not make room in my tiny space for another life—or yet another.

Another problem, related yet distinct, made me shy from marriage. There was vengeance in my soul. And almost as though I had willed it, the day after my high school graduation the rapist returned, showing up where I worked. He knows I'm getting well and wants to throw me down again, I thought, but the notion was unreal and passed unconsidered. I took vicious delight from his sudden appearance, the knee-shaking passion I had felt as a child while rifling Aunt Henni's drawers augmented a thousandfold. I would make him pay. I would wreak my revenge for the ruined dreams, the thwarted life. I would teach him to feel, would make him love and need me, and somehow I believed this would absolve the horror. Oh, it wouldn't be hard. I knew how to make men care, having sympathized my way into the confidence of so many by now. I knew when to hold and when to withhold, when to chase and when to run. My excuse for deserting others unkindly was that I had been acquiring skills. And now I would use them. This time I would win.

As before, my hands shook and coffee spilled, but it burned cold as the desire in my mind, a tiny pinpoint of light crowded by dark purpose. I was cool, so cool, refusing to recognize him until he brought attention to himself.

"Don't you remember me, baby? We had a good time together."

I ignored an urge to vomit. "Oh . . . you."

When he asked me out again, I demurred. "I'm going with someone. Too bad." I gave him a sultry smile.

One night when I had locked the diner, leaving the key inside for the morning manager, my car wouldn't start. I looked around for a telephone, then remembered that Brian was working late, unloading his brother's truck. I didn't think to call my father. I no longer thought of him as one of the resources in my life. I sighed and began to walk home. The air was warm and stars hung low. I was only a little afraid.

I had walked only a block when a car pulled up beside me. It was he. My heart stopped.

He rolled down the window. "Hey, a chick like you shouldn't be walkin' home. What if some nut found you?" His voice slipped and slithered.

My blood chilled, more with repulsion than fear. This wasn't what I had in mind. "Like you, for instance?" I walked more quickly. The car rolled alongside the curb, motor purring. I glanced around. Only dark stores, not a house for blocks. How could I ever keep the upper hand in a place like this?

"Listen, baby," his voice was soft, almost pleading. "I won't do anything you don't want."

I bowed my head and clenched my hands in my uniform pockets. I mustn't let him know I'm afraid of him. I forced myself to slow down. But he had stopped the car and leapt out silent as a cat. Now he had hold of my elbow, walking alongside me. "Whatsamatter, baby? Your car won't start?"

I looked up at him. "How did you know?" Then it hit me. "What did you do?" My heart stuck between beats as though processing shards of ice.

He grinned. "Just a small problem. I'll fix it in the morning. If you'll let me drive you home."

"You bastard. What did you do that for?"

"I had to do something. You wouldn't go out with me."

I shrugged. "There's other fish in the sea." I'm cool, I thought to myself. He doesn't know I'm afraid. I'm not afraid.

"I can't stop thinkin' about you. Just had to put my arm around you once more. See? That ain't so bad, is it? You gonna marry this creep you're goin' with?"

I wondered if he heard my teeth grind. "I don't know. I guess it all depends. . . ." I let my voice trail suggestively. "But you have a way of taking whatever you want. And I like to give things away."

He grinned salaciously. "Yeh. But I'll be good. Let me show you." He jerked his head at the car.

I considered. It was clear that he would not let me go. I would be better off to go along with him. I believed I could control him now, playing cat-and-mouse with words, for I was not drunk and I was not feeling weak. The desire for vengeance pumped strength into my veins. When I was a child and Danny had told me that there was a wolf in the cubbyhole, I had made myself go upstairs in the dark house so that I would not have to sleep in Aunt Henni's bed. I could do it again.

"All right. But you'll have to behave yourself."

He didn't take me home, of course, but drove to where the sagebrush rimmed the western foothills. We parked and looked down on the lights of the city. When he pulled me to him, my nails flashed and I was ready to bite and scream. A thrill of terror passed over my heart. Perhaps I would never make it home—my body would be found here with the jackrabbits and the last rattlesnakes and lizards. I wondered what my father would do. Would he cry? Would he be sorry?

I pushed against him. "You'll be sorry," I warned. "I told you I only give things away."

"You'll never give it away," he sulked.

"Oh . . . you don't know. . . ." My voice was heavy with promise. "You haven't seen anything yet. Look, I can't make love with a stranger. Not until I know something about you."

With this information I planned to plot his demise. I would make him love me. Then I would drop him. But he was curiously unemotional about everything: his parents, his brothers and sisters, his time in reform school. Nothing excited him except sex—sex and the fights he had been in until he was too old to escape being sentenced for assault.

We drove and parked, drove and parked, me probing, trying to find one chink in the armor. In return I submitted to the vile rush of his hands.

But he didn't tell me he loved me. He told me he was married. He laughed when he said it. He laughed when I told him I wouldn't go with him again. He laughed when I told him not to visit me where I worked. He laughed when I insisted he take me home. He laughed when I slammed the car door and started walking home.

Brian had seen the two of us parked at the end of my street. He pulled up alongside as I walked down my street, and my heart nearly strangled me. I got in the car beside him. I knew I had to confess my entanglement or lose Brian forever. I told him the story of the rape.

"I can't understand it myself," I told him, weeping. "It's like there's two people in me, and one of them is beyond control. Oh—not like you think! But I *had* to make him respect me . . . don't you see?"

Brian gritted his teeth. "Vermin respect nothing. Vermin ought to be exterminated. You'd better make up your mind. You'd better get control or you won't be seeing me anymore."

I didn't realize Brian's frenzy that night, that he had seen my car in the cafe parking lot and then had waited near my house, fuming and frightened, thinking me dead or gone forever—lost in any case—and then had seen me return at four A.M. with another man. I didn't know that Brian had called my mother and talked to her for an hour or more, that he had told her he loved me but that he, like her, didn't know what to do with me.

Next morning Brian dropped in at the diner—a surprise, because he didn't like me waitressing.

I took my break, setting two cups of coffee down as I slid into the booth. "I'm so glad to see you," I said.

"I didn't come to chat," he said abruptly. "You can have your midnight lover. I only came to tell you that I joined the Marine Corps. I'll be leaving for boot camp on Pioneer Day."

I gasped. "Brian! You're kidding. Please tell me you're kidding." I was suddenly trapped in a darkness far deeper than the shadows I had known before. I waved my hands, trying to brush his words away, trying to awaken myself.

There was no changing it. My most eloquent promises held no weight against the Marine Corps papers Brian had signed.

He left on schedule, July 24, 1967, marching with the customary Utah Platoon in the Pioneer Day Parade along with thirty-nine other youths, an illogical echo of the Mormon Battalion that Brigham Young pledged to fight in the Mexican War when Utah was first being settled by Mormon pioneers. Despite the U.S. Government resistance to Mormon dreams and doctrines, the Church committed five hundred troops, hoping the gesture would prove Mormon patriotism and soften persecutions sponsored by the government. The United States had accepted the help but returned no favors. Even while the Mormon Battalion marched, Church leaders were harassed for living polygamy.

As I watched Brian board the plane, kissing Miss Utah with thirty-nine others, helplessness infected my mind. I wondered if he, like half the Mormon Battalion, would never return to Zion.

When my tears were spent, the nightmares began. With the Vietnam War in full operation, Brian wrote that there were two kinds of Marines: those who had been and those who were going.

Night after night I was awakened by the sound of gunfire and artillery blasts in my ears. Along with the crack and boom of munitions was evidence of death: groans, shrieks, rattles, the stink of loss and destruction. I dreamed of Brian blown apart, his legs in fragments, his arms flung into the air, and I could not awaken but was transfixed by the dream—forced to walk through it, sorting his parts, impaled by my own vengeful spear against the wall of sleep.

At last my mother came to me and placed a cool hand on my forehead.

"Darling. You're having a nightmare. Wake up."

"Oh my God," I whispered. I wasn't taking the Lord's name in vain, not this time. I threw my arms around her. "Oh, Mama, Brian will be killed over there. And it's my fault. It's all my fault."

Chapter

11

The apartment was too expensive. I knew that when I took it, lying to the owner about my job. I had told my mother I'd be sharing expenses with a girl from the university, another lie. On the balcony was a glass-top table surrounded by wrought-iron chairs, where I sat over coffee this November morning.

The French doors were slightly open, and through them floated the sounds of Brian splashing in the bathroom. I had been awake for hours, waiting out this golden morning in heavy thought. I shifted impatiently, wanting to walk in the neighboring foothills or drive through the resplendent canyons, or rake leaves beneath the bright autumn sky, anything to send air stinging through my lungs, to send thoughts flying.

On the balcony I felt seated in a sandbagged balloon floating above the foothills checkered with neat cottages and the spired dome of the state capitol. Directly beyond, a statue of the Angel Moroni, son of Mormon who inscribed the Golden Plates, trumpeted captured sunlight from his pinnacle atop the Mormon temple.

Westward stretched the Great Salt Lake—the New World's own Dead Sea—fed by our own Jordan River, a silver ribbon rumpling south to join freshwater Utah Lake. Because of autumn winds the air today was clean and clear enough to sight the salt beach, a glistening edge on the horizon. From the balcony everything seemed orderly and beautiful: Promised Valley, City of Zion. But all was not "well in Zion."

And all was not well with me, although Brian was home on furlough and we planned to be married. I had made the decision almost unconsciously, writing the words before I thought them: "I want to be married before you go to Vietnam. I want to have your child." He had telephoned his assent immediately.

But there was still the question of our parents. We were not even officially engaged, but we were living together.

Brian interrupted my thoughts, easing through the French doors, a coffee cup in one hand, a cigarette in the other—incongruities below his shining, boyish face, made younger and more vulnerable by the GI haircut. What would my father say?

Although we pretended to be happy in this apartment, the strain of knowing it wasn't right stuck with us like a spiritual gumshoe. Suddenly the bright day was out of focus.

"Brian . . . I've been thinking. Maybe it wouldn't be such a bad idea to get an engagement ring after all."

He looked up, surprised. We had decided to spend our money enjoying the few days we had together, dispensing with old, empty formalities like engagement rings. "My mother didn't have one," I had told Brian. "If a plain gold band was good enough for her, I guess it should be good enough for me."

But now I had changed my mind. "It might convince our parents that we're serious, that we really want to be married," I explained. "Then maybe your mother would change her mind about us and give her consent."

He nodded and smiled vaguely. "You pick it out." He returned to the kitchen for more coffee. When he came back he was preoccupied and restless.

The silence bore down like a thumbscrew. "Brian, if you don't want a ring . . ."

"It isn't that. I've been wondering how we'll swing it. You know what my wages are in this Green Machine? Thirteen cents an hour. In a month or two I'll be getting combat pay, a big twenty cents an hour. Now how am I gonna support a wife on twenty cents an hour?"

"Brian, don't worry about it. I can work. I'll make the ring payments." This proposal embarrassed us both. I bit my lip.

"I don't like you working," he said, predictably. "Even with your scholarship you'll have to pay for books, and now the apartment." He paused. "You know what you ought to do while I'm overseas? Move home. It'd be better for everyone."

"I . . . I can't do that, Brian. It's true my folks haven't said anything about us. I suppose they believe I'm living in the dorms or with a girlfriend like I implied. But I can't be sure. And if my dad knew about us, he'd disown me—if he hasn't already."

Brian bowed his head. Then he turned to me. "What makes you think your father would even care if you came home? You could live with your mom and go to your room when your old man comes around. The last I heard, there wasn't much love to be lost between you two."

Suddenly I felt hot and twisted. "Will you quit trying to run my life? And don't call him 'old man'! He isn't so old. And he does care about me. He loves me. I know he does!" My breath came in sharp, painful spurts. "When I was a little girl, he'd hold me on his knee and pat my hair and call me 'princess.'" My voice was shrill, defensive. Suddenly I began to sob. "He does love me. I know he does. Besides, we could be married right now if it wasn't for your mother!"

Brian's eyes flashed and then he sighed, cheeks and chest imploding. "Yeh. I've got to do something about that. I'll call my commanding officer tomorrow and see what kind of pressure he can put on her. OK?"

Monday, after my zoology class at the university, I went looking for a ring, walking through town with my head bowed, pausing only to run my hand across the rough gray conrnerstones of Temple Square. The iron fence, ten or twelve feet high, makes gridwork of the trees and buildings beyond, but the spires of the temple tower above, Angel Moroni gleaming in the haze with the insubstantial felicity of a remembered dream. I wondered if I would ever see the temple from inside. "Sealed for eternity"—that phrase, that dream had been dangled before me a hundred times. If I could not marry in the temple (because of the Principle), then I was to be "sealed" to my husband forever by the power of the priesthood. This sealing would insure me the blessing of family in the hereafter—a husband to take care of me, to resurrect me from the dead, to ensure my eternal progression; plus my children to walk beside me always, enhancing every stage of growth through the milky corridors of the universe.

Temple marriage! I opened the apartment door and went to the bedroom. A tight ache in my stomach tugged me into bed. Temple marriage! I laughed hollowly and blew my nose. I didn't have a civil license, let alone a temple "recommend." Brian and I were as illegitimate as ever.

Brian came home from rabbit hunting with my brother Danny, smelling of autumn air and sagebrush.

"Did you look for a ring?" he asked when Danny was gone.

I shook my head. He was so good-looking and such a big man—it was hard to believe that I was the only woman in his life. Sometimes I felt guilty and greedy, half-believing I should share him and then at once chalking it up to the way I was raised.

Before I had agreed to marry him, Brian had been the jealous one. Now that I was committed to him, I knew what it felt like to be uncertain and wary, almost as though Brian had infected me with his sickness. Or perhaps I had always felt it but kept it hidden from myself, feeling shamed that such a selfish attitude could take root within me. Jealousy was one of those negative feelings we were taught to smother. The mothers would sooner die than admit to jealousy or envy or any form of rivalry. "School your feelings," my father had said whenever any of us expressed a sentiment that disrupted the smooth flow of family. And now I couldn't bring myself to tell Brian how I felt about marriage and eternal commitment. I couldn't bring myself to tell him that I had fears and expectations and ideals unmet.

"Well, why didn't you buy one?" he pressed about the ring.

"Well . . . I don't want to buy my own . . ." I flushed.

"Get dressed. We'll go get one."

His abrupt, practical manner reminded me of what my father had done one March when he breezed into the kitchen and my mother presented him with a kiss, a gift, and a "Happy Anniversary." My father looked dumbfounded, then fumbled in his pockets. He withdrew a small ceramic fish on a keychain, a bit chipped in one corner. "Happy Anniversary, darling," he said magnanimously, as if it were studded with diamonds.

But mainly, I wanted Brian to get the ring, to choose a perfect moment, then remove it from his pocket and the velvet case, placing it on my finger in the grand manner. I wanted another beginning, a cleansing of this dark, gyroscopic fear that whined in my heart. Why didn't he know how to do it right: ritualized, with moonlight and soft glances and some element of surprise. Why didn't he know how difficult, and important, it was to translate all the moments of my past into this moment?

As it turned out, Brian bought the ring without me, came home and caught me napping. I sat up and received my engagement token in a stupor, my hair tousled, my eyes half-shut, in my bathrobe.

On Tuesday, I went with Brian to tell his mother that we would be married, with or without her blessing.

— 185

"You're too young," she said flatly.

"But I'm old enough to fight a war!" Brian's voice was already hysterical; this was the way he and his mother talked to each other.

Her jaw was set and she stood broad-hipped and broad-shouldered, a hand on her waist, as firmly seated as any of the granite promontories above us. Suddenly Brian's hysteria became real, and my heart flooded with panic. This was a stubborn, strong-minded woman, and we were trapped in her resolve. The state law dictates that a man must be twenty-one or have his parents' permission to marry; but although we were both eighteen, I could marry anytime. This was Utah, where women are expected never to reach the age of accountability.

In a few short moments Brian's mother had reaffirmed that we couldn't get married, had threatened to expose our living arrangements to my parents, and had suggested she might well have the ring repossessed.

"I'll do whatever I have to do to make you see what a mistake you're making. You can get married in a year or two." But I believed she intended to keep him for life.

"The same thing happened with your brother," Brian's mother continued. "He took up with that girl—"

Brian's face was livid. "She's not like that!" And he glanced at me. But his voice trembled uncertainly, as though he half-feared I would be unfaithful. I was on the brink of tears or suicide. "Look, Mom," Brian tried again. "I love her. She loves me. You know we should get married. Even the Church says so."

Her lips folded like paper as she handed him a yellow military envelope. His orders.

"These came yesterday." She watched him open it, her expression almost smug.

"I'll be shipped out within three months. We've got to get married, Mom."

"When you get home from Vietnam," she intoned. "If you still want to by then." Her mouth closed with the finality of a coffin lid. She gave me a pointed look.

Amid the ferment in my brain fear took a shape. If she found out about my parents, she would never let us get married. And perhaps she would endanger my family, catalyzing another raid.

Suddenly I was afraid that my past would reveal itself in my posture, in my half-bowed head. I pulled Brian toward the door.

"Let's go."

We left without his mother's blessing. "I don't need it," Brian said. "I've never had it before. No reason anything should be different now."

He squeezed my hand. We had reached the crest of the hill above the city. He pressed my fingers to his lips, kissing my knuckles just above the diamond ring.

The day before Thanksgiving my mother phoned. "Honey," she said in her sweet voice, "the family is meeting for Thanksgiving dinner at Uncle Andrew's garage—you know, where we used to have our meetings until the 'school' was built. Won't you come? And be sure to bring Brian along."

I had not told my mother that Brian and I intended to marry, afraid that something would go amiss, as indeed it had. But she knew that what lived between us was serious. She didn't need a diamond ring to prove the premonition that had overpowered her when she first met him: that he would be the man to marry her daughter. Now, as she spoke, her voice welcoming and insistent, I knew that the time had come for Brian to meet my family.

Yet by Thursday morning I was mildly frantic, wet palms clutching my knees as I sat smiling and chatting at the breakfast table. From Brian's somber mood I assumed that he, like me, had spent the night in terror of my family. But when I suggested that we skip the gathering, Brian turned and smiled sadly.

"It isn't your family. Don't you know that?" His eyes were deep and empty.

I hurried off, muttering about being late. I didn't want to talk about his fear or the source of it. I couldn't even deal with my own fear.

I showered thoroughly. I gargled, to wash the odor of coffee away. I put on my longest dress. I cautioned Brian not to smoke.

The garage, originally built to camouflage our religious meetings, was packed with long tables, stacks of hymn books, noise, odors, and people.

Over crying babies and shrieking children, I yelled an introduction. "Aunt Sarah, this is Brian." Soft arms enfolded me, brown eyes communicated, It's forgiven, Jeannie—whatever you've done, we love you.

While Aunt Sarah chatted and joked with Brian, I glanced

desperately around for my mother. She had been my only envoy to the family for so many years, I hardly knew how to relate to them without her.

My father was seated in the only overstuffed chair among legions of folding chairs, looking prosperous and at ease. Since the ulcer operation, he seemed healthier—almost complacent. He wore a good brown suit, and with his hair gone silver-white he at last wore the dignity of his calling. In all the noise he was reading a familiar green book, my grandfather's justification of the Principle.

"Daddy," I said softly, but his eyes continued on the page. Good grief! He had read this book a dozen times if he had read it once. And how often had I come to him in the last five years? Once, maybe twice. Now a voice within spoke out, clearly, angrily: It's my turn now! A telescoping of concentration revived from childhood the sense that my father and I were the only two people in the room.

For a moment I studied the back of his head like a crazed phrenologist, finding in each node and bump a link with the continuous hum of the room, people shifting steadily as wind on sand, oblivious as ever to my happiness or lack of it. Children and grandchildren crawled between his legs and over his feet, tunneling cities of the earth beneath a body spreading slowly with age and power. Yet in the lean, sharp planes of his face was the essential evidence: like me, he was singular; even in all this love, he was alone.

At last he looked up at me from the bottom of the page.

"Hello, dear." His eyes, vague and otherworldly, threatened to return to the page.

"Daddy, look at my ring! I'm engaged!" And I immediately nipped my tongue for its fatuousness.

He smiled benignly and nodded. He didn't take my dangling hand or examine the diamond for size and authenticity. He only gazed for brief seconds barbed with wisdom.

"I'm not surprised," he said, and his eyes returned to the book.

Relief and rage battled for space within me. Then suddenly, I undestood that all he wanted, all he had ever wanted, was that my life would work, that I would achieve happiness and fulfillment with a minimum of difficulty for him and others. For one blinding moment I understood that he was a man, not the idol of my childhood days but a human being! Then the moment was gone, reality veiled by warped reflections—fears, hopes, dreams.

Now Aunt Lisa flitted past me, trilling that she must save the sweet potatoes from scorch. Half-consciously I noticed that she was expecting again and wondered how Brian would react to the fact that my father, in his sixties, was still procreating. Brian! I remembered, and searched the room for his brown head and broad back.

Across the room Aunt Gerda had Brian by the arm, exploiting the vulnerable tilt of his ear, exercising her seniority as usual. She could scare him off forever, I thought, and hurried toward him with all the ruffled indignity of a mother hen.

Aunt Gerda saw me coming and put out her other hand. "I was just telling Brad that he must come to our meetings. They are so inspiring. He'd love them, I know he would."

"His name is Brian, Aunt Gerda," I chirped querulously, knowing she wouldn't hear me as she strode away.

A child ran in front of me, bare feet slapping the cold concrete. One look at the pale, pinched face and I knew whose child she was. Her mother was just behind her, a baby on one arm, grasping a third child's hand with the other.

"Hello, Leora."

She grinned broadly through sharp little teeth—what was left of them—and threw an arm around me, crushing her baby between us. I was stung by the sallow cheeks, the deep half-moons under her eyes. She wasn't that much older than I, but she seemed so drained! Most of her life she had been caught in the tug-of-war between her mother and Aunt Gerda. I had hoped her life would improve after marriage.

"Are all these yours?" I asked, indicating the children.

She cackled. "Some of mine! I have five."

My mouth dropped open. "Taking after your mother, huh?"

I introduced Brian to Leora, watching him take in her thin hair and blue organdy dress with puffed sleeves and uneven hem, an early 50s evening gown unearthed in some thrift store. He smiled down at her beautiful blue-eyed children, then drifted back to her, staring. "Does she moonlight as the Blue Fairy?" he muttered for my ears only. He was polite, but I felt him wince, then withdraw, seeing me with wider eyes. He didn't know about the bonfire, how Leora would clap her hands and shout as the fire blazed high, or the soft, slow peace in her eyes as she shared the last bites of her potato. He didn't know these things—that Leora and each of them owned places in my heart long before I knew him. I really should have told him, prepared him.

— 189

I showed her my ring. Her eyes widened, a brief twinkle reflecting the diamond. She oh'd and ah'd and crowed, displaying it for her little girls, her rough fingers sandpapering my white, pampered hand. Then I noticed that her band was simple gold like my mother's, the ring of a second or third wife.

"You be happy," Leora whispered confidentially, patting my hand and backing away as though to give me the room I have always wanted. I felt stripped and cracked open, my selfishness exposed.

I sat down on a folding chair and stared numbly. Slowly I realized that the worst was over; if Brian was going to change his mind, he had already done it.

For a brief, panic-stricken moment I wondered why I was getting married. Then Brian squeezed my hand, his eyes touched with humor, and acceptance in his smile—how could I have forgotten!

Chairs jumbled and clanked as loudly as my thoughts. Everyone settled at the long tables, and my mother rushed in to take the seat across from me.

She saw my ring and smiled brilliantly.

"Beautiful!" she mouthed. I nodded, but my gaze traveled to her plain gold wedding band, and I hid my hand beneath the table.

Not until dinner was over and Brian motioned at the door did I realize that my father had not spoken to my betrothed. He had not given me away. I grabbed Brian by the hand, but as we neared my father, Brian fell back, suddenly awkward.

I leaned forward to be kissed. "Good-bye."

"My princess." My father took my face in his hands and looked into my eyes. I lowered the lids quickly, afraid he would read my thoughts. "Take care of yourself. We love you very much."

Surprise welled within me, dangerously fluid. What was this? This mercy, this acceptance? Some alien being in my father's body? Where was angry Jehovah thundering destruction from the sky? I blinked quickly and pulled away.

Brian and I left in a flurry of good-byes, a shower of hugs and kisses. "We love you!" my family called. "Come back soon." I turned to see my father watching us, his index finger lost in the leaves of Grandfather Harvey's book.

Friday passed with the smooth, rounded architecture of a dream. We lay on the bed, planning our future as though it was certain as sunlight. We chose a name for a child: Eric if it was a boy, Rebecca if it was a girl.

Saturday I awakened to the sound of Brian's voice. He was talking low and tense on the telephone. I went into the kitchen in my nightgown, my feet bare on the tiled floor. I touched the short hair at the nape of his bent neck, but he didn't raise his head. I kissed his cheek, but he stared straight at the floor. At last he hung up and sank his face into his hands. I waited, the chill of the floor joining at my feet with a deeper, eternal cold.

"She won't do it. She won't sign the papers." His voice was heavy and chill as the morning air.

"Brian, what can we do?"

"I just talked to my CO. He can't do a thing without my mother's consent. I asked for more leave to work things out; CO says it's out of the question."

For a long time I stood stiffly beside him, waiting for a miracle. But tension grew around us, until I wanted to dart at the ticking clock, tearing the hands from its obdurate face.

We drank coffee in silence. We dressed in silence. We packed Brian's clothing, carefully creasing the new uniforms, muttering only the necessary words. We drove to the airport and waited in the cafe for his flight to be called; we drank more coffee in silence. All this time I was thinking one thing: Brian didn't really want to marry me.

"You could do something if you really wanted to," I whispered hotly as we waited in the airport restaurant for his flight call.

His eyes flickered, then shrank behind their shrouds.

"You promised me you'd think of something. You said it would be all right."

"Jeannie . . ." He swallowed, shaking his head. "What do you want me to do? Look, if we're married in our hearts, does it really matter if we wait a year for a piece of paper? If it's supposed to happen, it'll happen."

I looked down at my blurred fish-eyed reflection in the coffee cup. "And what if . . . what if you don't come back?"

His eyes were rimmed with pain. The murky banks of a lifetime seemed to rush by as I waited for him to talk. He had to give the right answer . . . the right answer . . . the perfect answer.

And when he did speak, his words were soft, fragile, seeming to float on the steam of his coffee.

— *191*

"It's odd. I joined this Green Machine to prove that I didn't need anyone. But that's changed. And now I don't want to die."

I watched him closely. "You really want to marry me?"

He nodded and I believed him.

"There must be something. Some way." It was nearly plane time.

"Sure. We could get married in Mexico. All you'd have to do is hop in my seabag . . ."

"Mexico! Of course!" I was nearly shouting. People stared at us, smiling. "My grandparents were married in Mexico!"

The idea caught fire and I gulped for breath. "The law was against them, too. It must be the way for us! It is! I know it!"

"Hey, be reasonable. We're both broke. I don't even have money for lunch in Vegas unless I hit the nickel slot." He gazed at me and squirmed. "I can't ask my mother. You know what she'd say." He stooped and slung his seabag over his shoulder. "What about your father? Would he give us a loan?"

My breath caught. "Oh, he's never given us . . ." Then I grinned. "He's never actually disowned me. And he is my father."

We stopped at the gate. Brian looked down at me. "Well, baby, this is it. What do you think?"

There was a huge, tightrope kind of ache in my solar plexus. If I could walk this through, I would have everything. If not, if I failed, I would fall forever. I looked into Brian's eyes.

"What if he says no? What then?"

"Try," he whispered, kissing me. He strode to the ramp. "Try!" he yelled, and I nodded and waved.

I entered the terminal and realized that for once I was not crying. I sat in a chair before the observation window and watched the wings of Brian's plane tilt, pivoting in a large slow circle before straightening southward. I stared at the blank blue of the sky and tried to think.

Saturday night was usually my mother's night. I found my father planted at the kitchen table over a game of solitaire, his way of winding down, the way some men drink.

After amenities I sat at the table across from my father and set the car keys noisily between us. The table seemed miles across as he glanced up. Before crowds my father was an orator, a speaker of eloquent, ethereal phrases. But when faced with a moment of one-to-one, he was wordless.

As I stared at his furrowed forehead, my carefully contrived story dissolved in a wave of love. Perhaps he didn't want to know the truth. I wouldn't expose him to it unless he asked. But neither would I lie. I had done enough lying.

"Daddy, it's important that Brian and I get married soon. Vietnam . . ." The word nearly strangled me.

My father said nothing. His forehead knitted.

"Brian's mother won't let us get married, and he needs her permission. We'll have to go to Mexico. I'll need five hundred dollars for a plane ticket. Will you loan me the money?"

He looked up and met my eyes, his smile shattering, the deck of cards clutched fiercely in one hand. "Don't you think your young man should ask my permission?" His voice was gruff.

"Oh, Daddy." My eyes stung. I didn't think you cared, I thought. "He's in San Diego by now."

My father nodded slowly and tapped his deck on the table. "Meet me at my office on Monday morning. We'll go to the bank together."

Suddenly my arms were around him, and I was almost sobbing with relief. Apocalypse, like a great, fiery bird of prey had circled, then moved on. "Oh, Daddy, I love you."

I kissed my mother. "What will you do?" she asked. "We don't want you to be alone while Brian's away."

"Can I move home?" My mother nodded and patted my back. My father shuffled the cards and smiled to himself. It seemed that he always won in the end.

"We'll be happy, Mama."

"I'm sure of it, darling. You'll do just fine."

I turned back to my father, but he was laying out his cards, so I picked up my car keys and said good night. I would drive back to the apartment, pack my things, and leave during the night so that the apartment manager wouldn't harass me about a two-week notice. As I wheeled onto the freeway, with white lights guiding me through the darkness stretching ahead, I sang out to my father what I could not bring myself to tell him, what he wouldn't hear: "Thank you, Daddy, thank you for setting me free."

Chapter

12

We were married by a justice of the peace who slouched before us in his undershirt, the gray hair on his chest turning his dark skin dusty and ancient. His wife had curlers in her hair and smiled with her gums; her dentures floated in a little glass on the coffee table. None of our parents was there, of course. All through the little ceremony I was overheated and sick to my stomach. I wondered why Brian kept grinning like a fool.

If only I hadn't been so willful, doing things my own way all my life! I could have wed in style, a ceremony warmed and legitimized by well-wishing relatives. Perhaps after a period of repentance my father would even have sealed us for all eternity, bonding beyond death.

"Till death do you part," the JP said, hacking. And death was all around us.

Soon after we were married, Brian returned to his military base but went AWOL a few weeks later, spurred by my threatened miscarriage to join me in Salt Lake.

We were awed and terrified by my pregnancy, at once humbled and proud by the wish-come-true. I let my sudden fatigue and early-morning sickness speak the news to my family, hoping they would see past my misery to the new brightness of eyes and rosy complexion.

Brian and I spent nervous evenings in my bedroom, listening to records or reading, bolting upright each time my mother's telephone rang.

We rationalized our situation: "I tried to get CO's permission. Those lifers can't understand. . . ."

"You don't belong there anyway. You're no killer. You belong here with me."

And when Brian's eyes went dark, I blurted a platitude from my childhood. "Sometimes you must disobey the law of the land to keep a higher law. Brother Musser said so." I nodded perfunctorily in Aunt Henni's way as though Brother Musser had ever been my paradigm of highest good.

We tried to escape our situation, visiting Danny in his hospital room. A short time before my marriage, he had fallen thirty feet down an elevator shaft, just as my father had done about forty-five years before while hoisting a hod to a scaffold. But my father had merely wrenched his spine, a condition corrected by the chiropractor who later became his mentor and father-in-law. Danny's fall broke both legs badly and crushed four vertebrae. Doctors didn't expect him to walk again, but a fused ankle and a fighting spirit soon had him in a wheelchair and out of the hospital.

"It's a blessing in disguise," Danny braved, sounding so much like my father. "I was getting ripe for the draft. Now they can't touch me." He grinned at Brian and teased, "They wouldn't want me now if I was stupid enough to join up."

Brian often picked up Danny on our way to the university, coaxing the wheelchair up the basement steps, then lifting my brother like a child to set him in the car. With a start and a swell of feeling, I remembered Danny lifting my father into the car before his ulcer operation. Now I felt privy to an eternal moment, visionary of a cosmic pattern.

While I attended classes in literature and psychology at the university, Danny and Brian drove through the surrounding countryside and shot at quail and magpies. The two had formed a deep bond based on frank talk, sneaked cigarettes, and a mutual love of sports. I was abysmally shy and self-conscious of my rounding figure; when my classmates at the university spoke to me, I couldn't meet their eyes. Again I was an alien, an imposter from another world. What could these tweed-suited and sweatered professors know of my past and my present? These languid sorority girls with their monthly checks from Dad, secretly sharing apartments in town with long-haired musicians who protested the war on street corners—what could they possibly know about morning sickness and AWOL panic? And so I sat lonely on the steps of the Student Union or the physics building, studying distractedly, waiting for Danny and Brian to pick me up, the stone cold and unforgiving beneath me, my heart aching to flee.

Afterward we drove to my mother's house, where we ate lunch and played pinochle with my father. He played with fierce concentration that surpassed his usual will to win, as though something metaphysical was at stake in this game, where queens of spades and jacks of diamonds ruled all but double royal families. He took time from his regular office schedule (to Aunt Henni's frustration), and I became his partner because Brian, new at the game, shrank from his exacting standards and because Danny refused to play across from him.

"It spoils the game to get so serious about it," Danny remarked. "Besides, it's more fun to beat him than be his partner."

Now the hours I had spent watching the game in my early childhood paid off. I rarely botched my father's perfect game, but when I did make a mistake, his mouth twitched, his forehead furrowed, and he let loose sarcastic remarks that made me cower.

Danny was equally determined. "He wants to win so bad, he cheats when he's losing," he said of my father as we drove to my mother's.

"Danny! That's not true. Daddy wouldn't cheat!"

Danny chuckled. "You watch. Watch today and see if he doesn't cheat."

I watched. Once he sluffed a card when he should have played trump. When my father left for his office, Danny said gleefully, "Did you see that? He sluffed. That's cheating."

"Anybody can make a mistake," I demurred. But I knew he had been cheating; he had played the game too long to make such errors. Why then was I defending him? "And what if he was cheating?" I put in angrily.

"Yeh," Brian said, stretching. "He's human, just like me. I cheated twice on the third hand."

We soon ran out of money, for the Marine Corps stopped my allotment as soon as Brian was reported AWOL. I borrowed from my mother's meager reserves, but she had barely enough to buy groceries, especially with an extra mouth to feed. And Brian couldn't ask his mother for help, nor would I ask anything more of my father. Somehow we felt that such requests would be an admission of a bad marriage and of Brian's cowardice.

Cowardice. Brian's word, not mine. In my mind each day he was AWOL was another day he stayed alive. We talked of going to Canada. Rumors filtered through the newspapers that young men called for the draft were ducking across the border. The draft-dodgers were regarded as deserters by the Johnson administration. I remembered that the Mormon polygamists had fled the United States to live what they believed without breaking the law. Why couldn't Brian and I do the same? I proposed it one day as we drove aimlessly about the city, discussing our predicament.

"Do you want to go?" He watched me closely, his eyes darting from the road to my face.

I nodded, then cringed. I thought of my baby growing up without grandparents or relatives and buried my face in his parka. Spring rain pelted the roof of the car and echoed in my heart. In two more days Brian would be officially classified a deserter. His name would appear on wanted rosters, his picture in post offices. MPs would visit his mother's house, looking for him.

"Will she tell them where you are?"

"I don't know." He stared out at the gray-swathed mountains.

I sighed a deep, shuddering sob.

"Anyway, I can't hide out at your parents' place. I couldn't bear to have them come for me and cuff me in front of you and your mother."

"Would they do that? Treat you like a criminal?" I thought then of my father, led handcuffed through the streets of Salt Lake City.

Brian moaned. "Don't you see? I am a criminal. A deserter!"

"But you can't go to Vietnam! Can you, Bri?"

"Can I what?"

"Kill people. It's a sin. 'Thou shalt not kill'!"

Brian shook his head. "I wouldn't kill unless I had to."

"What does that mean? Killing is killing."

Brian stared at the window. "I could if I had to," he said at last. The air outside was gray and foul-smelling as a dirty sheet.

"It . . . it sounds as though you've already decided."

He looked surprised. "I guess I have."

"You're going back. Oh, why? Why?" My chest burned.

"Because I made a commitment."

"A commitment! To who? The Marine Corps? They don't care about you! You made a commitment to me, to our child!"

"But I committed to go. Commitment's the only thing that keeps me from being like my father. . . . If I don't go and finish my time, I'll never be able to face myself again."

I sat sobbing softly, staring out at the rain.

He cupped a hand under my chin and turned my face to meet his. "I know you don't understand this right now, but you'd never be able to face me, either."

"You're wrong!" Then suddenly the fight was gone, and I felt limp and weak. I didn't want to go to Canada, not really. I was too young to be alone in a strange country with a new baby and a confused husband.

"You have to do what you think is right," I murmured, and noted that I could be long-suffering like my mother.

They held Brian in the brig for a month. He wrote that I shouldn't write anything intimate or send any photographs because the guards had a field day with anything personal. I thought of my mother trying to communicate with my father at the Utah state prison, where every letter was ripped open and scanned for evidence. I remembered how they refused to let her see him once they learned she was a plural wife.

Three weeks after release, Brian telephoned, his voice bitter and unyielding, as though he blamed me for allowing him to return.

"They've got me now. They only let me out of the brig because I signed an agreement to leave for Vietnam immediately."

"You mean you could have stayed in jail? Oh, Brian, go back! It's so much better than killing—or being killed!" My father had spent an extra thirty days on death row for breaking parole to live with all of his families. Why couldn't Brian suffer the same for his life?

"Go back to jail?" Brian's voice was rough, angry. "No way. I'd die first."

He flew to Vietnam in June shortly before my birthday, when lilacs burst on the trees outside my bedroom window and the first primroses were opening. He sent pictures from Okinawa. Then his unit shipped to Vietnam, and I began my daily ritual of watching for the mailman.

I planned to give birth in the hospital, one of the few in my family ever to do so. I explained to my mother that the Marine Corps had assigned me to a particular hospital under the care of a certified obstetrician, the only way the birth would be covered by insurance. It was a lie to protect my father's feelings. I couldn't bear to have him deliver my child. I was afraid that with him in the room all my nerves would go berserk, my muscles seize up, and I would fail.

He had delivered the babies of his other daughters. At the shower Aunt Sarah threw for me, my sisters spoke of how grateful they were for his calm, soothing presence.

"I know everything's all right because Daddy's there. I couldn't do it without him," Annette announced as we sipped green Kool-Aid from mock-crystal cups.

One of Aunt Sarah's girls, Erin, put in, "Right after I went into labor, I told him I didn't know if I wanted to go through with it after all. He got such a kick out of that! He laughed and said, 'You should have considered that nine months ago, daughter.' "

I smiled and said nothing about my hospital plans, amazed by their pure and placid attitudes. What was it that made me shy from such intimacy with my father? I had loved and trusted him so much! Daddy, what happened?

A feeling, shadowed and uncertain, made me tremble when I thought of him examining me like my obstetrician, a kindly ex-Marine who had served in Vietnam himself. He joked about the distension of my body, yet made me feel womanly and beautiful in my husband's absence. My eyes stung with sorrow and gratitude as I left the office of this stranger. Did my father do those things— explain to his daughters why their breasts changed, how they should rub lubricant across the pelvis to prevent stretch marks? Did he examine them monthly, or even once before the final date? Did he treat their pregnancies as brusquely as he had treated my broken arm? I could not imagine him as my doctor. He was my father. And I believed it was my failure, believed that not enough light or purity dwelled within me to endure his care.

And so my baby was born in the hospital. Danny sat with me through much of my labor. I was horrified when he suggested that he take Brian's place in the delivery room. I didn't want him, any more than I wanted my father watching as my secret places opened to admit new life.

And I didn't fail. "It isn't a Marine," my doctor commented as he threw the wet, wonderful little creature on my stomach. I was ecstatic. White fibers of light wove through me, and I sat up, grinning. Although my legs and hands trembled from exertion, I wasn't tired. I wanted to jump up and parade through the halls of the hospital with my beautiful daughter. I wanted to show her off to all her relatives.

What joy to participate in creation! No wonder my father loved to go on baby cases, regardless of the time of day or night! No wonder he had sired forty-eight children and growing numbers of grandchildren and had delivered as many of them as possible! Life, pure life! A bulwark against Brian's death; even should he die, I would have something of him here, in my arms. I telegraphed the news through the Red Cross, hoping his daughter would bring him extra incentive to live.

One night two months later I huddled beneath the blanket, drawing into myself, trying to dispel dark thoughts of Brian. After awhile, I knelt and prayed for his safety, then hazarded another prayer, that I would see him again, alive and well. How I missed him.

An hour later I awakened from a dream in which I had been talking to Brian on the telephone. He had told me to meet him. He had told me that he loved me, that we would be together soon. I would see him in Hawaii.

I shook my head to clear the ringing of my ears. Then I realized that the phone was ringing, had rung twice at three o'clock in the morning. It must be a call for my father, another baby case. But he didn't answer the phone; I remembered he was with Aunt Henni.

My heart leapt and I rushed for the phone, praying it wouldn't stop ringing.

"Mrs. Solomon?" The voice was far away, crackling through static and buzzers.

"Yes!" I shouted into the din.

"Wife of PFC Brian Solomon?"

I caught my breath. I had heard of phone calls made when the man was wounded and shipped to Japan. "What's wrong with him?"

"He just wants to talk to you, lady."

His voice came through a sound-maze of switches, beeps, and more voices. "I'm OK." It was Brian! Alive! His voice garbled through thirteen thousand miles of interference.

"Did you hear me? . . . R and R?" He was still talking.

"Meet me. . . ." His voice was lost in static. ". . . seven days."

"We've gotta stop now. We're tying up some important channels," the radio operator broke in. "Anything you want to say?"

"I love you, Brian!" My head was spinning. Why had he called? He wasn't wounded, thank God. He was talking again. "What? I can't hear you." I replied.

The operator spoke. "He says he loves you!"

"Oh." I flushed and laughed. "Brian? Are you there?"

The radio operator's voice was kind. "He's gone, lady. Go back to bed and get some sleep."

Some sleep. How could I sleep?

"What did he want? Is he all right?" My mother was beside me.

I nodded jubilantly. Then I frowned. "I'm not sure why he called. He said something about R and R. I think that's leave. I think he wants me to meet him. I'm not sure." Then I remembered my dream. He had told me to meet him in Hawaii. I was astonished. The dream had come true, except for the static; in the dream Brian's voice was strikingly clear.

Now, with thirteen thousand miles of static and a war zone separating me from Brian, I had only my dream. It directed me to make plane reservations two weeks hence and to fly to Hawaii and Brian. I followed my dream, borrowed money against the credit I had earned in paying off the loan arranged through my father, and met him at the Honolulu airport. He was so thin! We rode together on a transport bus across the island, refrained from kissing before the other troops, and secretly eyed each other. After the military briefing we went to our hotel room, which we scarcely left during our six days together.

I discovered that it hurt to feel again after letting my need for Brian dehydrate—like putting on a pair of loafers that have dried before the fire. But after he showered away the musk of Vietnam—a deep, old smell of something rotting—we were deep in love again. In an hour I lost my independence; my stern self-control reduced to shimmering, molten love.

We stayed awake far into the night, talking of Vietnam and reviewing current events on the mainland, where I had attended student protests against the war. Brian whistled low, "What a deal! Me in Nam and my wife calling me down." His eyes were perplexed, yet wizened.

"No! No, I'm not. I want you to come home alive. I want this war to end."

"But the hippies . . . they say we're wrong."

I studied the silk figured sheets. "They cite some nasty rumors about the real motives behind the war. And about what goes on there. . . ."

"Oh, I know why they'd think we're a bunch of savages. Nothing's clear-cut in Nam. What we have to do to say we've won a position . . ." He stared at the ceiling for a long time.

When he spoke again, his voice was constricted. "There was a boy, about as old as your little brother. The kid came running at us. He was holding something." Brian stopped and drew in his breath. "I was riding shotgun for a truck carrying about forty men. Just a week before a kid blew up a troop transport with sixty men aboard; he threw a grenade into the hold." He shook his head. I could see beads of sweat on his upper lip. "No one else saw him coming. I had to do something. I wanted to stop him, wing him. But I missed—or rather, I hit, dead center. The way these rounds work they tear a tiny hole when they go in, but they take half the organs when they leave."

I looked down where he lay on the pillow. He gazed deeply into my eyes, trying to see past the shadows, waiting for my response. I flinched.

"Did you shout for him to stop?"

Brian nodded.

I thought of my father jackknifing newborn babies to get them breathing. Hard-starters, he called them. But he never gave up on them. Not till the body was cold. A rank taste invaded my mouth.

"Did he have a grenade?"

"Yeh, but the pin wasn't pulled. He might have been coming to trade it for candy. He might have been just a kid, any kid—your little brother or one of his friends—playing a war game." Tears streamed down his cheeks now, and he covered his face with his hands. "I didn't know what to do."

I touched his hair in a confusion of pity and fear.

I could feel something happening as he spoke, a softening of the shield that had been all around him when we first came together, once the door was closed and the suitcases thrown on a shelf. I sensed that what gave way was his armor, his way of surviving, just as I had hardened to survive the months without him. And suddenly I was afraid for him, afraid that by encouraging him to talk, to feel human again, I had betrayed his capacity to survive the war. I pressed my fists against my forehead, wishing they held something sharp, something to dissipate the recurring vision of a dying Oriental child.

When I spoke it was in carefully measured tones. "You did what you had to. You have to fight to live, any way you can. I want you to come home to me. I need my husband. Our daughter needs her father." Then my strength dissolved in tears. "But it isn't right! We know it isn't right! Killing little children! It can't be right!"

We held each other tightly. Shadows seemed to nip at the corners of our togetherness. He told me of other horrors—of strafing villages supposedly evacuated by all but Viet Cong, then finding tiny bodies in bunkers mortared into rubble. He told of missions into the forbidden Demilitarized Zone and Laos, from where he had carried back the cold body of his sergeant, his only companion on the mission. "I carried him across my shoulders for ten miles of jungle. The toughest ten miles of my life."

Brian told of his own miraculous escapes from death. "We were passing a ruined temple on mop-up when machine-gun fire burst out of the thicket. Every man with me was killed. There were holes in the temple wall directly behind me. I should have been dead, but I wasn't touched. Somebody up there wants me to survive. I just can't figure out why. I feel guilty—and terribly . . . chosen . . . for what only God knows."

And when all words were spent, we lay beside each other watching moonlight flicker across the ocean beyond our window, trying to piece together the divided parts of ourselves and the self we had formed in our coming together. I searched for golden threads of love and understanding, but I was too split within myself to offer much, too divided between my desire to see that my husband survived and my sense that this war was wrong, its methods and motives depraved beyond the inevitable corruption of war. I felt divided between my wish to rekindle his love and respect for life, to share the birth of our daughter, and the sense that I should leave well enough alone, leave him with the grit of his survival instinct.

The six days passed almost without our notice, for we slept at odd hours and ate only when we had to. I tried to get Brian to eat more—he had lost about fifty pounds—but he seemed to have no appetite. After hearing his war stories I too lost the desire to eat. The milk in my breasts dried up.

On the fifth day Brian went out and bought some twiggy marijuana in the open marketplace. Back in our hotel room we smoked it together. My first experience was one of joy and terror, a realization of paranoia, of having no control over my own life, and a sense of impending loss. Whether high or not, throughout our stay I heard the remote, terrible rasp of a saw drawn across a bone, the relentless inevitability of our separation.

Brian gazed at the ceiling. "I just wish I could have accepted your need to work things out. . . ." The air tensed. "Well, I've had a whole bellyful of revenge. You don't know how many times I've killed him over there. I sometimes think my hatred for him kept me alive."

I nodded slowly, comprehending. I knew then that war begins with individuals. Nations only provide the scenario for hate.

The flight home was so tinctured with pain I couldn't fully open my eyes or lift my head. No one greeted me at the Salt Lake airport. My mother was shopping with Aunt Henni, as usual on Wednesdays. My in-laws brought the baby when I called, but she didn't know me and refused to nurse. Helplessness stifled me; I sat on my bed, holding her tightly, rocking back and forth, back and forth.

Weeks passed, then months. From the tone of Brian's letters I discerned that his survival instinct had taken over as he settled into the war, stationed near the DMZ, where he'd stay alert and battle-hardened, living from one minute to the next. Often, while lost in the bush or isolated on some remote firebase, he was the only one who knew what to do.

"They call me Moses," he wrote, "and I don't even know why. I have no idea why or where I'm leading them."

During his tour of duty he was promoted and demoted eleven times. Washington couldn't keep pace with his shifts in rank and pay. I was always misaddressing his letters. He wrote to explain: "Some upstart lieutenant, new in country and out to get promoted, storms in and starts flashing orders that'll get us all killed. I won't do it. I won't sacrifice a lot of lives to somebody's ego. So I get busted. Then lieutenant gets killed strutting his stuff and there's no one to take over, so headquarters promotes me by radio while they scare up somebody else. It's a circle, a crazy circle. And I'm in the middle of it. Not too many can stay alive where we are."

My professors mouthed phrases about the horror of the war, but they didn't really know anything about it. It was an abstraction to them, only as real as the rest of their philosophizing. Their lofty ideas seemed parallel to my father's formula for living: the rules and guidelines, the doctrines and defenses were all very high-minded, but when it came to living such perfection, to applying their beliefs, that was another story.

One afternoon I drove home from school feeling tired and cynical. Glancing in the rear-view mirror, I saw my forehead knitted much like my father's and noticed that small lines of worry had begun to form around my eyes. I was only nineteen, but I felt ancient, as though my life were nearly spent.

I must have some fun, I thought. Or someone to talk to, someone who understands. I hadn't had a friend like that since Brian had left, and before him, since junior high school and Jeanne Stanton. Perhaps I could call Jeanne and tell her quite plainly that I was desperate for companionship. Perhaps I could imbibe some of her tranquility. I had run into her once at the univerity. She seemed carefree, delighted as always by life—the way life should be. I knew that she was busy with her sorority and her fiancé. When she came to see my baby, gifting her with a white hairpin-lace sweater, intricate and lovely as my feelings for Jeanne, we had talked. Yet I kept her at arm's length, not wanting to tarnish her tiara of wholeness nor her delight in my new life.

Now I half-listened to the radio as I drove and thought, so I scarcely noticed when the music broke to announce a fatal accident on the new belt-route freeway across town. Then I realized that the announcer had said Jeanne's name.

I don't remember driving home. I concentrated on believing there was some mistake. I went immediately to the telephone and called the number that had been engraved in memory since I was twelve. Foolishly I asked for Jeanne; the voice at the other end burst into sobs.

But she had scarcely lived! Newly in love, virginal, about to exercise her kindness on the world. The world needed more people like her, fewer people like me with my confusion and failure and my ancient heart. Why hadn't it been me instead of her? I held little Becky to me and I knew the answer.

I went to the viewing, although I had vowed to avoid mortuaries while Brian was in Vietnam, superstitious that any acknowledgment of death would invite it to creep into my life. And it had come, anyway, from an utterly unanticipated quarter.

In April, with only two months left of his tour, Brian wrote a long letter, devoid of light, heavy with grief. His desire to live was gone:

> They told us not to make friends over here, but sometimes you can't help it. The two guys I was closest to—I've written about Canada and Henry—are dead, killed within three

days of each other. That's why I haven't written. I hope I didn't cause you too much worry.

It makes no sense. Henry caught a mortar round. He's the black dude I told you about. He had a girl and a mother, both of them counting on him to come home. I had to write to them. What do you say? How do you tell them that you'd have gladly gone in his place?

Two days later Canada was walking point for me—it should have been me, I was senior man, but the skipper sent him forward to take my place because he wanted to see me. I was coming back to relieve him and reached out to touch his shoulder when a sniper got him. He took my bullet, the bullet meant for me. His brains blew all over me, into my mouth. I can't tell you how it made me feel. It should have been me instead of him. It should have been me.

A great, terrible ache burned within me. I wanted to hold him and pummel him all at once.

"Death to your death-wish, Brian," I told the photograph on my dresser. "Now you are legitimate. Your mortal rights are sealed with the flesh of your friend." And I wanted to rock him until the horrible taste and vision were gone forever, blotted clean by my love.

In late May he wrote that they had pressured him to reenlist. "They need guys who know how to stay alive. Of course my decision depends on you. How do you feel about it? It would mean three thousand dollars on the spot, a raise in pay, and thirty days leave before my second tour."

I was horrified that he would even think of staying in that hell and keeping me in mine. "No!" I wrote. "Come home!" I was deeply shaken that he would be vulnerable to such an idea, and I wrote a long letter denouncing the war and the waiting. "I couldn't live through another year of this," I declared. "And neither could you."

A week later, before my letter had time to reach him, I received another letter saying that he had decided against reenlistment but that his rotation date could be delayed indefinitely.

"They aren't happy about my decision. They want to keep me. I think that's why I was framed. . . ."

I read the details hurriedly, feeling I was in a nightmare.

He had showered in a rear area camp where he'd been sent to await rotation, had put on a freshly laundered set of utilities, picked up from the base laundry. Then he walked toward his bunker behind a group of blacks who were "jiving," as he put it, and smoking grass, marijuana.

Then an MP jeep came up behind us and they threw about a dozen "partypacks"—little plastic bags with about ten joints each—into a nearby field. The wind caught them and they scattered all around, like confetti. The MPs saw it, of course, and when they picked up the guys with the dope, they picked me up, too. I was clean, for a change—nothing on me, not even my wallet. But they took us to headquarters and searched us again. They let the blacks go and held me while they called my station. Then they searched me again and found a roach in one of the pockets. It wasn't mine—I swear it. You know I wouldn't lie. It could have been mine. But it wasn't.

I didn't know whether to believe him or not. In Hawaii he had confessed about the drug world of Vietnam. I had worried. "It'll throw you off-balance and get you into other stuff," I warned. And from what he said, there was plenty of "stuff" to get into, and most guys did.

I waited. My birthday came and went. July passed slothfully. Brian stopped writing. Each date brought the fear closer, louder: He would die in Vietnam. They would hold him until he died in Vietnam.

I wrote letters, made phone calls. I contacted troubleshooting programs and public service organizations.

Brian's mother and I made daily comparisons of our mutual effort. We called our congressmen and senators in shifts. We made trips downtown to the Marine Corps recruiting depot. We filed protests and broadcast our complaint on radio talk shows. In a rush of blind faith and panic I even wrote to President Nixon. Two weeks later a letter came from the Oval Office: "The President regrets to inform you . . ."

The answers were always the same. "We've requested more information . . . a military zone. We can do nothing. The situation is in the hands of your husband's CO."

The baby's first birthday came and went. Summer waned. My fingers trembled all the time. The nightmares returned of Brian dismembered, emasculated, dying. I woke up weeping. My fault, my fault, my fault.

One night I awakened and knelt by my bed. I had prayed for Brian all along, but the prayers had become mechanical, chanted again and again. Now I waited, searching my heart. I began to feel that his deliverance was contingent on me somehow. I closed my eyes and listened. The baby breathed softly. My own lungs and heart beat out soft rhythms that seemed to have a function independent of the universe.

But you aren't. No human being stands alone. To be, to live, you must be part of the Great I-Am. The voice spoke clearly. It will not be easy to guide him back to life. Even if he were here, would you be equal to it?

How can I be equal to it? What must I do? I'll do anything. I'll do Thy Will. I give my life to You for Brian's life. Bring him home, now, and I am Yours forever.

This is the way to fulfillment and happiness. Come to Me. Discover the Tree of Life.

Dawn crept forth, but I stayed by my bed. The baby slept peacefully. My mother fixed breakfast. I stayed on my knees, praying.

The voice had stopped. I became aware of the magnitude of my sins: how my indecision, rebellion, faithlessness had jeopardized life. I repented. I wept, fearing I had lost Brian. He really was my life, not just any life saved, but my life saved. Perhaps, then, each life was equally precious. My hands shook and I covered my face with them. Suddenly my father strode into my room, without knocking, something he'd never done before.

He lifted me to my feet. "Tell me, daughter, what is it?"

I blurted it out, sobbing, told him everything, including my fear that Brian was indeed using drugs. I told him I had tried everything humanly possible, believing it was enough to do all I could do, that I could bring him back by myself. But it wasn't enough, wasn't enough. And now I was helpless.

"What can I do, Daddy?" I sobbed against his shoulder.

"We will ask the Lord for His help. Stop crying, darling. We'll bring him home."

Next morning I visited a medical doctor, a friend of my father. He examined me quickly, then asked me into his office.

"Your husband is in Vietnam?"

I nodded. I told him about the legal hold, about the drug charge, about the trial that refused to take place.

He scribbled a prescription. "Satan's war," he muttered. "The cream of our youth sacrificed . . . civilians, women and children . . . our leaders involved . . . all for the Almighty Dollar. We'll bring him home. With the Lord's help."

He handed me the form. "Take these three times a day. You realize, of course, that you are on the verge of a nervous breakdown."

I nodded, believing him.

"I'll notify the Red Cross that he must be flown home immediately, on emergency leave."

The Red Cross sent the telegram to Quang Tri the next day, the same day that Brian, responding to some prompting of the spirit, tied himself to a triangle of trees beneath the thick canopy of Vietnam and went through heroin withdrawal. It took them three days to find him.

Thirty-six hours later he was home, his bloody utilities in a duffle bag purchased at the San Francisco airport and stuffed where civilian eyes would no longer stare. He was the last one off the plane that landed in Salt Lake City, disembarking five minutes after everyone else. He walked reluctantly down the ramp toward me and his baby daughter. I held my breath; he stood alive and whole before me—thank God, yes—but with an iceberg ocean of pain in his eyes.

Chapter

13

Brian burst through the front door of our tiny apartment, holding a newspaper, his tie loose, his eyes fierce and red—from anger, drinking, smoking grass, or all three, I could never be sure anymore.

"You hear about that bastard, Nixon? Four students in Ohio shot."

I felt sick and sat down. "Are they dead?"

"Oh, yeah!" His voice taunted, challenging anyone to an argument. "These are only the ones who died. More were wounded. Bullets, clubs—you name it, the Guard used it. Suckin' weekend warriors." He paced the small living room, kicking a porch chair someone had lent us when we moved in.

I coaxed him to sit on the mattress covered with an India bedspread—our "sofa." "As if enough people haven't already died for that damn war," I muttered.

Brian lit a cigarette and resumed pacing. "I'm so frustrated I could kill somebody, starting with Nixon."

I grabbed his arm. "What a thing to say! Can't you see that's what's wrong here—killing for some far-out notion of what's right? Maybe those students didn't ask for it, but the more radical groups are just as ready to kill for what they believe as the government!"

"Yeh, well, it's time we started shooting back. Killing unarmed students—that's too much."

"Brian, it doesn't matter which side you're on. It's the killing that's wrong."

"Oh, yeh?" Again his voice taunted. "Something I learned in Nam is sometimes you gotta kill to have peace. If you don't get rid of that sniper in the bushes, nobody can do anything."

I retreated to the kitchen to get a Coke, but the last bottle was empty; his friends had finished it off the night before. Each night

I emptied ashtrays and threw away beer cans and wine bottles so that our daughter, Becky, wouldn't see them next morning.

"I'll go for more Coke," Brian offered.

"We can't—we've already gone way over our budget. It isn't easy to feed and entertain all those extra people."

Brian's face went cold and hard. "You want us to go somewhere else?"

"I didn't say that," I hastened to answer. I didn't want him hanging around in bars with the single men who let me wait on them as they swapped tall tales of their exploits in the military or with women, taking advantage of the hospitable attitude I had inherited from my parents. But in my mother's house no one smoked or put beer in the refrigerator or took the Lord's name in vain. Everyone knew what my parents stood for. No one knew what I stood for—least of all me.

"I'm going for more Coke," Brian said.

"Don't you have to get back to work?"

"I'm not going back today." He slammed the door.

Since Vietnam he had been like that—impulsive and erratic and restive as a caged animal. The first night home he rose at midnight, urging me to dress so we could drive through the city.

Like my father, Brian loved to drive, but Brian drove when he should have been working at the bank. Because he was a veteran and had scored well on the tests, they were grooming him to be a loan officer, but he wouldn't submit to initiation rites. One day he had lent a man six thousand dollars on his signature, no collateral. While the bank president sputtered, Brian said implacably, "He's good for it. I've learned to recognize people who can be trusted." The man repaid the six thousand as promised, but Brian was moved to the collections department, where his ability to recognize honest faces couldn't make much difference.

He spoke of quitting work to keep vigil near military recruiting stations to dissuade young men from enlistment. "Young men"— it was strange hearing him say that. He was young, barely twenty years old, but he was old inside. "I'm senile," he told me. "I've forgotten why I'm alive."

All organized effort seemed dangerous to him: institutions of learning, big businesses, governments, religions—especially religions—were suspect.

I longed to help Brian deflect the guilt that woke him, breathing heavily, in the night. I would reach out and find him wet with perspiration, his pillow soaked. I wanted him to reach out to me, to reach out to someone, with his nightmares. Perhaps if he could share them, they would stop.

But he refused to open, refused to recommit his trust. I soon realized that our life was dull and anticlimactic for Brian. Nothing I did—no dress I put on, no couple I invited for dinner, no conversation or movie or hike—matched the pressure and crisis of Vietnam. Even lovemaking, our primary communication, didn't reach the climactic terror of the war. In Vietnam, Brian explained in an unguarded moment, his every sense had been poised for survival; faculties he didn't even know he possessed were in operation. But here in the city all the learning and the consciousness seemed out of place and useless, a lot of energy contained in a tiny space with nowhere to go, a time bomb destined to explode at some indeterminate moment.

Brian spoke sparingly, making only oblique reference to the war. He seemed to have allied himself in spirit with the hippies he had resented so much while overseas.

I was studying education and literature at the university during this time, and I identified strongly with the killings at Kent State. Yet I was too rewarded in my studies to turn my attention to student protests for very long. George Leonard, Carl Rogers, and Abraham Maslow encouraged me to regard a broader world with a brighter future created by free and responsible human beings. The Elizabethan poets, Sidney, Greville, and Shakespeare, urged me to reach for the heavens yet keep my feet on the ground.

Ideas chattered incessantly as I washed dishes and fed the baby. Feelings welled up in me—of hope and optimism and something I could almost call God. I was deeply in love with learning and I was deeply in love with Brian, despite a dangerous edge that at once thrilled and terrified me.

On the day I decided to abandon psychology to become a schoolteacher, I went and snuggled close and told him of my plan to teach high school.

He stared at me for a long moment, then pulled away from me. "Of all the rotten institutions in our decaying culture, schools are worst of all," he stated. "Look what they do to kids, forcing them to reason against the grain of imagination, obliterating natural curiosity, molding them into 'good citizens.' " After a pause, he spoke again. His voice dripped sarcasm. "Well, I saw a lot of 'good citizens' kill people and dig it. One time I came up on this guy—he was in my unit, a regular dude, didn't smoke grass like most, but he seemed OK until we swept this village. When I found him, he was raping a Vietnamese girl—she was about fourteen. I nearly killed him. When he looked over his shoulder, he had somebody else's face—you know who I saw when he looked at me?"

I knew then that Brian had not stopped hating. I believed he hated even me, for my part in his enlistment and simply because I hadn't been there in that hell-on-earth.

I didn't know how to make up for the part I had played in his torment. I waited on him, indulging his every whim.

I stayed up late with him but arose early each morning to clean the apartment before studying for classes: washing on Monday, ironing on Tuesday. . . . How had my mother done so much for us? All those children along with her nervous breakdowns and piano lessons.

In our third year of marriage Brian and Becky and I abandoned apartment life, but I felt that our rented house was haunted, the air seeming muddy and tinged chartreuse. We soon learned that a convicted rapist had lived there with his sister, both of them violated by their father while young. I wanted to move. Instead we painted over the yellowed wallpaper, hung curtains, scrubbed floors, and shoveled garbage out of the basement. Then we dumped disinfectant everywhere until the house smelled the way the mothers' houses did when someone was having a baby. But the odor provided only an illusion of cleanliness. A friend said the house had "bad karma," and even I could feel the dirt deep in the cracks and timbers of the old place, the soil of human degradation.

We often had dinner with Danny and Dierdre at their house or ours, putting our little girls in bed together when dinner was finished and returning to the living room to play pinochle or engage in long conversations, many of them focused on the family and my father.

In recent months Saul and my father had exchanged letters, stifling their heat and passion behind a quasi-reasonable format. The correspondence involved Saul's research into Church doctrines, in an attempt to "gain a testimony." But I believed Saul's truest struggle was for the sense of identity he couldn't gain without moving outside my father's overweening vision. Saul's research revealed disturbing contradictions: for instance, notorious Mormon apostates, the Tanners, insisted that the Principle of Plural Marriage was founded on Joseph Smith's concupiscence, a doctrine invented to justify his embarrassing and dangerous extramarital affairs. Detractors contemporary to Smith had called him a "glass-looker" and referred to the early nineteenth-century popularity of "seer-stones" to discredit his translation of the Golden Plates of Mormon. All in all, Saul's obsession to "find the facts" resulted in his disillusion with Smith and disregard for the Church.

Saul had composed a letter of some length, working on it for months, gathering footnotes, revising statements, amassing an arsenal against my father's position. His statements went something like this: That my father had entered the Principle to fulfill an inner wish for authority; that every man has the right to free and democratic thought, and that my father had tried to violate Saul's integrity; that my father accepted little, if any, responsibility for cultivating his children and preparing them for life; that he had neglected my mother through his overextended dedication to the Principle; that Saul loved my father anyway and hoped that he would love and accept him in return despite his doubt and disagreement with the Church.

Before the final version Danny offered to edit the letter and suggested a revision. "His love? You don't want his love—what's that worth? His respect, maybe. His love, no."

And so Saul deleted the statement about love, offered a course of mutual respect, and summoned courage to mail the tome. My father sidestepped the suggestion, stuck to his doctrines, pulled out bigger guns, and questioned Saul's filial loyalty.

Saul, who was president of Zero Population Growth for Northern California, wrote back and accused my father of having an irresponsible attitude as a member of the species and a citizen of the world.

A round of correspondence followed, volley upon volley of words, each bombarding the preceding letter. The spirit of the exchange was disturbingly similar to the correspondence between my father and his father, Grandfather Harvey. My father had been Saul's age when he wrote to dissuade Grandfather Harvey from publishing his book in support of the Principle. But unlike my father, Saul wasn't converted, and soon the letters petered out.

Saul came back to Salt Lake that summer, the summer of our haunted house, of Becky's third birthday, and of my graduation from college. I was excited, yet frightened about entering "the real world," for I was vaguely aware that most of what I had learned was theoretical, unfounded in anyone's experience. But I was proud of myself, too, feeling that I had effected some sort of conquest over my background. I knew that Saul was proud of me and that my mother was pleased. I wasn't sure about my father.

Saul and his wife, Danny and Dierdre, and Brian and I planned a celebration. We all ate dinner at Danny and Dierdre's, speaking of the letters and of the family's response to them. Danny theorized that Saul had been dubbed a son of perdition, a soul beyond redemption, because he'd rejected Daddy's version of the gospel. "He insists on absolute obedience in thought as much as action. And no harping on reality can open him up. He's a little tyrant, that's all." My mouth dropped open.

Danny had left the Church, in spirit if not in fact. His professors at the university argued that existential modern man must not be distracted by childish fantasies such as religion but must keep a clear perspective on the absurdity of the universe. Danny, the fisherman who never got skunked, swallowed it hook, line, and sinker.

"Absolute power corrupts absolutely," Danny stated, with my father's inflection. "Look at Mama. She's suffered for years because of him. She's a sensitive, sensuous woman. She should have had a husband to herself."

When I said Mama was blinded by love and nothing else, Saul clenched his jaw until the angry muscle pulsed. As soon as dinner was over, he went to the phone. We overheard him talking to my mother, his voice desperate and passionate.

"I'm not just worried about your health, Mama. If what biographers say about Joseph Smith is true, then Mormonism is just a big con! And in that case I fear for your soul!"

His theologizing didn't dissolve my sense that Saul battled not with Mormonism but with my father. From earliest childhood Saul had been my mother's "little man," as she said—her companion and confidant, a solver of problems, a source of strength and support, a surrogate father to her younger children in the premature maturity forced on him by the Principle. I thought of the Nevada years, of the extraordinary closeness between Saul and my mother, of how he escorted her to a playing engagement or a community banquet—she so fresh-looking, just out of her breakdown, that some mistook them for husband and wife.

I knew that she was vulnerable to Saul's words, almost as open to her eldest son as to her husband.

Recently, when my mother had been asked to take the Church position of stake organist, she felt obliged to remind stake authorities that she was officially excommunicated, though certainly they must have known. Whenever she played for the Primary's yearly performance in sacrament meeting, she always refused the sacrament when it was offered to her, a good excommunicatee. Shortly after her confession to stake leaders, the bishop called her into his office and said that pressure was being put on him by highest-level authorities. One of the apostles had insisted that she be dismissed from her calling in the ward Primary.

I told Brian and Danny and Dierdre the story. "I hope Saul's not too hard on her. The Church and Daddy have put enough pressure on her this year."

"Well, she's not a member of the Church," Dierdre clipped. "You break the rules, you get excommunicated. That's what it means."

"But she loved the Church. She was raised in it, and it was hard to let go. She has some rights, doesn't she? That one little job meant so much to her." I swallowed.

We could hear Saul pontificating in the kitchen. I wondered if it was my father's night at my mother's, and wondered if he was listening in, waiting to go to work on her, blaming her for "the failure of your children" when Saul was through.

I painted every room in our rented house, polished the windows, and scoured the steps. I worked toward an unconscious goal: Becky's third birthday, when I'd invite my parents to dinner. As I worked, I imagined the five of us in the white living room, with its stained-glass windows and dark oak woodwork, eating, talking, laughing, playing pinochle, quilting the pieces of our life together. I made plans without consulting Brian, thinking he wouldn't mind, or if he did mind, he'd be less resistant on the day of the celebration.

But Saul's letter haunted me as did the house. Just as when I entered the upstairs study, a claustrophobic boxlike room whose fresh coat of yellow paint couldn't dispel the sense that something terrible had happened there, I would stumble upon memories that somehow, for all their brightness, filled me with remorse and foreboding. Prospects of Becky's birthday dinner magnified in significance. I wanted my mother and my father to know that I stood separate from Saul and Danny, that their judgments were not mine and Brian's. But the morning of Becky's birthday Brian told me that he'd be fishing till dusk.

"Brian, I made plans!" I put down my scrub brush and looked up at him. Bad enough he wouldn't help clean house but to desert me at a time like this!

Brian's face was immobile. "You should have checked your plans with me."

"But it's your daughter's birthday. I thought you'd . . . "

"That's what you get for doing your own thinking."

Tears prodded the corners of my eyes. The bucket of gray-brown water reminded me of the general state of our relationship. But I didn't want to fight with him, not today. I wanted Becky's birthday to be perfect, something to remember, as my mother had made birthdays special even during our worst times.

I swallowed. "How'd you manage this?"

"Danny's inspiration. He knows how hard it is to talk to your dad."

"What will my parents think?"

"Let them think the worst. They do anyway."

"They do not! My parents love you, Brian!" I knew that was true. Despite his long hair and the ubiquitous odor of cigarette smoke, they treated him like a long-lost son.

When Brian had gone off with Danny, I put on a long dress with puffed sleeves and a flowered skirt. I wore almost no makeup. I sprinkled disinfectant in the basement one last time to give the impression that births, not deaths, would happen in this home.

Seated on our India-bedspread sofa, my father looked so undignified and out of place with his feet stuck out and his back against the wall that I felt I'd somehow compromised his integrity.

"Please let me get you a chair, Daddy."

He refused, an aura of watchful humility about him as a man will wear in a room full of strangers. "You've done very nicely with this place, daughter. I hope this marks the beginning of a long and happy life for you and your young man."

I bowed my head. "Thank you, Daddy."

My father was unusually quiet, leaving most of the conversation to my mother.

At one point he sneezed and, as always, shook the windows. "Excuse me, dear," he said, looking up.

I was startled. He'd never apologized for sneezing before! Suddenly it struck me: he was ill-at-ease! I made him as uncomfortable and wary as he made me. How to put him at ease, to make him at home in my home? I was no good at punning and utterly unprepared to discuss the gospel in the way our relationship demanded: me asking the questions and he giving fullscale lectures.

But my moments with him were precious in their rarity, and the impulse to exult was overwhelming.

"How's everything at the ranch, Daddy?" I blurted as I poured lemonade.

He unfolded his legs and balanced his hands on his knees. "The brethren are starting businesses in the area. A great deal of money is involved. Many of the men have invested their life work in them. We're praying that they'll succeed and afford our people a way to stay alive. Unfortunately, the people in nearby Trinityville are catching on to us. They're reluctant to hire our young men."

A man named Thom Pearson had joined the group and was a strong support to my father, urging the brethren on the ranch and their families to live the United Order.

"The whole ranch?" I marveled. "How's it working?"

My father sucked his teeth, then made the clicking sound that we always took as a signal to be silent because he was about to speak. "It works—in a way. People join the Order when they feel moved. Brother Pearson wants to get everyone involved, but I've advised against too much pressure." He thought for a moment, then suddenly: "It works about as well as it has in my family."

His comment had a double edge. "And are the people happy with it?"

He didn't look up. "As happy as they'll let themselves be."

Now my mother chattered about people in the group—some I knew, some I didn't—talking on and on in a frenzied way entirely out of character. I noticed lines around her eyes and mouth that hadn't been there before the summer began. Suddenly I realized that my mother was covering up something with her incessant talk; something was terribly wrong, something she was trying to hide from me, from my father, from herself.

"Shall we eat?" I was serving Mexican food Japanese-style on the coffee table. My life was a similar hashing of beliefs and values—yoga and rock 'n' roll and turn-of-the-century novels. I felt sorry for my parents, should they try to understand me.

My father sat straighter and looked at Becky. The solemnity

and distance in his face suddenly burst into a gleaming gold-filled grin. "Will you ask the blessing, Becky darling?"

I froze. Although the blessing on the food had been among the first of my sentences, I didn't even know if Becky could say it. I had given up prayer at mealtimes, and regular meals as well. Brian was never hungry for dinner, eating sandwiches or fast food at odd hours. That was typical of our life—nothing had shape, the traditions and rituals of my paternal household blighted by Brian's restlessness. Why didn't I have the strength to officiate, to create order in my own household?

But Becky smiled complacently, folded her arms and closed her eyes, "Dear God, thank you for my birthday and for my party." She opened one eye and simpered. "And thank you for my grandma. And that my grandpa could come. Jesus Christ. Amen."

I was astonished. Chip off the old block, her grandfather's granddaughter.

My mother smiled proprietarily. My father beamed. Perhaps they had taught Becky while my mother tended her. I felt a rush of gratitude for their structured, predictable life, the life that had seemed so suffocating a few years ago. How naive I had been, expecting that my life with Brian would be easier, freed from my father's dictates and the stringent expectations of the group. Brian had offered only drugs and cynicism to replace my family structures.

Now I studied my father's face, trying to imagine him in the days when he and Aunt Susan were young, just starting out their life together. Had that knot of wrinkles between his eyes formed when he let her go? He had described the divorce as feeling as though limbs had been torn from his body. How could a belief be more powerful than love of spouse?

After the song and candles and birthday cake my father stood. "We must leave, dear. Patients to check on our way home."

I stood at the door waving as my mother always did when we went away, until the car was out of sight.

That autumn I was immersed in my new teaching position, teaching language arts and literature to ninth graders. I often felt that I was strapped to the White Whale, determined to tame it but in no position to do so; every day brought a new dousing in the oceans of classroom reality. My background in permissive education left me curiously lacking in common sense. I went home and complained to Brian, and he gave me some methods that might have worked for him but not for me. "Why didn't you ever learn to street-fight?" he asked.

I loved my students desperately and longed to help them through the crisis of adolescence, the rites of which I had never completed, leaving a thick shadow of irresolution in my wake. And so their rites became my rites. I longed to nurture them all, to feed each soul and heart as well as each mind. They gaped at me like starving baby birds; with a dim horror I realized they would never get enough.

Several weeks passed before I found the time or nerve to visit my mother, settling at her kitchen table to brag about how easily I'd netted my teaching position, getting on the dean's list and then braving my way past a squad of secretaries straight into the personnel supervisor's office to take my pick of jobs. I felt the need to exaggerate my success ever so slightly, as if the real accomplishment wasn't enough, didn't measure up to what she'd sacrificed for her children. Then on to share the cute things Becky said and did. At last I mustered the courage to ask her, tentatively, what was wrong.

"Nothing's *wrong*." She set her mouth in that fixed, too-bright smile that I remembered from other times when she merely recalled joy rather than felt it. Then, after cautioning me not to tell anyone just yet, she revealed that my father had taken two new wives, widows of a man in the group who had asked my father to look after them when he died.

Something close to jealousy roiled within me. How unfair that the mothers would have to divide his time still more minutely after sharing him for so long! With poverty and children behind them, didn't they deserve some years of reflection and pleasure? Couldn't my father stop moving, stop incorporating people into his fold? "Does he *sleep* with them, Mama?" I asked without thinking.

She flushed. "Well, no, not that way. He doesn't *live* with them." And for the first time she explained to me about the Law of Chastity, how in the Principle sex is forbidden except for procreation.

A few days later Brian and I met Danny and Dierdre for dinner, and somehow I let it slip out about the new women. There it was again—Danny and Dierdre could get me to share my deepest secrets, then leave me with the sense that I'd loaded the gun they pointed at my head. Perhaps it was because they had so carelessly discarded their own secret vows, indiscriminate as the temple garments that Dierdre now used as dust cloths.

As we played an after-dinner round of pinochle—the last vestige of our family traditions—Danny started in on my father, appalled that he would take on more responsibility and cause more pain for the mothers.

"He's only counseling them," I explained about the new wives.

"I'll just bet he counsels them," Danny snickered. I put a fist to my big mouth, wishing for a cork the same size. My mother had warned me not to say anything.

Dierdre quipped, "Sure he counsels them, right there on the couch with them like any counselor."

But I couldn't bear to think of him that way, making love to strange women. I couldn't bear to think that of him any more than I could think that of Brian. No, he wouldn't do that; he was my father.

"Daddy wouldn't do that," I murmured. "Would he, Danny?"

"It's power he's interested in, not sex," Danny pronounced. "Those people follow him like sheep. They're under his spell and they'd do anything he asked."

I flushed. "He wouldn't ask them to do anything wrong. Good grief, Danny, he's our father!"

"Well, you can't choose your family," Dierdre said blithely. "But you can choose your friends. We like to think of you guys as friends rather than family." She looked at Brian.

Danny might as well have said it, for he and Dierdre mouthed each other's phrases until it was impossible to tell which of them thought what. Suddenly I felt sick and dirty, my mouth dry, my head pounding in the right temple. "Is it such a bad family?"

"When you consider it's headed by Hitler . . ." Dierdre said.

"Hitler!"

"He's just as power-mad. It's evil, the way he brainwashes people."

"Of course he isn't evil!" I blurted. Perhaps, thinking of my mother's pain, I feared Dierdre was right. But a need deep as oceans demanded that I renounce this thought. "Sure, he makes mistakes—he's human. But he's no more evil than your parents, following the Church leaders blindly as anyone in my father's group follows him. Just because he had the courage to act, you accuse him. All right! Judge him by his acts. 'By their fruits ye shall know them.' Remember? Or do you figure you married into a rotten branch?"

The silence stagnated before Brian spoke. "Finish you guys off another time. We'd better be going now."

"What do you think?" I asked Brian when my tears had stopped long after we got home. "Is Daddy power-mad like they say?"

Brian looked at me and said nothing.

"Look at Mama," I snuffled. "She has suffered! And for what? So some lonely widow can enjoy his company! What about Mama's loneliness?" I sobbed for a long time. Finally I blew my nose and sighed. "Maybe they're right."

To my surprise Brian moved close to me and took my hand. "It's really presumptuous of anyone to judge your father. Dierdre and Danny's lives aren't so perfect that they can sit in judgment—and neither is yours."

"Oh, I wasn't saying my life was perfect!" I said. "I'd never dream of saying anything as preposterous as that! Look at us!"

"Look, Jeannie, everybody everywhere hurts over something—it's part of living. You can try to escape suffering—I'm always trying to escape it. But it's always there, waiting, when you come back to reality. Your mother would probably suffer if she lived monogamy. Maybe in a different way, but the pain would still be there." He took a deep breath. "Obviously, I'm indebted to your father. In a way I owe him my life. But that isn't the reason I'm defending him. Your father believes what he lives. Take the word of someone who knows hypocrisy inside and out."

"But Brian, he does govern their thoughts!"

Brian nodded. "And they love him for it. It's the outsiders who complain. Somebody has to lead, and at best it's someone who's right for the job. Your father knows what he's doing. Oh, he fouls up, we all foul up. But he does a better job than most men with one wife and no followers."

How true, I thought, and stared at the carpet.

"Look, there's always someone to poke holes in the man with the power. Some ambitious young buck to challenge the old one. In Vietnam I had my critics. If somebody died, guess whose fault it was. But if we escaped, I was Moses, the deliverer. I could do no wrong; I was the hero. Over there."

He sighed, trying to shift the weight, and his voice became heavy. "Jeannie, your father tries to be fair—you've said that yourself—and he's done a damn good job of doing what he set out to do. I hope I can say the same about my life when it's done."

And so we struggled through my first year of teaching and into the summer. I blamed Brian's continuing nightmares and my preoccupation with my lawless, free-spirited students for my restlessness, for the times I wanted to leave him, escaping to another man or another life, wanting most of all to elude the apocalyptic imminence of Vietnam.

What a terrible paradox that I had longed for monogamy—a man dedicated to me and our children, someone to cultivate my life, someone to fill the gap where my father should have been, someone to bind the two halves of myself together. But Brian depended on me in a frightening, flop-house way, and rarely fulfilled my needs. He was gone much of the time—if not fishing with Danny, then exploring parts unknown. He quit work the day I started teaching and sporadically attended classes at the university. When we were together, he competed with Becky for my attention.

Ed strutted into this milieu one summer afternoon, phoning unexpectedly from the bus depot. Brain and I were more excited than we'd been in months, for Ed had buddied Brian through boot camp; "like brothers," Brian described the two of them. On first leave, he and Brian had binged and buffaloed each other into getting identical tatoos: "USMC"—"Uncle's Sam's Misguided Children," joked Brian and Ed. I had been horrified by such indelible rebellion (Mormons bent on temple endowments don't get tatooed) but was later mollified by Ed's portrait, Brian's look-alike only darker, and by the concerned, cheerful letter he wrote to reassure me before they left for Vietnam.

The two had lost touch in Nam, and Brian had sometimes quietly wondered if Ed had "bought it." Now Ed was in Salt Lake City, to find a job and start a new life.

My skin tingled with premonition as we drove to the bus station. Ed was as goodlooking as his picture and again I was astonished by the resemblance to Brian in features and manner. I knew immediately that he loved and respected Brian, even idolized him.

I had loved and respected Brian before the war. Now I only loved him, the way one will nurse a broken limb. How long would the goodwill between Brian and Ed last? I wondered. How long before Ed discovered the holes, the wounds that didn't show?

Perhaps because Ed bore similar battle scars, his interest quickly transferred from Brian to me. "How'd you ever land something like this, man?" he teased Brian. "The lady's got class."

We stayed up late talking peripherally of Vietnam and more directly about our failing society.

"The establishment's gonna crumble," Ed predicted, passing a joint to Brian. "You can see it in L.A."

Brian nodded without expression.

"My father predicted this for a long time," I told them. "He's been saying all along we were heading for trouble because we've forgotten to serve the Lord first and ourselves second." The two men looked at me and said nothing.

After a long while of tokes and staring into space, Ed said, "What I've got in mind is to buy some land in the country. Buy a cow, some seeds, some equipment. We oughta do it together, man. We always got on." But he was looking at me.

"Yeh," Brian said. "After you find yourself a woman."

"What about her?" Ed grinned. "You woman enough for both of us?"

I blushed, reveling in the attention.

"Really," Ed went on. "People are trying out all different ways of living—communes, group marriages. They know we gotta stick together or it's the end of the line. We could gather some people around us, hand pick them, you know? Like they're doin' in L.A."

Brian snorted. "California really is falling into the ocean."

The three of us got high together and wandered through the valley, the canyons, and the mountain dells above the Wasatch Front. Ed had an eye for beauty, for fine architecture, especially.

"These Mormons must really be something, holding onto the past. Those far-out buildings! You won't find old houses like these in L.A.—they were torn down thirty years ago. The people there are crazy, they float around like seaweed. You know, you gotta hold onto the past. Something has gotta have a past."

"Yes," I murmured. "Nothing can grow without roots."

Brian sat silently, watching sidelong with the eye of an eagle.

I glowed with Ed's appreciation of my Zion home. He never tired of hearing acout my father, my mothers, my brothers and sisters. "Phenomenal," he said. "All those people pulling together."

And he loved my mountains. Over the years, my sense of their beauty had faded—the red and orange of mineral rock and flowers, the purple and azure of stones and streams had all gone gray, colors clotted into terrifying masses threatening to topple and bury me beneath. But through Ed's eyes, I saw my mountains in beauty once again.

Ed delighted in minnows nibbling at his toes and in watching water skaters race. He tried to name trees and animal tracks. He seemed to partake of the joy that Danny had once shared with me. I wanted Ed to stay in my life, to be the brother I feared I was losing. I wanted Ed's companionship and constancy, a hand to help me from the whirlpooling influence of Danny and his wife. Ed saw God in everything. Lately, Danny saw God in nothing.

Something of my voluptuousness returned; I regained the weight I had lost while Brian was at war, color returned to my cheeks, sparkle to my eyes. Sometimes, on an early-morning hike or while watching the sun set across the valley, I could feel my breasts nipple with the sheer pleasure of being alive.

I loved Ed because he loved the Salt Lake valley, and because he loved Brian and me. For him I radiated my wittiest, my most perceptive, my best-informed self, curiously oblivious that my flirtations were taken seriously. Ed's overtures became increasingly seductive until the Fourth of July evening when we went to the canyons for our celebration—Brian and Ed and I and all of Nature. Brian's mother took Becky to watch fireworks, and I was free and lighthearted, motherhood outdistanced by childlike ecstasy.

Suddenly I began to run through the picnic area and up the mountainside, then down again, leaping in my bare feet, disregarding the slash of rocks. I imagined myself to be a deer nearly flying as she broke for . . . I didn't know what. Was she running for or from something? I stopped all of a sudden in front of Ed and looked into his eyes.

He held out a primrose. "Smell it."

I thought I had never smelled such delicacy, such sweetness. His eyes held promise of the same.

"One kiss," Brian's voice broke in, "and all the flowers and wild animals will disappear." His voice lay claim to my private forests.

The three of us walked to the bridge and watched the rushing water. It seemed to me that the river's small channel held the melted snows of a thousand winters, the liquid ice of a hundred wars. Ed stood at one end of the bridge, Brian at the other. I could walk to either one of them—or I could jump. I wanted to jump.

Shame overtook me. My mother, my mothers, would never find themselves in such a situation. Their clear-cut lives acknowledged no purpose in a woman having two men. A man had more than one wife because he could procreate through many at one time, offering more souls a mortal body. But a woman normally bore a single baby within a term; if she had more than one husband, she would only confuse her fidelity, would wonder who was the father of the child she carried.

How had I allowed even the hint of this confusion to grow? I asked myself, gazing at the churning waters. My husband's dearest friend—perhaps his only friend—was inviting me to bed with him. Probably the real reason he'd stayed on, instead of returning to California or drifting down the road.

I felt Brian's anger like hot wind. I felt Ed's desire with the awe of someone who watches fireworks—remotely.

"You ever experienced déjà vu?" asked Ed. He was speaking over my head, to Brian. "This feeling we've been here before?"

"Yeh," Brian said scornfully. Then his voice softened. "We've all been here before, all right." For a time there was only the roaring silence of the river, and then, "Last time it turned out in war. She's the one who decides."

I felt myself to be a plot of ground being bartered until Brian's words echoed through my soul. "She decides. I wanted no more war."

I broke from Ed's gaze and went to Brian like a penitent child trying to regain approval.

"I love you," I said, looking up at him. My voice trembled with the hint of a lie. How could one love and mistrust at once? How did one love two men at once? How did one love men of God like my father and yet love warriors and alcoholics and even rapists? I loved the entire valley, the world, and each star in the heavens. Could such monstrous indiscrimination be considered love?

I sat beside Brian as he strummed his guitar . . . better, it seemed, than he had played before. "You've got to love everybody. . . ." he sang. How did one love everybody? If I loved Ed the way he wanted me to love him, I would lose Brian. If I loved Brian exclusively, we would lose Ed. My heart burned with shame and confusion. I loved too much—too much altogether.

Suddenly I felt lifted on eagle's wings. The river below was inviting, cool, exciting. But the swift current would drag me like driftwood until I drowned in the ocean. There must be a way to love without drowning! I gazed at the deepening shadows of the mountains. The spirits of my grandparents seemed near. I wouldn't plunge; I would climb. Anything else would be spiritual suicide. A halo of light surrounded Brian and me, proof that our love was not gone, only hidden somewhere, like the Golden Plates in the mountainside. Someday each leaf would be revealed again.

"It's cold," Ed complained.

I gathered wood while Brian struck a fire. The two of us sat together on a stone and watched for awhile as the shadows encroached on our little blaze. Brian's face was chiseled clean by the last rays of the sun, his eyes transparent blue. A powerful sense of eternalness returned, and my skin lifted in goosebumps, as I saw his blue eyes again and again, on one plane of time and space after another. I looked into his eyes and saw all the paternal beings within me: Jehovah, Jesus Christ, my father demanding, expecting loyalty, a wellspring of fidelity. My heart swelled and overflowed. I touched his shoulder.

"It's lonely here," Ed complained from the other side of the fire. His face, carved in shadows, appeared coarse and animal. I felt guilt; somehow I had misled him.

Now Brian's face was red with firelight, his ears flaring in points of fire, the sharp slant of flames intruding on his eyes, his features. He was smoldering, angry.

"Wood," he said. "Stubborn stuff. People don't resist like this. They crumble." His face seemed to be the face of Satan, the face of repression and loss and destruction.

He looked across at the dark hulk that was Ed. "People burn fast. Doesn't take much—just a little cannister of white phosphorus or some well-directed napalm and in ten or twenty minutes they're ashes and light. Ashes and light."

Ed was silent, his face only a silhouette. Love and guilt waxed and waned with the fire.

"I love you," I said to Brian. This time I meant it. Despite the doubts, despite the blackened landscape of Vietnam, despite clouds of shame and confusion, I knew in a way that I hadn't known when I said my marriage vows that here, with Brian, would be my heaven and my hell.

The next morning, Ed took a bus to L.A. to attend a Rolling

Stones concert. Several months later he wrote to tell us that he was married and had become a Jesus freak.

The episode in the mountains had somehow reinforced the evanescent knowledge that I was an individual in need of my own divine connection. I dared not follow literally in my father's footsteps, nor could I in conscience merely live my life to please him, not with this sense that I had my own purposes, my own reason for being. There was much my father owed me, much I certainly owed him, for our bond was strong—a bond of soul and of body. But I somehow knew he hadn't created my spirit, nor had he breathed life into my immortal soul. My earthly father could not be one and the same as my Heavenly Father.

God had shown Himself at last—not His face, certainly, but I had glimpsed how I, how we all, rest in His benevolent hand, each breath, each thought, each feeling, proceeding from Creation. Now I felt how He held me, suspended from a string, challenging me to climb. But how, I wondered. A promise, I had made a promise. I couldn't remember having made it, didn't know how I could keep it, but the Lord was telling me to pay up. I just didn't know how.

In that moment of divisive wholeness I began to understand my father. And I understood this about myself: that I loved him and wanted to be near him, regardless of our differences.

When my mother returned from an Independence Day celebration at the ranch, I visited her; while I was there, my father showed up.

"Did your mother tell you about Joel LeBaron?" he asked, right off. "I think you should know that he was murdered."

"Murdered? How? Why?"

"His own brother, Ervil Morrell LeBaron, is responsible. He had his henchmen do the deed."

"Ervil killed his own brother?"

"Joel was bludgeoned with furniture—a chair leg, I believe—and cut with beer bottles. Some of his followers told me about it."

I was speechless. My father went on. "Ervil calls his following The Church of the Lamb of God. Such irony when they've sacrificed a lamb themselves. Joel did no man harm. He was misdirected, but he was a good man."

As a child, my brother Jake had followed Joel around as he tended the garden that fed my father's entire family in Mexico.

"I thought the LeBarons had another church. I mean, didn't Joel call you to be a counselor—what was the name of his church?"

"The Church of the First Born in the Fullness of Times. Yes, he called me to be his counselor. But he had no authority to do it. The LeBarons believe they received the mantle of Joseph from their great-grandfather, Benjamin Johnson. But the patriarchy isn't passed on that way. The Lord is the one who passes on authority."

I nodded dumbly. Why is he telling me all this, I wondered.

"The first mistake the LeBaron brethren made was in forming their own church. There's only one true church on the face of the earth today. Some day that church will be set in order and we will be welcomed at the temple gates with open arms."

I cleared my throat; the time had come to say what was in my heart. "Daddy, I . . . I want you to know . . . I want you to know something. I . . . I know I've been difficult. I've made a lot of mistakes. But . . . I can see now what a fine thing you've given your children. So many of my students have no structure in their lives. They come from broken homes. They don't see their fathers at all, and they don't have anyone to place expectations on them. It breeds a slothfulness of mind and soul."

My father wouldn't look at me. He shuffled the cards for solitaire.

"You've given us a lot to work with," I went on. "You've taught us to love a higher good. That's a lot, Daddy."

He smiled his tight smile and looked up, his eyes squinting into mine. "That's commendable, darling," he said at last. "I'm deeply grateful that you're returning to the ways of the Lord. But . . ."—he shuffled the cards and was silent for a long moment— ". . . all the love in the world won't hold your family together without the priesthood sealing those bonds." And he quoted Christ, saying that what is bonded on earth is bonded in heaven, and what is loosed on earth is loosed in heaven.

I studied the table; my heart was pounding. Nothing had changed. He would be satisfied with nothing less than a "sealed" marriage, if not by him then at least in the Mormon temple.

"Daddy," I said with elaborate patience, "the bond *is* love. Besides, I can't insist on something Brian's not ready for . . . something that mystifies me."

He shook his head slightly. "It will always mystify you, will mystify all of us. Only God truly understands these things. We can only obey His commandments."

I felt the blood leave my face, then return in a rush. Which commandments, I was thinking. But I said, "We've done the best we can. We've been as honest with ourselves as we know how to be right now."

I opened my clenched fists and felt my stomach slowly sinking. All my humbling and love and appreciation had earned only disapproval, as always.

I wanted to explain that eternal bonding was an impossible topic, that lately Brian had refused even to discuss it. Before the war he had spoken of temple marriage. Now he saw religion as hocus-pocus performed by hypocrites trying to maintain the fabric of tradition. I agreed that churches stifle creativity and free thought. Besides, I wasn't sure that I wanted to spend eternity with someone who inspired so much fear and distrust in me.

But how could I say these things to my father, whose face and speech, indeed his entire manner, told me, "Live up to it."

"I'm moving as fast as I can, Daddy. As the spirit moves me."

He grimaced. "Sometimes our fastest isn't fast enough. Sometimes we must move by faith and let the spirit catch up later."

I pressed my lips together, thinking of old wounds. "I'd better be getting home," I announced, kissing him quickly. "Brian will be wanting supper."

It was a lie. Brian wouldn't be home for supper. He hadn't been home for supper in a long time, coming in as late as he pleased and having already eaten. I drove across the valley, my heart torn with thoughts of brotherhood and betrayal, of families and individuals, of all the many ways in which life is conceived, then divided, then brought together again—only to be split once more.

Chapter 14

The bed quaked as Brian settled himself. "You were a burned-out bulb tonight. When are you going to stop being such a drag?"

I bit my lip, my throat too full for reply. Danny and his wife had come for dinner, toting a record of *Jesus Christ, Superstar*, to spin an evening of innuendo, a web to capture the human frailty of Jesus.

"An idealist, that's all," Danny had said.

And Dierdre: "A masochist is more like it."

And I, wincing: "Whatever He was, the entire world has to deal with Him. Everyone draws identity from Him, for or against. Even curses are a kind of homage." The idea formed in my mind but came out garbled, and they laughed, unconvinced.

Everyone put in kind words about the chili and homemade bread, but no one valued my thoughts. I was stupid, an ostrich like the people of the group. Fitting metaphor: ostriches were polygamous, too, No individual identity. Why couldn't I pull my head out of the sands of illusion and face reality? Why not give up these silly thoughts of God and Christ? Why keep picking at myths like the gospel and the Principle? Danny had smiled pityingly. I was like a child, scratching a scab on my soul until it bled.

Finally Danny and Dierdre had left, yawning, saying I should read more and ruminate less.

Now I turned to Brian, who was nearly asleep, and spoke in a trembling voice. "Do you believe in God?"

He turned over and looked at me. "You know I do."

"What is His name?"

"I-Am."

"You believe in Christ's divinity?"

He grunted.

"Then why didn't you stop them?"

He sat up, irritated. "Why didn't *you* stop them? There is no stopping them. They won't listen to either of us. They think they're right and there's no other way. Like most people. Besides, belief is a very personal thing."

"Aren't you your brother's keeper?"

Brian turned away, his face dark. "I can hardly keep myself," he said.

The air fell silent. I felt blocked from stars or sunlight, stuck on the cold, shadowed side of the moon.

"I'm going to sleep." Brian switched out the bedlamp. Soon he was snoring.

I put on a robe and crept downstairs, settling at the kitchen table as the night grew quiet. Then I began to write, almost unconsciously, with only Becky's spaniel curled over my bare feet and a cup of tea for warmth. Some hours later, when my hand went stiff with cramp, I read what I had written.

In passage after passage about polygamy and monogamy, about my father and God, an unavoidable message dominated: that it matters less what one believes than how one lives out that belief. To live monogamy in dedication, to live polygamy in good faith, to live in constancy and fidelity, whatever the way of life—there was the challenge I couldn't meet because I didn't know what I believed.

Like many Mormons of Zion, my father and the group assumed that our unique position as "God's chosen" would automatically lead us to a better life. An attitude more than a belief, this rigidity had afflicted many of my people with a sort of braggadocio toward the world.

"The command to live plural marriage is founded in reason, like all of God's laws," my father had announced throughout our lives. "Eugenic breeding is part of God's plan to improve the race."

His words goose-stepped through me now, and I cringed as memory spoke with unmerciful clarity. We had believed that our salvations depended on him, this magnet of perfection drawing us all toward completion and light by example or through our mere kinship to him. All we had to do was follow, stepping neither to the right nor to the left, treading carefully in his footsteps. Then we wouldn't fall.

But if we stepped off the path, dared to think or choose for ourselves, we would likely be hewn down and thrown into the furnace, a corrupt branch bearing corrupt fruit, destroyed to save the family tree. Was this what my profound self-doubt meant? Was I being cut from the family tree?

I knew then that I had to find out. I must travel every dark vein, searching out the diseases of selfishness and hypocrisy and untruth. I must pursue light above all, no matter how it seared my heart and burned my soul. I would be purified by fire. I would sort all my own attitudes, would smelt them from the bedrock of reality. No use blaming parents or circumstances for my confusion.

At the same time another realization emerged from my crowded pages: the complacency of the group and of the Church in presuming that sin can be closed out along with the world was ill-founded. I had an inkling that sin begins in some dark hollow of the individual, when fear merges with the desire to control. Even if it were possible to shut out the world completely, sin would proliferate until that bitter marriage of fear and pride was dissolved.

How ridiculous to try to keep the world out anyway, as one local polygamous sector had done, erecting a ten-foot wall of concrete around their acreage so that it looked like a ghetto. What folly to pretend that any one group, that any one individual is exempt from the workings of the race! Nuclear weapons empirically proved John Donne's declaration that "no man is an island." Despite my parents' attempts to make the world go away, they had gone to prison, had lost homes and jobs and citizenship. Each day I abandoned the pure perfection of my yoga meditations to confront 220 hormone-crazed adolescents. Our illusions of superiority and insularity had only left us unprepared to cope with reality when it bore down on us.

I couldn't return to my family, nor to the Church, nor could I entrust my soul to Brian. Not until I could stand alone, apart from them all, knowing who I was in my own eyes and in God's, could I relax my vigil. I must attend to my soul myself.

My family was in trouble. That much I had learned from my mother's innuendo. But the causes and degrees of difficulty remained mysterious until the weekend my father and Aunt Henni went north to the ranch and my mother called, her voice thin and volatile as ether.

"I feel so peculiar, all trembly and odd. My heart's acting up again. I wish your daddy was here."

A moment in our Nevada home flashed from memory, my mother at the hall phone, her hand over her heart and face pale as the collar of her temple garments rumpled at her throat. She cried quietly into the receiver, describing her symptoms to my father who was stuck in Salt Lake with his patients. I had hugged her desperately, praying into her bathrobe, "Don't die, Mama. Please don't die." And later that night when the symptoms passed and there was no heart attack, I was at once relieved and angry with her for frightening me so.

We had always been terrified that we would lose her, that her heart, weakened since childhood by rheumatic fever, would someday be strangled by tension. Now the terror of my childhood clawed at me again, cutting my breath, raking my stomach.

"Call a doctor, Mama," I ordered.

"No . . . no. Your daddy would be hurt." And again, "I wish he was here."

"Why? He hasn't been able to help you, anyway, has he?" I wielded my fear with brutish honesty. She wept on in soft, plaintive mews; guilt roared through me.

"Go lie down, Mama. I'll be there soon as I can."

When I arrived, my mother was wringing her hands and pacing the kitchen.

"I don't know what to do. My nerves. My heart. My whole body's gone haywire." Her face mirrored the woodcut Saul had made years before that he called "Woman in Anguish." I realized with a start where he took his model.

I took hold of my terror and smothered it, sitting calmly at the table and urging her to do likewise.

"Your father says how crazy it is that he's cured so many people. 'Everyone but my own wife,' he says. I know it makes him feel badly. But I can't help it."

"He can't cure you because he's part of the problem, Mama."

Surprise and comprehension flooded her face. But she continued to pace, her gestures frenetic as a snared animal's.

Suddenly I realized the source of her agitation: with her keepers—my father and Aunt Henni—gone, her dependency loomed undeniable as a predator. How had it happened? After her victory over her illness in Nevada, when she had learned to create her life without them, she had lost the bloom of independence on our return to Salt Lake City. Her thoughts and feelings had merged and tangled with Aunt Henni's and my father's. My mother, lost in the confusion of identities, had lost the will to self. Thinking of how her relationship with Henni and my father had promulgated her condition, I felt my old rage rising; I determined to free her if I could.

"Come downstairs where it's quiet." She led me downstairs into the music room.

She stretched out on the carpet alongside her piano. I didn't touch her but spoke soothingly, applying the principles of relaxation and positive imagizing that I'd learned from yoga. She responded like clay, centering her whole being around my words, trusting each direction I gave, shaping herself to my thoughts. The sudden sense of power paralyzed me for a few seconds, as I realized that I had become her protector, that she would do whatever I said, for or against her well-being. I had become my mother's mother. I trembled for her in her innocence and for me in my knowledge, for all those so trusting and trusted, trapped by power. Understanding for Aunt Henni glimmered briefly, then faded like a firefly. My mother breathed deeply, gently, and I sensed the great weight of consciousness lift from her and fall on me.

She awoke much later, eyes hazy and bewildered. We went upstairs to the kitchen where we sat over instant coffee, my mother taking hers with aspirin, the strongest narcotic my father would recommend. "Since that nap I wouldn't need this, except for my back," she explained gratefully.

She talked for awhile of her youth, tales I had heard long ago, which I now absorbed with matured awareness. Unlike me, she hadn't mottled her early life with broken commandments and periods of willful rebellion. On the contrary, she had lived with exquisite placidity, obscuring her own depths, content at the surface with her life dominated by the notions of others. At fourteen she had succumbed to her first nervous breakdown, after a childhood fraught with illness. During the parallel period of development in which I had insulted my father and was dubbed a hussy, my mother had reclined on a cot in the school infirmary, enduring her writhing nerves.

She had been reared in poverty more discouraging than ours, with no end in sight. Her father, heart-diseased since she was very young, died before she married. She and her mother and sisters spent their years scrubbing away the accumulating shame of being "on relief," scouring away the soot of impoverishment that might tarnish their will to shine. Their agents of dignity were love of family, faith in God and His priesthood, devotion to Mormonism. And now, in her fifties, eyes dim with sorrow, my mother searched for a truth that lay beyond these perimeters. For, like me, she felt that my father had betrayed her.

She didn't say he had betrayed her. She wouldn't have said it had she thought it, which she probably didn't. But an aura of implosion surrounded and invaded her. She had lost weight. Her skin wrinkled with the delicacy of a drying leaf. Only her eyes were full and red-streaked, the pupils dilated with disillusion.

She began describing my father's many difficulties, as though trying to prepare my heart with understanding. She revealed that the council had invested hundreds of thousands of dollars into businesses near the ranch, businesses that were failing.

Nearby Trinityville residents banned Sprucewood's attempts to establish a new township and refused the young polygamist men employment, even to the point of boycotting their private enterprises. Some of the young boys in the group had been caught using drugs and stealing from the general store. Group patriarchs responded by holding them captive in a dark root cellar for three days.

My mother shook her head sadly and gazed at her hands. As though seeing them for the first time, I noticed the heavy veins and muscles that protruded, knobbing her wrists and fingers. Her strength was in her hands! All the strength I thought Aunt Henni had taken from her—had it actually gone into her music, the voice of her mute passion?

In addition, some of the newcomers that Brother Pearson had brought into the group were causing dissension. One of them, Ronald Ellison, had pursued notoriety, marrying several beautiful young women and breaking the fundamentalists' cardinal rule that plural marriage be lived in discretion. But then he wasn't really a fundamentalist. Newly converted to Mormonism, his faith seemed to be a mixture of opportunism and dilettantism. Sometimes he wore Lamanite (American Indian) clothing and carried a silver pistol. He said that the Principle of Plural Marriage was a political issue rather than a religious one.

"The Lord is supposed to give a man his wives," my mother sighed. "If it doesn't come through the proper authority, then it isn't really a marriage. When your daddy reprimanded him, and told him he couldn't take any more wives on his own, Ronald said, 'Rulon, you taught me by your example that if a man knows what he's doing and his leader won't sustain him, he should go ahead and do whatever he wants!' He's just capitalizing on the old split in the group—which he knows nothing about. When your daddy didn't go along with that, Ronald left the ranch." Her voice dropped to a scandalized whisper. "Now I hear he talks with God and claims he's head of some new church. And he takes young women into his family left and right."

Most of the women I associated with at the university and through my teaching and even former friends from high school were separated, divorced, or desperately unhappy. My women friends envied even my crippled relationship with Brian and despaired of finding "a good man" who would father their children and provide for them. From this perspective Ronald Ellison's wives seemed fortunate, and the wives of men in the group—kind, predictable men with steady incomes and stable morals—seemed luckier still.

My mother reported that a feeling of competition had developed between my father and Brother Pearson, who had undermined my father's power on the ranch.

"I think that's part of the reason your daddy has taken more wives. Brother Pearson has so many, and these men believe their worthiness is judged by the number of wives the Lord gives them. There's not a word of scripture to support it. But Joseph Smith had so many in later life and . . . "

Her voice trailed away.

More wives. More wives. "More than the two widows?"

She nodded, her face out of whack somehow, contorting to keep composure.

"But Mama, he has more than enough now!"

My mother nodded. Then her eyes filled with tears. "I couldn't tell you while it was happening. I felt so ashamed of my feelings!"

"You were trying to get Saul and Daddy to reconcile," I whispered, my voice heavy with realization. "And then Daddy . . . "

She hung her head. "I guess I felt your daddy already had taken on so much, maybe too much. Saul and the other boys had complained for years that they didn't see enough of him, that they couldn't depend on him. They didn't feel close to him. And that hurt me. You know the parable of the lost lamb. Why couldn't he have taken time to find Saul and bring him back? The others would have been all right."

"You feel Saul didn't gain a testimony because Daddy didn't help him?"

She shifted her shoulders ever so slightly. "I just wanted him to give the boys more . . . time and attention. Lots of the children have been lost in the shuffle, not just mine."

My mother sighed, but the tension hung on. I could feel it crowding her soul, the residue of feeling that no burning could reduce to ash. "The Principle has always been so beautiful, so easy for me until now. I didn't know how much I was taking for granted."

"You never felt any jealousy or competition? Really now, Mama." I was thinking of the insufferable heat in my chest when Brian came home too late.

My mother shook her head. "The only time I felt any distress was when Lisa and your father had been married for quite awhile before I guessed it. And I felt so foolish! But otherwise my feelings have been in accord—until now. I never thought I could have such feelings. I've tried to school them, but . . . I have this dream that I'm trying to throw these terrible, mixed-up paintings with nauseatingly garish colors out the window. And they keep coming back at me, like boomerangs. What bothers me most of all is realizing that the devil can have his way here, too. I always thought we would be safe from this sort of thing."

"What sort of thing?" I imagined Jezebels seducing my father, the one man I thought of as being beyond seduction. My voice must have communicated my horror, for my mother quickly informed me that, to the best of her knowledge my father didn't have conjugal relations with any of the women.

"If he did, he'd be breaking the Law of Chastity. They're too old to have children, with the exception of one. And she's divorced."

"But Daddy had vowed that he would never marry a divorced woman, that it would be committing adultery," I reminded her.

My mother gazed at me sorrowfully. "Why do you think my heart aches so? Several of the new women were married before . . . mostly widows. And we're not sure who they belong to now, their former husbands or your father. They're not sure, so how can we be?" Again her voice shook with the force of her feeling.

"And now this divorcée. He always said he would get our consent. When a woman marries into the Principle, she marries the sister-wives too. She didn't seem to care about how we felt at all. She'd get into his family—or else!"

"Did Daddy want her so much?"

"I don't know. I don't know. All I know is that we opposed it, and he said, all right, he would tell her no. 'I don't know whether she's unworthy of us or we of her,' he said, 'but her schemes and dreams will come to nothing.' And then she said, 'You introduced me to the Principle, Brother Allred, and if you don't help me live it, you'll bear the weight of my damnation!' "

"But she comes from another way of life," I cried, starting up so that our coffee cups rattled. "It doesn't apply to her!"

So she had circumvented my father's iron will. By his own standard he had become no better than the man who married his Susan, reaping a harvest in hell. This new woman had manipulated him into a position of self-contradiction by using his own ground rules to the gospel. I wanted to know more about her.

My mother described her as striking, with long straight hair and good features, but "worldly."

"She paints some. In your daddy's office, I notice she has taken down Saul's painting of the white house, set it on the bookcase in the back room, and in its stead hung one of her own. Also, she told someone in the group, 'It's about time Rulon married a woman who is his intellectual equal.' "

My heart raged. Intelligence equated with brazen manipulation! Intelligence equated with self-aggrandizement! I rose from my chair to put my arms around my mother. "Don't let her get to you, Mama. Intelligence is relative. It doesn't matter how much you've got; it's what you do with it that counts."

My mother had no sooner dried her eyes than she began to cry again. "I don't mean to blame her—I don't mean to judge. It's me, it's my own feelings that I can't resolve. I just can't believe that anyone could force her way into . . . into our citadel, our home."

"Well, isn't that how it's set up?" I asked coolly, wanting to bring her out of this lake of sadness into realization about the situation. "The man in the Principle always has the final word and the woman follows it, unless she's like this new woman or a couple of others we know, and tramps right over the rules when it suits her."

Years later I read in my father's journal about his *nuit blanche*, of how he had gone at midnight to his office and had prayed about the woman, and of how he had confronted himself, acknowledging his own frailty, realizing that he had entered the Principle at the price of great pain for himself and his first family. Now, these many years later, with the biblical promise of many houses, wives, and children fulfilled, he stood at the altar, ready to pay the price again.

So the marriage inconvenienced his long-time wives and the children already lonely for his companionship. It was nothing new. So age sixty-six seemed a strange time to begin new relationships; age thirty had seemed no less strange at the time. No matter that his darlings would be hurt; they would grow from the experience. As indeed they did.

In later years, when my father could not speak to set the record straight, the new woman claimed that an angel of the Lord had visited him that night in his office and had ordered him to go against the will of his wives. In his journal he wrote nothing of angels and midnight visitations, but he married her in April. She reaped the bittersweet crop of having what she wanted and then wondering if she really wanted it. She shared her wedding with a widow who also yearned to partake of my father's magnanimity.

In the fall my mother called with news that fit, horrifyingly, with the feelings of betrayal that surrounded my family. It was as though gentle, tractable Isaac had been selected to appease all the silent cries for justice and restitution.

Isaac hadn't entered the Principle at the outset of his marriage, for Teresa was set against sharing him.

"Don't tell me anything about it," she had pleaded, half-laughing, when Aunt Henni tried to teach her about the Principle. "If I find out any more, I'll be under obligation to live it—and I don't want that." But there was a note of dead-seriousness in her voice that everyone, including Aunt Henni, respected.

Aunt Henni contented herself with fasting and praying for them during her day off work from my father's office. Meanwhile, Isaac moved to California to teach school and there met my father's oldest son by Aunt Susan; the two men attended the same wardhouse, and both were active in the Church. Isaac was delighted to meet his brother, Monroe, but the older man was remote, burying his bequest of bitterness beneath a polite crust. For years he had been told that his father had run off to live a life of lust and self-indulgence, hiding his perversity behind outlawed, outdated Church commandments. Despite Monroe's resentment, he was compelled to follow in his absent father's footsteps, the only one of my father's twenty-three sons to become a doctor. Isaac's friendship with him didn't last long, for Isaac soon returned to Salt Lake City, moved by his testimony of the Principle. His California sojourn achieved at least two purposes: One, that of acquainting him with the deepening corruption of the world of drugs and crime beyond the group (he had left Utah with one overriding goal, "to prove Daddy wrong," but like his father before him, veered back to the footsteps of his ancestors); and two, that of placing my father in contact with his first family, a loose end grasped toward the final tying.

When they returned to Salt Lake, Isaac's Teresa was still reluctant about the Principle, but her sweet nature coupled with a certainty that she didn't want to find herself in a position similar to that of Aunt Susan, the shriveled woman whom she had met a few weeks before leaving California. Life without Isaac, rearing their children alone, would be so bleak. . . . She began to pray for a testimony. One night she dreamed that she gave to Isaac two women who were currently married to a Mexican member of the group. When Teresa awakened from her dream, all conflict and jealousy had vanished. She gave Isaac her consent to choose another wife.

A couple of weeks later the husband of the two women in Teresa's dream died in an automobile accident, and Teresa's dream came true.

The son of one of these widows, a rebellious and high-spirited teenager caught in a strong sense of identification with his people, the Lamanites, silently disapproved the marriage. He had let his dark hair grow long and took to wearing it in braids or a headband. Isaac tried to persuade him that this style contradicted the well-groomed appearance valued by members of his family. He promised to take the boy deer hunting if he would only submit to a haircut.

I imagined Isaac entering the kitchen with scissors and comb in hand, just as his mother, Aunt Henni, had done each Saturday night before bath time. Isaac insisted that the hair be cut or the boy couldn't hunt deer with the men. The boy had agreed to this taming of his long locks, but his dark eyes burned with resentment. This man had taken his father's place with his mother before his body was fully cold in the ground and now tried to take his father's place in his own heart. Loyalty is strong in the young; the boy was no exception.

Isaac approached him, speaking in low reassuring tones. Great anger flashed in the boy as Isaac touched scissors to hair. The knife, the long knife he intended to take hunting, appeared suddenly and Isaac grabbed his side, the scissors and comb clattering to the floor.

As I imagined it, the realization and incomprehension of betrayal seized my heart, the shock and horror inscribed on cells innocent of any wish to harm. And I could see Isaac's kind face contorted with pain for the boy as much as for himself.

"Will he be all right?" I asked my mother. "How is Aunt Henni?"

"She and your daddy have gone up by private plane. Your daddy is sure that Isaac's life will be spared, but he's still in great danger—of losing his kidney, or liver, or both. They've asked for prayer and fasting among the family."

My father did nothing, nor did the Trinityville police, giving the incident the character of an accident. Isaac had requested that the boy be left in the family's custody. After much prayer, fasting, and administering by the priesthood council, Isaac underwent surgery to have his kidney removed. During the operation my father promised the Lord he would never play pinochle again if only Isaac might live. It was the only corporeal vice he could evict from his ascetic life, offering it as a sacrifice in return for the life of his son.

When Isaac came to consciousness, he described his beautiful visions of the spirit world. And he told my father of a dream about Saul. "We were wrestling in such fun, with nothing but love and goodwill between us. I feel certain we can win Saul to the ways of the Lord."

Isaac recovered to head the table at his family's Thanksgiving Day feast. When the teenage offender hung back from joining the family at dinner, Isaac went to him. "I have endured my surgery, son," he said quietly, so that the others couldn't hear. "Now you must endure yours."

One night I dreamed I was imprisoned in a government building by the same authorities who jailed my parents. And then I escaped, following directions Saul had sent to me and flying on great white wings toward the ranch, where I would meet Isaac. Somehow a voice diverted me to a mountain peak of breathtaking vista, where I could write letters of truth and freedom to my loved ones— my brothers and sisters all over the world. "Brothers and Sisters," I wrote. "I come to remind you that the truth shall set you free and you must be free to love. You must be free to make clear choices. You must be free." In the dream my letters grew eloquent and fine, beautiful words and phrases woven together, colors and textures I couldn't have found except for the influence of a great, divine light.

I awakened with the feeling that I had walked the Milky Way, that a million crystal bells had chimed for me, that a billion lights had shone for me.

After the long time of searching, of trying to teach school, of trying to train my clumsy hands to paint or throw pots or make candles or play guitar, I had found a form for sharing with the world. And more than that, I had found my calling, what Mormons called one's mission in life, supposedly foreordained in the Spirit World before coming to earth. Now I remembered the promise I had made when Brian's life was saved and knew one way to fulfill that promise.

From the dream I understood that the writing would besiege my life, would subject me to duress and isolation. But I knew that the call would eventually lead me to freedom. Already I felt that I had drunk at the source of some clear mountain stream and had been renewed. There was a completion of the senses; the old feeling of being "burned out" had disappeared.

In a moment of epiphany I felt that I knew exactly why I had been born into this family and why I had experienced such a multifarious, painful, and sin-filled life. I had been visited by angels; my ancestors had presented me with a precious blessing—and a great responsibility.

I knew that I would find a way to translate my life into something I could understand. Perhaps the world and my own people would also be able to see it—the message of individual freedom and personal responsibility so hard-learned for me.

Perhaps Brian felt the separateness and integrity of my new, secret dream, for one day he told me that he wanted to have another child. I was at once confused and delighted, for he seemed so disinclined to commit himself to me.

"I'd have to quit work," I insisted. "I don't believe in letting someone else rear my children."

He nodded. "I'll get a better job, something to provide for all of us."

In the spring of my second pregnancy, during Church conference, a Church official gave open address against the fundamentalists, calling them apostates and wolves that would ravish the flock.

My father's reaction surprised me. "With all the little groups and pseudo-churches that have sprung up, trying to pull good

Church members into their midst, we must understand the Church's stance. Ronald Ellison's group and the new LeBaron group that Ervil started are good examples of what the Church fears. And they should be feared, for they have nothing to do with the true spirit of Celestial Marriage."

As he spoke, seated at my mother's kitchen table, he put down his cards and took an apple from the basket on the table. He peeled it slowly in one long curl, then fed me slices from his knife tip. I felt at once homey and uncomfortable, sitting there with him discussing the state of plural marriage. If he only knew the things I believed about a woman's right to free will and self-responsibility! If only he knew how angry I was that he had hurt my mother and taken wives without her consent!

"Unfortunately," my father continued, "we get lumped in with the others. The Church has rallied against us to the extent that we can't finish our new home. They've reprimanded our neighbors for associating with us. They've banded groups together to deny us our water rights. Our building permit has been hard to come by; it took two years to get it. And they want to refute our right-of-way to the new property. It's a damnable situation."

He spoke of the huge new home planned on the priesthood's West Valley property. His dream was to bring all his family together as we had been at the white house compound.

My father's eyes beamed past me in their concentration. "But the Church is starting a new movement against us. One of our girls' bishops told her outright, 'I'm thankful my name isn't Allred.' And they've sent spies to the school"—he spoke of the new building where meetings were held and where they hoped someday to hold classes so that their children would be spared the humiliation and "indoctrination" of public schools—"and they've checked license plates of cars in our lot. If any worthy Church member is found there, he'll be excommunicated."

My father sighed, his brow harrowed with discouragement. "I've been excommunicated, but my name has not been stricken from the record in Heaven. I've not been excommunicated from the gospel, only from the Church—and not even that, in spirit. I've been called to keep the Principle alive, and the cost of that calling is that I must perform my duties outside the official Church. But my mind and heart are in complete harmony with the Church on all counts save one: the Principle. Some day the Church will be set in order and the Saints will be as One."

"You mean the Church still believes in the Principle, even though it isn't practiced?"

He nodded. "I've had private counsel with some of the brethren. They foresee that the day when these things are fully restored isn't too far off."

A piece of apple seemed to have struck in my throat. What if the Principle were no longer outlawed; how would I feel about it then? Would I want to live it?

"Meanwhile, we must strive to keep our own house in order," my father said. "Even my own children have committed crimes and left debts unpaid! And it is all the more troubling for us, because we hold an awesome responsibility."

This seemed my opening, my chance to let him know how I felt about my own rights and about the violation of my mother's.

"And yet, isn't it true that everyone must take responsibility for her own soul?"

My father nodded.

"But so many people come to you, trying to give you responsibility for their decisions."

He nodded again. "I'm blessed to be of service, but they would grow more rapidly if they'd do the deciding on their own. None of us escape our tests," he said.

"How is a Mormon woman supposed to take responsibility when she's completely subject to the will of her husband and the priesthood?"

He sprang up from the table and strode into the living room. My eyes stung and my heart pounded. I had offended him!

He returned with a green book in hand, a new compilation of writings about the Principle.

"In the Celestial Kingdom, a woman's place is one of queenhood. There she may reign in spiritual majesty from her noble pedestal, protected by her husband and the divine authority of the priesthood with the assurance that in the day of resurrection she shall be awakened from the sleep of death in full glory."

I could say nothing when he finished. It was his point of view, inarguable. I felt suddenly trapped by my swelling, weighted body and by the close summer heat of my mother's kitchen.

"Ervil LeBaron has been released from prison," he announced suddenly.

"He's only been in prison about six months, hasn't he? That's not very long to serve for the murder of one's brother."

My father's mouth withered. "Vengeance belongs to the Lord," he said after a moment.

My mother had come into the room and she said, "They say that he bribed the Mexican officials to set him free. His people came up with eighty thousand dollars. Where do you suppose they would get so much money?"

"I hear they got the money from our fundamentalist brethren in northern Utah," my father said, his voice strangely cryptic. "They threatened the lives of the brethren if they didn't turn their tithes over to Ervil's henchmen. I was told that one patriarch's car was blown to smithereens before the money was submitted."

Icy fingers caressed my heart. "I thought Ervil's church was just a pathetic little group."

"But they have one who helps them." My father picked up his black medical grip. "I must be going." He kissed the top of my head. "You take care of yourself—and give our love to your dear husband. We love him."

Despite his usual—and for me, irritating—use of the royal "we" I sensed that something was changing in him but couldn't say what it was. His words had been the same, his manner just as dogmatic, but he had softened somewhere, somehow. The shift in his character frightened me.

Pictures from the Bible stories book flooded my memory—of Cain and Abel, of Abraham standing over Isaac, about to render his ultimate sacrifice to God, of Christ on the cross. I thought of Isaac and then of my father. And as I returned to my haunted house, a scripture echoed in my head like a warning: "For in the last days, there shall be opposition in all things."

Chapter

15

Utah winter had just begun, the morning cold gripping like an elderly hand as I stepped outside. I mentally warmed myself against the frigid wind, thinking that it had been an exceptional year for Brian and for me. His new position, though not tailor-made for his tastes and abilities, provided him with more fulfillment than his previous jobs. We rejoiced together in the birth and growth of our baby daughter, Janelle. On the days when I taught composition or took classes in creative writing at the university, Brian happily changed Janelle's diapers and rocked her to sleep. The thought of him holding her protected me against the bitter white starkness of the morning.

I stuffed the last of the Christmas wrappings into a garbage can just as the morning paper was thrown, kicking up a fine powder of snow as it landed with a thud on the front step. I opened it as I went inside, glancing absently at the date: December 27, 1974. I intended to read only the political cartoons and my horoscope over a cup of Sanka—no caffeine or horror stories now that I was nursing—but a headline caught my attention and held it: "Polygamous Settlement Attacked." I read rapidly, incredulously, half-realizing that my vague fear for my father was legitimate, not simply the concoction of a writer's imagination.

The polygamous colony at Los Molinos, Mexico, was inhabited by some distant cousins and other members of Joel LeBaron's Church of the First Born. In the quiet of Christmas night their log cabins had suddenly burst into flames from Molotov cocktails exploding all around. As the stunned, sleepy people stumbled from their blazing homes, they were picked off by staccato cracks of rifle fire. By the time the aggressors left the ruined settlement, two First Born members were dead and twelve were wounded. Reporters speculated that the raid might be connected to the rivalry between the Church of the First Born—now headed by Joel's younger brother, Verlan—and Ervil's Church of the Lamb of God.

My heart thumped crazily and I went to the phone. My mother had already heard. One of my cousins had telephoned my father, warning him to keep a lookout. Since Ervil had bribed his way out of prison, he was calling himself the "One Mighty and Strong," who would usher in the millenial reign of Christ. It seemed that Ervil was so empowered by his delusions of grandeur that he took whatever he wanted—money, authority, followers, women. . . .

My mother said he was worse than his crazy siblings, including Ben and Lucinda. Then she told me that those who had conducted this firebombing and the subsequent shootings were only teenagers, some of them girls in their early adolescence. I realized then how cunning Ervil must be, to deduce that teenagers, if caught, wouldn't be prosecuted as severely or attract the outrage of adults. But why did he involve girls, I wondered. He must be some kind of hypnotist to get people to do such dirty work for him.

I offered to come to my mother's assistance along with Brian, but she declined. "I worry about your daddy. But as for myself . . ."—her voice a murmur—"sometimes I wish I was dead."

I promised to visit soon and knew that this was a promise I would keep.

I sat down at the breakfast table, warming my hands around the cup of Sanka and gazing at the headlines, lost in memory.

I remembered my mother's tale of how Ervil congratulated her on her piano playing and seemed sane enough, well-groomed, neatly dressed, and articulate. Then Ben stepped between them, hair sticking out in odd places and unshaven. He roared a rancid declaration in my mother's face, "I'm the Lion of Zion!" And rolling his eyes like a fear-crazed horse, he urged his brother toward the door. "Ervil ain't s'posed to be talkin' to wimmen." And Ervil allowed Ben to lead him away, shouting, "I told you a hunnerd times, a man of the priesthood don't bother with wimmen."

As oldest, Ben was also first to homestead that spiritual territory of the long-awaited "One Mighty and Strong." Indeed, the entire family of brothers, seven in all, claimed that peerless birthright, "the mantle of Joseph," which included the authority to seal celestial marriages and the supreme patriarchal seat in the house of Israel, trying to revive the nepotism long since overthrown by Brigham Young when he took the Mormon reins after Joseph Smith's assassination. Ben, Ervil, and Joel had staked their priesthood calling on their maternal grandfather, Benjamin Johnson, who received his authority from Joseph Smith. True, splinters of the Mormon Church proliferated, dating back to the Reorganized Latter-Day Saints Church sponsored by Joseph Smith's first wife and son, which outlawed polygamy. But the LeBaron group, with its history of violence and its hysterical declaration of holding the only true authority on the face of the earth, stood apart from the other slivers of the Mormon trunk; it used the holy scriptures to ordain bloodshed.

Of course the Latter-Day Saints Church had claimed all along to be "the only true church of God," an attitude sustained by my father. Yet some group members insisted that he was the only man who held all the keys of the priesthood at one time, despite his open statement that he didn't hold the authority to conduct temple ceremonies such as baptisms and sealings for the dead. But he had certainly believed in his own righteousness, in his authority to seal and practice plural marriages to the point of sacrificing his relationship with Saul.

Did these LeBarons believe in their "callings" to priesthood with the same wholehearted, single-minded intensity as my father? Where, then, was the line between divinely endowed responsibility and mad obsession?

To affirm his leadership and to discourage the ambitions of Brother Pearson, my father had taken several more wives, for some members of the group held that the man with most wives was most blessed and most capable. Joseph Smith himself had married somewhere between forty and 130 women, taking even wives of his counselors, on the premise that he was more worthy of them than men of lesser authority. This notion of equating many wives with greater magnanimity was counterpart mythology to the supposition that the woman with most children was favored by her husband and by God. Although few in the group questioned such assumptions, they made no sense to me. How could one produce quality people—the primary aim of the Principle—if one was too overwhelmed with quantity to invest each individual with a sense of worthiness and purpose? I wondered if Ben and Ervil had felt "lost in the shuffle" as I had. Had they seen life in two categories, powerful and powerless, and had they determined to become powerful, as I once had, to become "mighty and strong" regardless of the cost?

How different was my father's proof of position from Ben's bizarre ways of proving that he was the One Mighty and Strong? Uncle Andrew had chanced upon Ben LeBaron one day while crossing Main Street and refused to stop on the street and argue priesthood lineage with the hulking man. Ben promptly stretched himself out on the asphalt and held up traffic for half an hour while he did a couple hundred push-ups to prove that he was filled with righteous strength. "I'm the head of Israel," Ben roared between push-ups. "You tell that to Rulon!" And then, swiveling his head to address the gathering crowd, he yelled, "And tell that to David O. Mackay, too! He may think he's the president of the Church of Jesus Christ, but I'm the One Mighty and Strong! I'm the true head of Israel!"

I remembered then that Ben LeBaron had recently died in Arizona's state mental hospital. Over the years he had sent letters in his childish scrawl, demanding that my father repent and recognize his "true priesthood." But Ervil did more than write notes and perform histrionics. The things that Ben only threatened, Ervil lived out. The schizophrenic thrusts of Ben's sick and insecure mind had become pillars of the universe to his younger brother. Unlike Ben's, Ervil's insanity didn't show; that was what made him so dangerous. I remembered him as a dark tower with deep-set, burning eyes, a presence almost as charismatic as my father's. Ervil had even developed a doctrine and had written books and pamphlets to translate Ben's delusions into realities.

I had heard about Ervil's doctrines, vanity-pressed booklets stating that God demanded immediate execution of "criminal religious leaders," his phrase for people who led without the proper authority. He talked about "legal ecclesiastical courts" and a theocratic form of government headed by the "Patriarch of Israel"—none other than Ervil himself. Another pamphlet subscribed him to Blood Atonement, an obscure doctrine exhumed from the early Church annals when saints were driven from one state to another, losing lives and property to mobs. Joseph Smith had placated his people with the promise that one day their lands, red with the blood of usurpers, would be returned. Perhaps being driven beyond the law had brought out the Mormon "outlaw"—the rugged individualist who will fight to the death for his freedoms.

My mind swarmed with contradictions, each protesting its own validity and virtue. The U.S. government had disregarded freedom of religion in disallowing polygamy. Then the Church had abrogated its own article of faith, ignoring the law of the nation in pursuit of the "the higher law." Later, when statehood loomed, the Church abolished the Principle that had spawned so many lives and eventually turned on its own, driving us from our homes, leaving us jobless, exiling us from our native land. Then my father, who had taught us to keep all the laws of God, insisted that we tell lies rather than incriminate the family for living the fullness of the gospel.

Where was the line between legitimacy and illegitimacy, between in-law and outlaw? In most ways, my father was a law-abiding and kindly man. But what of the consequences of his life and the torment of mine in thinking that my mother never would have married him, nor I have been born, had it not been for Aunt Henni; or in knowing that the ambient culture regarded me as a bastard, in feeling that my only earthly inheritance was the bottomless Gulf of Mexico?

My father had joked about his in-laws being outlaws and his outlaws being in-laws. With the new marriages, the possibilities had increased with the different types or degrees of marriage—some sealed for time, some for eternity, some confused about the nature of the relationship. One woman who had been sealed to another man, now dead, insisted that she belonged to my father, although they had been bonded for time only. My father said that "we must not rob the dead of their celestial blessings," but the woman's heart didn't change; she wanted my father. What of being torn between two men for all eternity, and what of the pain of the old wives— my mothers—whose sense of definition and appreciation for the Principle had been thrown into chaos? They didn't know why this invasion of strangers hadn't been repelled; they questioned why correct principle hadn't been followed. My father had gone back on his own word, had violated his own limitations. Where then was the line? Were there no magic circles, all life uncontained and dissipating like blood spilled on the ground? If my father's word couldn't be trusted, how then could my writings be trusted to perpetuate truth or health? How dared I trust myself if I couldn't trust my parentage?

My father had allowed us our free agency. But what kind of free agency was it: a choice of submitting to his dedication to God and fellow man, which far outstripped his capacity to serve and share with his existing family—or of leaving as Aunt Susan had done, to live a life sorrowing and yearning for him? What sort of choice was it, choosing him the ultimate and exclusive oracle of God or choosing one's personal relationship with conscience and with God? No wonder people called to ask him inane questions at midnight! They couldn't think for themselves; they chose my father as the direct connection to the heavens, instead of themselves! Just as I had almost done. I had accepted, actually accepted his estimation of me! I had become a hussy to fulfill his prophecy, to maintain him in his peerless position as oracle, even though he had never actually claimed to be a prophet of God. In a sense, he had given me permission to be my worst, and I had been. It was wrong, perhaps the greatest of my sins—idolatry or blasphemy—to make my father a god on earth. I had too much evidence of his humanity.

Now I wondered, did he realize how deeply his zeal had cut me, had cut the mothers? When he came to the crossroads between old and new relationships, the crossroads I had faced with Ed, he had chosen the new, had subjected his loyal wives of thirty-five years to the prison of loving him. Just as he had done to Aunt Susan. How different was he, then, from Ervil, from anyone who takes heaven by force?

Well, unlike Ervil he wasn't physically violent; his deeds were loving and kind. But wasn't there a kind of psychological violence in claiming to hold a monopoly on the truth, in separating people into piles of wheat and chaff, and holding the market on the wheat?

I remembered again that the difference resided in free agency— "the cornerstone of the gospel," he always called it. This was the difference between Christ, who wished to persuade men to come to God through love, and Lucifer, who wanted to force people into goodness. But a precious little cornerstone it seemed to be when I thought of the pain forced on women and children. What of Aunt Susan's terrible choice between sharing her husband with an indefinite number of women or losing him altogether? What of Aunt Susan's children, who had grown up without a father, or of children like me and certain others for whom my father had been as omnipresent and unredemptive as a bad conscience?

The solution to all these dilemmas, I recalled from my first writings, must be contained within the individual. No leader could be trusted absolutely. No mortal could hold a monopoly on what is right. Each person must be responsible to and for herself.

I was no longer blind to my father and couldn't submit to his leadership. Yet realizing his mortality made me love and fear for him all the more. There was no middle ground between pure good and pure evil, no stable bridge where we could meet and talk, where angels and demons could negotiate peace. The result was this: teenage girls throwing bombs and wielding rifles against aunts and uncles and brothers.

Terror and confusion spun together, and I had to get up, had to do something to stop thinking. I poured my cold Sanka into the sink and stared at the brown stain spreading across the porcelain. For an instant it reminded me of blood. I quickly turned on the water and let it run warmly over my cold, numb hands. I thought of my father, of the warmth of his lap, his arms around me. I began to shake, and I stood this way, weeping, with the water running over my hands and down the drain, until the baby awakened and screamed with hunger.

I couldn't calm myself to nurse her. She squirmed in my arms, nuzzling desperately, then tore away in frustration and yelled before she nuzzled again. Each tug at the nipple was an excruciating bite. My milk wouldn't flow. The baby screamed until tears ran down her cheeks. Finally I went to the kitchen and prepared a bottle, feeling desperate and helpless. I felt I was going mad. The world seemed mad. Mothers without the milk to nourish. People without the milk of human kindness. Brothers killing brothers. Brothers tying up sisters. Husbands leaving wives. Fathers turning against sons and sons against fathers. Fathers exiling daughters, daughters reviling fathers. The Church making a law of polygamy, breaking women's hearts. The Church outlawing polygamy, breaking women's hearts. Mothers and daughters holding each other, weeping, reaping the spoils of war as the sons without fathers became killers, wife abusers, child beaters, rambling dandies; polygamy everywhere in serial form—an affair, a divorce, another wife, another daughter, abandoned, abandoned, lost. My mind roiled and spewed images of violence and death; my father stood above me in a white robe, bloodstained. I heard my own voice as though it came from someone else, crying. "It's time to stop! No more sacrifice on the altar of fear!"

The baby stared up at me for an extended moment, her eyes wide and frightened. Then she began to scream. Sickness—at myself, at the world—rose in my throat. I put my hand over my mouth, set the baby down, and raced for the bathroom. Afterward, when all the tremors had stopped, I went calmly to the telephone and called the Salt Lake Mental Health Center.

One result of my visits with a counselor was that I stood up to Danny and Dierdre. Although I no longer counted on Danny's sanction, this sense that because of his influence over Brian my marriage rested in his hands made me uneasy. I had been fairly tiptoeing around the three of them, with the unwholesome feeling that I peered through a keyhole at the antics of some unholy triad that locked me outside with the children's bedtime stories and my mother's platitudes. I was left alone as she had been to hide my fears and to temper the fragile prism of my imagination.

Danny and Dierdre continued to include me in camping trips and yard parties, but I felt it was for the sake of appearance and to strengthen their hold on Brian.

One evening while we played our usual pinochle, Dierdre's warm foot suddenly caressed my leg. She blushed, saying, "Oops," and I thought it was Danny she'd reached for, until later when I put out my hand to squeeze Brian's knee and found Dierdre's bare foot in his lap. I froze, as tongue-tied and horrified as if I'd witnessed incest.

"What's going on here?" I cried hoarsely, damning the tears that always started when I was angry.

"Not a thing," Dierdre giggled. Danny grinned to himself. Brian studied his cards.

"Like hell," I said. They studied their cards in silence, holding secret smiles.

"You can't afford to take yourself so seriously," Danny advised after a potent silence.

I remembered then my father telling us how his schoolmates called him Elijah because he was so zealous in his moral and religious duties. Even then, at the age of fourteen, he had been dedicated, had already assigned his will to One that transcended the pettier works of man. Suddenly I understood the depth of his loneliness, and my voice came low, resolute. "Stop the nasty little games or you'll have to find another fourth."

The room had been terribly still. Danny cleared his throat. "This sounds like a scene from *Who's Afraid of Virginia Woolf?*" He tried to toss the comment off, but his voice trembled.

I wondered why, as Brian once asked, I had never before learned to psychologically street-fight. Why couldn't I trade insult for insult and stab below the psychological belt, probing the soft under-side of the subconscious?

"Yes. But I'm not the bitch at this table," I said.

Dierdre slumped in her chair and giggled nervously. Then her grin faded to a sneer. "Nobody calls me that and gets away with it," she said. Her voice held enough banter to sustain the atmosphere, as had all the insults, carefully sheathed in propriety and "honest fun"—zingers, they called them.

My primary weakness was that I couldn't stop sharing. I showed them my writing, talked about my spiritual experiences, opened myself to attack. One weekend when Brian hadn't come home, I had gone to Danny and Dierdre, confessing my torment. I had even told them about the rapist; now it seemed they used what they knew to humiliate me. It had to be a kind of rape in itself, using a trust to undermine someone's dignity. I wondered how I invited it.

I flushed darkly and stood. "I won't put up with this!" Tears burned my eyelids, and I started blindly from the room. I didn't notice Brian reach for me or feel his long fingers closing around my ankle until suddenly I was flat on the floor, my ribs aching, my breath gone, my face scorched by the carpet and humiliation.

Brian hunched over me, legs pinning me down. "I'm sorry, honey. You just shouldn't take yourself so seriously. Come on down to our level and have some fun."

"No!" I wailed. I put my hands over my face. Every nerve trembled. Memories came flooding back, of when Danny had sat on me just this way, holding me down, tickling my feet until I passed out, dripping water on my forehead until I screamed, hog-tying me and leaving me alone in the corner. Memories flooded back, of the rapist, heavy on top of me. I heaved him off and got up.

Brian clutched at my hand, but I shook him off and stalked into the bathroom without looking back. Then I gazed into the mirror at the thin face with great dark hollows under the eyes, the nose and cheekbones jutting sharp and uncompromising. Something had happened to transform the soft, fulsome girl I had been into a woman of distinct features, sharp planes.

There was a disturbing sense of familiarity about my face; suddenly I recognized the family look of suffering—the face of martyrdom worn by so many members of my family. I had even seen it on Danny's face from time to time. Then Danny must already be aware of my pain, of the confusions of my heart! Why would he make it worse for me? He laughed at the flirtations between Brian and Dierdre as though he enjoyed them. Couldn't he remember the dark brooding in my mother's eyes when my father disappeared into Aunt Henni's bedroom? Couldn't he feel the way words stopped in her throat because she didn't expect to be heard? Couldn't he feel that I was living out her pain?

Something I had heard in an undergraduate psychology course came back to me, something about children being compelled to select life partners who will help them play out the emotional patterns of their parents.

If I was suffering as a result of this compulsion, then Danny must also be suffering, however he tried to disguise his pain beneath an absurdist's mask. I thought of the nervous wink he developed during prelims, so like the twitch of my father's mouth when he was trying to please Aunt Gerda. Earlier in the evening Danny had stated that people were driven above all else to seek security, and I had argued that people were motivated by something finer and more powerful—by curiosity and a hunger for excellence.

Realization flooded my mind again, as I remembered something about the pathology of abuse: how the victims become victimizers, how the abused become abusers, pain begetting pain, the sins of the fathers visited upon the children ad infinitum.

Danny must be hurting terribly, participating as he was in my pain; he must be feeling so small and fragmented that he had lost touch with his native zeal and now believed only in some sort of primitive territorialism. I began to weep silently, not wanting them to hear my crying. "Oh God," I whispered. "Forgive him. Forgive us all."

I thought of the wars raging inside Danny and Brian. What could I say to them? How could I tell them what little I knew about the frenetic motion of the family group, all of us trapped in isolation, with the illusion that we dangled freely but still fixed to a single place in the heavens, always bumping into each other like a group of tangled marionettes. Somehow we had to free ourselves or we would all be as mad as Ervil and his crazy brother, Ben, doing push-ups on Main Street, roaring on Temple Square, shaking our fists at the existing order—what was left of it.

Somehow we must each establish a connection with conscience, an accountability for our divine capacities, must become responsible in the same sense as when we were baptized at age eight—creators of every sin and every good deed that issued from our being. No more blaming authorities and claiming their right to shepherd lost lambs; each must enter the straight gate by his own choice.

Then why pity Danny or myself—or anyone! While I couldn't erase the essential weakness in myself or others, I could overthrow the curse of Eve, disavow original sin, achieve self-responsibility. I would escape my father's oracle and receive my birthright of individuality. Redemption and forgiveness would torchlight the way.

I stood. My back felt straight and strong, as though the vertebrae had been rearranged by a heavenly chiropractor. I would banish the demons from the face of love, beginning with Brian and Danny and Dierdre.

Unfortunately, they had opened another bottle of wine. They were oblivious to my transformation.

One spring morning, before I'd dressed or finished my newspaper and coffee, my mother and Aunt Henni rapped at the kitchen window and motioned that I should open the front door. I dumped my coffee and slung into a bathrobe as I raced to the door. I glanced quickly around the living room as I turned the lock. No beer cans, thank heaven!

I kissed them both before I saw my father lurking on the porch. My stomach somersaulted. Of course the house smelled of cigarettes. My mother or Aunt Henni would never be caught in such a clutter of baby clothes, boots, full ashtrays, and dirty dishes. But they came in and spread out, beyond my control—my mother to pick up the baby, my father to gaze at the abstract paintings purchased from my artist friend. They would make no sense to him, of course. I paced agitatedly, picking up clutter as we chatted. I finished their sentences, failed to finish my own. I waited, wincing, for my father to make a sarcastic remark about how well we kept the Word of Wisdom in my house.

My father took Janelle from my mother. He was grinning at her, at my little simile. I watched for a moment as they played, watched her soft round face, eyes shining and demure, reflecting his. She didn't cry as he held her overhead, balanced perfectly on his palm, as though she could feel his trustworthiness. He'd taught us the Mormon doctrine about babies born with heaven's secrets inscribed on their souls. By the time most learned to talk, their memory of perfection had vanished, but a select few retained knowledge of truth and light—children of the millennium. For this reason we were taught to cherish babies because they are so close to the Creator and could be called back to Him at any time. My father always courted little babies, believing in their special influence with the Heavenly Father, as though their recommendations were worth more than the flattery of grown-ups.

He threw my daughter up and caught her as she rushed earthward, giggling. "You haven't seen the new house, have you?"

"No, I haven't. And I haven't met your new . . . wives, either." My voice went suddenly brittle.

"Then come with us. We're going there now."

I hedged. "I'd like to. But I haven't a car to get home. . . ."

"We'll bring you home."

I flushed with pleasure. My busy father, willing to travel across the valley to bring me home again! I ran upstairs and threw on jeans and a sweater, then stuffed the baby's arms into a jacket. "We're ready," I said.

"All aboard the Mayflower," he cried, flinging the car door open. He had always said that, as though each trip to friends or meeting or even the grocery store was a pilgrimage.

"Last Thursday not one of my girls spread a welcome mat for me," my father remarked as we drove. "I stayed at the office, hoping to find some peace." His mouth twitched and the creases in his forehead deepened.

My mother protested. "One of the new girls wanted to change her night, so we other girls are expected to change our plans. I had piano lessons and didn't even know everything was shifted until I was in the middle of them."

My father patted her hand. "It's happened before, and I expect it'll happen again."

I soon learned that Ervil LeBaron had shown himself again. The previous Sunday his sons came to my father's building during meeting and placed pamphlets on the cars. On my father's windshield was a scribbled note, charging him to "repent and live the Constitution of the Political Kingdom of God, lest the sword of the Lord fall upon him." The police would do nothing about the threat.

"We have one friend on the police force," my father sighed. "Perhaps that will be enough."

"How can it be enough? Daddy, you must do something to protect yourself!"

— 258

He shook his head slightly. "What would you have me do? A man can't walk in fear all his life and still have the spirit of God."

"But someone should guard you! Or maybe you could carry a gun!" Even as I said it, the notion seemed absurd. I couldn't imagine my father wielding a gun. He stood for life, not death.

"Don't worry about me, dear." His eyes bleared a little. "I'll go when the Lord wants me to—not one moment sooner."

We drove in silence for a time, turning down a lane and traveling some distance before reaching a private drive with several homes clustering along the dirt road. A big white house loomed ahead, stately brick with heavy wooden doors. My father had tried to recapture the white house days and gird against the future with this house. The smell of manure, the gurgle of turkeys and mawing of cows, the little blond children scattering as the car turned down the drive—my throat clicked and stuck and I saw through a blur of memory.

"Your mother would be happy here. Fresh air, farm animals, surrounded by loved ones."

"I'm at home where I live now," my mother said with stubborn resolution. I remembered that she had been pressured to give up her home to move here, but I knew she wouldn't do it.

"Mama has a mind of her own," I said as we got out of the car.

"Yes, I know." He ducked around a stand of poplars. "Did your mother ever tell you about the time she refused to marry me?"

"Mama!"

She smiled shyly. "Well, I didn't want to come into the family on Henni's skirts or because my father suggested it. I knew that I loved your daddy, but I didn't want him unless I knew he loved me the same way."

"She wrote a letter and said she wouldn't marry me after all. Certainly put me in my place! I had to write a couple hundred letters and make a dozen trips from Long Beach to Short Creek to convince her I meant business!"

My mother winked at me. "You know how these Allreds exaggerate."

"She's the only one who ever stood up and said no to me." He pulled her to him and kissed her. "Spunky little wife."

Spunky little wife! My shy, placid-mannered mother? So he had loved her all along! Aunt Henni and my grandfather hadn't forced the marriage! The passion and tenderness was genuine—my parents really loved each other! If my father loved my mother, then certainly his love for me was also real. We wouldn't be separated through the eternities, me caught in the terrestrial kingdom with all the monogamous people, while he ignored me from his celestial throne; love translated itself from one sphere to another! Perhaps, I thought then, my mind racing as we crossed the lawn, his label "hussy" had been no more than a reaction born of anger and concern and not a prophecy at all. I had never thought of the incident that way. The day glittered and my heart twinkled joy and hope. I felt that my lost birthright had been fully returned. Past, present, and future lay like a shimmering highway, inviting me to make my pilgrimage.

Basically a four-plex, the new house was much larger than the original white house. My father explained that it had been constructed by his sons and brethren in the group, and that it had been financed by the priesthood and two of his new wives.

"The Lord has promised that if we will serve Him with all our hearts, might, minds, and strength, all else will be added unto us. Here's proof that He keeps His promises to us." My father threw his hand out in a grand gesture.

But I knew that this addition hadn't appeared miraculously. Besides the difficulty with state and local building agencies and the opposition of the Mormon ward, much feeling fomented in the family regarding the cost and architecture of the building. Some of the new wives contributed heavily and therefore took a stronger part in planning the new home. My father's older wives were generally left out of the decisions, and I noticed that the new women used financial prowess to finagle more than their share of time with my father. And all the mothers but Aunt Lisa refused to live in the new house, feeling that it wasn't theirs in any true sense.

When I saw Aunt Lisa's sweet, girlish face, her long brown hair untouched by gray though she was nearing fifty still combed in ringlets clustered at the nape of her neck, I began to feel at home on these strange grounds. She led us through her apartment. The rooms were gigantic.

"You expecting all your married children to move in on you, Daddy?" I teased.

"In the last days, the streets of Zion will run with blood," Aunt Lisa reminded. "We'll have to stick together to survive."

"You really think it's that close?" I asked, looking from Aunt Lisa to my father.

"We're in the judgments now. The Jews have returned to Zion. Earthquakes and wars erupt all over the world. These are the signs of the times." He quoted Christ's words about the ripening fig tree.

After years of doomsday talk, it had come to this: literal preparation for the end. Another time I might have smiled indulgently or turned away in irritation that most of the group looked forward to apocalypse. More than yearning for the day when the temple doors would be opened, more than longing to see the Savior, they actually reached for it, perhaps even tried to create it. Life was so unbearable when the major focus was one of persecution and sacrifice, waiting huddled and trembling for the rampage of the wicked. Didn't they grow weary of expecting the mountains to fall, and from sheer enervation didn't they long to get it over with?

My father smiled complacently, surveying the walls and ceilings of his new home. Despite his obvious pride he didn't reflect the tender aspiration, the sense of security, the feeling of being at home that he had at the white house. The white house would always be home, while this place was a temporary sanctuary and a monument to his past.

We went upstairs to visit the widow from Maryland whose husband had been murdered in a robbery. She was a refined, gracious woman with magnificent white hair, who handed my father a quart jar of cloudy fluid and urged him to drink it.

"This will clear up that kidney condition of yours, Rulon," she pronounced. Then she urged us to sit at her kitchen table and partake of the bowls of nuts and dried fruits she set out.

"Fresh nuts and fruits are very good for you," the new woman said. I supposed she couldn't know that I had heard these words throughout my childhood. "We've been eating only them and a few herbs for several weeks now," she went on. "Your father says he feels much better."

I resisted an urge to roll my eyes. Each of my father's wives had placed him on one eating regimen or another, trying to save his stomach. I wondered if the extremes of diet had actually ruined it.

"I've been reading the Talmud," I said with nervous pride as we sat at the widow's formica table. "The similarity between Judaic teachings and the things you taught us . . ." My eyes darted

— 261

to the new woman. I didn't like her hearing what I had to say to my father.

"Yes." He nodded vigorously. "But you must remember—these are the words of men. You can only trust in the word of God."

"I read the *Bible*," I murmured, thinking of the incredible challenge of translating history from one age to another! But I said nothing about men and inspiration and error. Let my father keep his clear and narrow views. My wider stream of belief was marred with rapids and jutting rocks.

"But you must read the other standard works, too," admonished the new wife.

I swallowed my irritation with difficulty. She was a newcomer, couldn't know that I had been spoon-fed the standard works from birth.

"*The Book of Mormon, The Doctrine and Covenants,* and *The Pearl of Great Price.*" My father ticked them off as though I had forgotten. Four fingers, four standard works. I wondered what one did with the signifier of creativity, the opposable thumb.

"We'll go see Sister Madera now," my father said, calling his other new wife by her former surname. "She's well educated," he said pointedly as we made our way to another entrance. He seemed to emphasize that schooling and the gospel needn't be mutually exclusive. "She's well traveled, speaks many languages. She has quite a past."

"I'm a lady with a past myself," I murmured as we went inside. My father didn't seem to have heard me.

My mother had described the new wife accurately but hadn't spoken of her remarkable eyes: quick, intelligent, showing a tendency to anger. Her clipped manner reminded me vaguely of certain women friends who had grown up without fatherly affection because of Don Juanism or divorce or death. We spoke quickly and politely of her paintings, her pottery, her macrame wall-hangings, and of her first-time struggle with the tomatoes she was canning.

My father paced nervously at the door. It was clearly time to go. As we reached the highway, I took a deep breath. I was learning the lesson at last. The only way to overcome fear is to confront it and be done with it.

"Daddy, I know that Mama's children have caused you a lot of grief. But we aren't total miscreants. We have learned things from you. A sense of order, a stringent kind of caring, a capacity for commitment." I swallowed and went on. "And a community motive that transcends our own selfishness. You know, Daddy, in some ways we're more like you than some of the other children in the family."

My father's smile tightened until it threatened to break. "And how is that?"

"You're the soul of independence! You always insisted on making your own way, on following your own conscience. At one time, you had no intention of living the Principle."

His eyes screwed up. "I remember."

"I know you were devoted to Aunt Susan, just as my brothers are devoted to their wives. Daddy, in a nation where marriage is a dying institution, that's something to be proud of!" I was thinking of how easy it would be for Brian to leave me.

He nodded slowly. "I'm pleased that they honor their bonds." He pinched his lips and stared silently at the highway.

"Remember, Daddy, when you were searching for your way, you wrote to your own father, and quarreled with him, just as Saul did with you?"

I saw his Adam's apple bob, but he said nothing.

"Like you said, Daddy, God has something for each of us to do. If I followed directly in your footsteps it would be a violation of my personal compact with God. I have my own covenants to fulfill."

Still he didn't speak. I cleared my throat and plunged on. "Something could happen to you, Daddy. Then what would everyone do? How will they know where to go? So many people can't make a decision without you—how will they survive? Would you have me be like them, helpless without you?"

He chewed the inside of his bottom lip. "It's all very good to be self-reliant. But when we forget to rely on the Lord, we lose our sense of direction and purpose in life."

"Relying on God and relying on you aren't always one and the same, Daddy."

He darted a swift look at me, and his face changed, the inscrutability falling away to naked emotion: doubt, fear, love, tenderness, regret, hope. He swallowed and coughed.

"Most of the children in the family are content to follow you. And I'm not saying that's bad . . . for them. But for me . . . it's too late to change what I've learned. You defied your own father until you were convinced he was right. And then you defied the

Church and the United States government and now Ervil LeBaron to worship as you see fit. Daddy, I admire you so much for that!" Tears made my voice crack. "And I have the same rights. I have the same freedoms. In that way, I follow your example, footprint for footprint. Even though I am a woman!"

I braced myself for the lecture, for the anger swathed in reason. He would tell me that all my rationalizations were very fine, but I'd still be damned if I didn't change the way I lived. He would tell me that I was trading a million dollars in eternal blessings on the shiny penny of the present. He would tell me I was for him or against him. And I would tell him that I was Cordelia, loving him according to my bond, and that he, like Lear, was drunk with his own importance. In another moment we would return to the long-ago confrontation, and he would banish me to celestial glory with the thieves and murderers.

The mask of inscrutability was in place again. He nodded, squinting. "Free agency is the cornerstone of the gospel. I hope you'll find happiness. But if you don't—or if the spirit prompts you—remember the ways of your father and grandfather, of your mother and grandmother. They preserve family bonds like nothing else. And the Lord approves." He swallowed again, and I could see tears glittering in his eyes. I knew that he couldn't give up his way of seeing to perceive with me, not even for a moment, so I didn't tell him about my writing, about it being a corridor to my family and all the treasures that resided there. How could I explain to him that I embraced it all, that I didn't know how to discriminate my faith? At least he had accepted my need to search, and that much was like riches falling into the empty coffers of my heart. We reached across my mother and grasped hands. Love passed, electric, between us.

"Watch out for Ervil, Daddy," I choked.

His face lost its tender appeal and he let go of my hand. "I can't change my attitude to suit him any more than you can change yours to suit me."

Realization flashed like lightning, and then I couldn't think anymore. The day had been too much. I felt dizzy, hyperventilated. I kissed my parents good-bye and went into my ramshackle, rented house.

Chapter

16

No longer did I dream of being tied up in the back seat of a driverless car heading over the edge of a cliff. No longer did I dream of courtrooms and prisons. The doors of judgment had unlocked for my father and me, inviting us to meet at the humble, translucent portal of mutual acceptance.

Healing seemed more important than doctrinal disputes regarding the plan of salvation. When I saw my father on the street or at a wedding, I was warmed by our greeting. When I found his car parked in my mother's carport, I didn't feel the urge to drive away. Our confrontation had somehow freed me to love him openly, to love them all—every mother, sister, and brother.

The times were also freer, more healing. My father now traversed the front lawn in broad daylight, going from my mother's to Aunt Henni's, unafraid of the neighbors' rancor. The world had grown permissive, common-law marriages everywhere, polygamy only another deviation from a dissipating norm. Teenage pregnancy proliferated, group marriages abounded in California, and people rationalized all sorts of behavior under the vast umbrella of self-discovery. Sometimes it seemed that my father and his followers were the last bastions of strict principle, of clear definition.

My father had relaxed in another way as well. In 1975 he had cooperated with Utah State University in compiling an oral history of polygamy. During one interview he repeated Saul's words in an earlier letter, speaking with perplexity and pride, as though the battle to determine who was right had somehow earned him a Purple Heart: "My own son said, 'I might have to thank my father for my life, but I don't have to follow him for it.' My own son said that. He called himself a bastard because he couldn't cope with the social embarrassment, the stigma of his polygamous background. He was ashamed of his father and of his origins, and so he turned from those who love him most." In my mind's eye I could see my father as he spoke these words onto tape and could read the thoughts inscribed in the deepening lines of his face: my own son turned against me. War in the king's household, among his wives and children. Absalom, Absalom. My son, my son. Another item on the long list of persecutions.

In the spring of 1976 he became spokesman for the Mormon fundamentalists in a televised documentary about modern-day polygamy. In the black-and-white film, he seemed thin and old, but his voice reverberated with authority and self-assurance.

"There is nothing sinister about the truth," he declared to the world. Then he explained that the Principle is very demanding for all concerned and that he and his group weren't proselytizing or looking for converts. Then one of my handsome brothers and his two young, lovely wives spoke blithely of their living arrangements and of their human problems, as though all was easily overcome. When the interviewer asked my brother why he had chosen this way of life, he responded, "I was raised in it, reared to it, and I owe my life to it."

"Would you die for it?"

He nodded vehemently. "I would die for it."

Breakers of feeling washed over me. How strange to see my secretive, suspicious family announcing their beliefs over the media! Touched by my brother's claim, envious of his testimony, admiring of his dedication, and understanding of his sense of obligation, I sat before the TV, reckoning a renewed sense of kinship. I wondered about the difference in my dedication to life and my younger brother's, between his devotion to good living and Saul's. But most significantly, the broadcast broke the circle of secrecy about my family. My guilt about writing the family stories was stilled for a time.

Partly in response to my counseling and to the new realization of my individuality, I experienced a new openness to life. I was wrestling with my early stand against divorce, and conceded that Brian and I should be freed of each other if we couldn't promote mutual growth. I was terribly unhappy. Brian seemed to augment my loneliness rather than alleviate it, and no friendship had filled the space where my family belonged. The consonance of my childhood seemed irreplaceably lost. That white house haven had produced few dispersions of spirit such as those posed by my life with Brian.

I was overwhelmed by Brian's ways. He preferred fishing alone on a Sunday afternoon to taking a drive with me and the children, putting even my shallow dreams of monogamy to rout. We disagreed about everything. I had become the focus of his rebellion, merely replacing his mother as a wall of resistance.

There were times when I wished for someone—another woman perhaps—to share the balance, break the unwholesome tryst. Another person dedicated to family, someone to deepen our commitment and help it endure.

I thought enviously of how the mothers relied on each other even more than on my busy father. But I couldn't share such thoughts with Brian or my friends. Outsiders didn't understand my loneliness; they had nothing to compare my experience to. They couldn't understand why I fell apart over hiring a baby-sitter outside the family. They couldn't understand why the house rattled its emptiness like old bones.

When I grew weary of washing clothes and preparing meals and doing dishes, I subconsciously waited for someone to spell me, free me from the rut of daily responsibility. I waited for someone to share the feelings and thoughts that Brian was unable to receive.

In the beginning I had never intended to share him, not even with his own mother. Now I was almost certain that I was sharing him without my consent. Time, which often became the mothers' measurement of my father's love, became my yardstick with Brian, and our time decreased in quality and quantity. When I telephoned him at work and found that he wasn't in, my heart ached with a premonition of loss. I put my hands against my temples, trying to push away the image of him with another woman. I told myself I had it coming because of my prolonged affair with the rapist. Then I couldn't accept even this rationalization and told myself instead that some men are by nature polygamous, and I thought how much plural marriage had to recommend it. To be able to lean on "the other woman" for support instead of regarding her as a threat or a direct hit on one's identity—what balm that would be! To arise with a gentle prodding to meet the challenge of being one's best self each day, instead of awakening to depression, serving breakfast with shrewish, suspicious words . . . to strive for excellence, not for the sake of narcissism but for the good of all . . . to join together as children with a loving parent, the rivalry restrained and kind, the limitations clear . . . most of all, the comfort in knowing that the arms that held Brian (if indeed other arms held him) would hold me too, in an eternal embrace of sisterly love.

It wouldn't be easy; it had never been easy. I knew that from experience. As I'd been told, "Many more will be damned by the Principle than saved. . . ." But if the Principle could save a marriage, save a soul . . . if people could have multiple relationships and yet love, love eternally, love traveling full-circle with no deceptions to break the magic ring of trust . . . that would be celestial, indeed!

One summer night as Brian and I sat together on the front porch, my thoughts and feelings swelled until I felt I must open the floodgates. I took a deep breath and plunged in: "Brian, you should know . . . I've sensed something. . . . If you ever felt you had to have another woman, the Principle is the way to have her—legitimized in the eyes of God. But you'd have to take care of her and give her children, just as you do me. And we'd have to be in agreement. I'm . . . I'm not saying I want that," I added hastily. "But I'd rather you made a woman part of our lives than that you had an affair. You, of all people, should know that affairs are illegitimate. They're wrong in the eyes of society and in the eyes of God, and they end in loss, whatever way they go. But the Principle produces growth and requires commitment. People encourage each other to transcend their pettiness. I'd much rather you had a plural wife than a mistress or some casual . . ." I broke off, out of breath, out of courage.

Brian was silent. I could feel him smiling in the dark. I felt that he had seen through me.

After awhile he took my hand. His voice was patronizing. "Jeannie, I honestly don't think you'd be happy living plural marriage. It's more conceivable, really, that you'd have two husbands."

I opened my mouth in protest, but he put up a hand. "If I ever took another wife, you'd have to be the one to find her. Either that, or the Lord Himself would have to order me to marry again. You're all the woman I want." His eyes, glimmering in the moonlight, mixed pity with amusement.

— 268

Words and tears stuck in my throat. I wondered if he was lying. My feelings bottlenecked. What was I saying, encouraging him to think of plural marriage? As if the Principle was some kind of convenience, a diathermy machine to warm the hearts of the lovelorn. As if I had the social skills and selflessness, let alone the conviction, to share my husband. I felt that I had betrayed myself or that I was utterly paranoid, just as Danny had asserted months ago.

Late that summer Brian and I planned a vacation in the woods of the Pacific Northwest. It was a last attempt to heal our marriage, to lessen the almost commonplace talk of separation, to diminish the growing gap of divided interests and attitudes.

Brian bound his fishing pole and our camping gear in a canvassed lump atop our station wagon. We left town at midnight, planning to journey directly north, where we would visit briefly with my brothers and sisters who had colonized the ranch. I longed to see Isaac and the other siblings who had peopled my early life. And the ranch had lived long in my mind as a symbol of family unity and harmony. How I needed that ideal now!

The people in nearby Trinityville grew thin-lipped as we asked directions to the ranch. They eyed us with puzzled expressions, for we didn't fit the mold of the typical Sprucewood visitor. Brian's hair was too long, mine too short.

Most buildings were in varying stages of construction, for living conditions could improve only when other priorities were met. The residents laughingly called their unfinished homes "Sprucewood Modern" and seemed not to mind cement walls, wide-open fireplaces, dirt floors, and plywood exteriors while awaiting better fortune. Honeybees buzzed everywhere among dusty-smelling purple weeds.

We sat in a trailer with Aunt Sarah, cooling off. She didn't say the words I'd traveled so far to hear, didn't provide the acceptance and harmony I'd imagined. In fact she spoke with an edge, almost defensive when I asked about the conflict with Brother Pearson and the problems with the young people.

"These things happen, Jeannie. Even people dedicated to the Lord's work are human. It'd be better if we didn't say any more about it." And Aunt Sarah turned the conversation to talk of us, of our lives. We bore her scrutiny and insight with general discomfiture, Brian furiously tugging at his moustache and me winding my purse strap into a knot.

When we spoke of my writing, Aunt Sarah said abruptly, "I imagine everyone has her point of view—whatever *that's* worth. I've done some writing myself, but I wouldn't show it to anyone. Too many feelings would be hurt." By the tone of her voice, I felt that I had somehow offended her.

Isaac was away, working in another state, where employers didn't know about his religious colony. I felt incomplete in not seeing him before we left. Of all the people in my family, I felt he would understand my contradictory longings, how my need to belong strained against personal destiny. As we traveled the winding road to the highway, I felt that I had failed, that I had let myself and everyone else down with my mighty dreams, my glorious expectations of the ranch. It was, after all, another remote community peopled by human beings with flaws and frailties and flashes of greatness.

I had dreamed of the ranch before we came. I had stood in a desert, the land bare except for gravestones and piles of bones. A large wolf faced me, warning me away with his eyes, with words I understood through feeling rather than hearing. "There is only death here. Loneliness and death. If you stay here, you'll become like me." Then, suddenly I was on a verdant mountainside like the one I witnessed now as we drove west. In my dream, a tiny log cabin stood invitingly open. Inside were my father, my mother, and Aunt Henni. They sat watching a movie that my father projected with his vision. "What about your own vision?" I asked the mothers, and they smiled at me, their faces lamblike, their eyes downcast and humble. "We chose this," they replied. "It is all for harmony, all for love."

When I awakened, I felt that a fusion had occurred, a connection between dream and reality, between my need to belong to the family and my individual purpose. I had come to the ranch to live out that fusion, but the ranch, like history, was a dusty disappointment, a fragment of the dream that breaks and splinters beneath the crushing weight of reality. My life still was not whole. My only home was within the upright, constantly watching figure that conversed with both wolves and lambs, that faced both life and death, both harmony and dissent, the being who witnessed the lonely truth of individuality and the reactive power of group communion. Somehow I knew I must permit the paradox to live on within me. But right now I felt it would twist and chafe until something broke.

We stopped at Flathead Lake next day, and I squatted on the shoreline where I had once waded in to be baptized by my father. I remembered how I had looked up to him that day, how he had seemed a bright, shining messenger or perhaps a god himself, his right hand raised above me in a command to uphold. . . . I flinched suddenly. A bee resting on my arm had stung me awake.

Late in the afternoon we traveled through Sandpoint, Idaho, remarking the beauty of the countryside. I remembered that my grandfather had nearly bought the heavily wooded hills north of the mile-long bridge. He had made the down payment and had even traveled with my father and all their possessions in a boxcar to build a house for his family. After spending a night on the forested land, he concluded it would make tough ranching, and they returned without even unloading the boxcar.

We spent a day traversing Washington, taking our time, nearing the Oregon border.

"Where do you want to camp?" Brian asked.

"Eagle Creek," I said as though the name had jumped off the map and into my mouth. We found it at dusk, a tiny river with a single campground. The trees seemed tall as redwoods, ramrod thin, gaining height rather than breadth in the close forest.

We stayed the night with the echo of owls slurring in the trees and the shrill cry of nighthawks ricocheting off pines. The wilderness felt more comfortable than home, yet there was an undercurrent of perpetual motion, as though we followed a prearranged course or a path already beaten. Brian must have felt it too, for as we lay awake, listening to the forest speak, he whispered, "I'm not worried about tomorrow. I don't know where we're going, but I know that we'll get there."

I nodded, and he slipped his arm beneath my neck and drew me to him. His breath was clean and sharp as evergreen. We made love, enveloped in the rustling sleeping bag, and I felt clean and light, as though the shadows of otherness had been lost somewhere, left on the roadside leading from Salt Lake City.

The streams and rivers were rich with trout. Brian stopped at least once a day to flick a dry fly across the ever-changing water, having caught the fishing madness of my brothers, who inherited it from my father. I doodled with a stick in the sandy banks or looked for smooth stones to skip behind him—never ahead, where the fish would spook; Saul had taught me well. I tried to identify plants and wildflowers from comments made by my father so long ago, realizing now that he had really known most of them, part of the herbology he studied for his naturopathic degree. I didn't mind waiting in the wilderness as Brian fished. My mind teemed with the sense of arriving, of being near the end of a very long journey. Sometimes I wrote, and the words were not dead bones but flowering branches and slim, bright children playing in the sunshine.

The warm feeling grew as we crossed and recrossed the Columbia River. Sometimes we stopped the car to revere its full azure, its uncommon width, its sharp and colorful gorge.

"I've been here," I whispered to Brian.

He looked at me sharply, eyes veiled. "With who?"

"I . . . can't remember. I . . . know I've never actually been here, but . . ."

He pulled in breath as though hooking a fish, quick and sharp. "I know. I feel it too."

As we moved along, the highway narrowed to a strip with ravines on either side. I had the sense of tightrope walking, of mincing at the edge of a volcano. I felt I was approaching the place where my family's special brand of hell began.

I couldn't explain the feeling except by tracing it as we warped south into the dry plains and sagebrush of inland Oregon, curving alongside rivers without names until we began to climb again. Pines appeared, and great porous rocks studded the countryside like oversize sponges. As we mounted toward Crater Lake, so did my fear— an unconscionable, ridiculous fear, I told myself. But its rib-cracking power crowded my heart. I couldn't move, couldn't turn to look at Brian, although his face had been peaceful and unclothed all morning. I feared to see something—a wounded animal or a person dead on the roadside.

I wasn't sure where I had heard it, but I knew that my father had asked Aunt Susan to marry him here, at Crater Lake. She had been a doctor's only daughter. The summer she and my father were engaged, he had been logging at nearby Lake Hebron to help support his father's family and to pay for the diamond ring ordered from a Sears Roebuck catalogue. Her family planned to vacation with his family at Crater Lake, approving the warmth between the two young people. During their separation, he had grown taller, tanner with logging work, but Susan's image must have assumed mythical proportions in his dreams as her brown, young body became the epitome of desireable womanhood. When at last he saw her, he disappointed everyone by declaring, "Susan, how small you are!"

I stood beside Brian, staring into the water. It was lovely, no longer a pustule erupting on the earth but crystalline and pure. Clear as Brian's eyes. Pale-blue shade of my father's. Impertinently blue and clear, almost challenging the sky in purity. Deceptive as romantic love, anointing the heart with rapture, inducing two to hope, to turn from all the world to find consolation in a single orb, a solitary sphere—when, in fact, it is the mouth of hell in disguise.

"Nothing can live in it," Brian told me.

"No fish? No plants?" Why couldn't I remember what I had learned and relearned about illusion, the way the mind sees more than is really there when the heart is stunned into silence. But I asked Brian anyway, feeling like a middle-aged debutante. "Why not?"

"Too cold. It's all snow water."

Once, perhaps, it had been a mountain peak, a green-treed pinnacle reaching for clouds and eagles. They had been happy the first year, she working so that he could go to osteopathy school to become, like her father, a doctor. It was a small enough sacrifice; someday she would return to the way of life she had always known. But their first child had died, and the second had been sickly. My father spent most of his time on church activities, traveling to the Mesa temple to do work for the dead, or in the genealogical library doing research, or presiding at one meeting or another. She hadn't realized he was so . . . zealous. She was lonely at home with the children, another and then another. Although my father graduated from college with a degree in naturopathy, he was seldom around to treat his patients, always on some church work or another. Susan had no money for groceries; she had to call the genealogical library or track him down at the wardhouse to take care of a waiting patient. They quarreled bitterly.

And then came the final straw, my grandfather's book on the Principle. My father, staunch supporter of the official church, called his own father to repentance and accused him of "kicking against the pricks" of righteous authority. A deluge of correspondence followed, and when my father converted, Susan and her mother—a woman who gave no quarter of belief to plural marriage although she was Mormon by birth—were incensed. Susan threatened to leave with the children several times, came close to accepting the Principle, then did leave, perhaps hoping to shock him out of his allegiance.

The separation grew into a divorce. The yawning hole was never healed for either of them.

I knew how Aunt Susan felt. I knew of the black hole that followed the death of one's dreams. I had a similar hole—a pinpoint of darkness that sometimes expanded like a dilating pupil and threatened to swallow me whole. I felt it when Brian was away from me, or when he held a restless silence, or when he was quietly angry. From all reports Aunt Susan's life had deteriorated after the divorce. Although she married again and raised the three living children, the black hole had grown.

During a visit to my father's office, I had learned of his correspondence with Aunt Susan, following decades of silence. Later, the mothers filled in the details, and much later I was privileged to read the letters.

It had actually begun as a communication between my father and his oldest son, Monroe. When Isaac had met Monroe and Aunt Susan in Southern California, he had urged a meeting between the two of them and my father. Monroe and Susan coolly declined.

Then, in the summer of 1976, on the fiftieth anniversary of his mother's marriage to my father, Monroe had telephoned Aunt Susan, knowing he would probably be the only one besides her to remember the day's significance. He wanted to wish her well, to fortify her fragile psyche against the onslaught of painful memories.

But she hadn't answered the phone. He called and called, then jumped into his car and drove the forty miles to the trailer court where she lived alone. He found her still in her nightgown, slumped on the bed, staring vacantly at the ceiling, her face tear-streaked, her breath coming in hoarse, wracking sobs. Her short, small frame seemed scarcely more than a lump on the cot—a mound of earth with life leaving it.

Monroe called to her, then splashed cold water across her face. Even though he was a doctor, trained to meet such emergencies, he was terrified that she was dying or mad. Once he had completely roused her, he called in a neighbor. Then, instead of heading back to his practice, he drove east, across the Mojave in mid-day heat to Salt Lake City, arriving as my father finished with his last patients.

Fuming, he waited on a folding chair, wondering what he would do when he saw his father—the first time in perhaps forty years. He wanted to hit him. He wanted to see the agony on his mother's face where it belonged—on the face of the man who had deserted her.

But when at last the older man came out—rushing, delighted, having discovered who waited to see him, the fine head of platinum hair surrounding a lean, angular face, bright eyes, kind smile exuding warmth—Monroe only held out his hand, and then they embraced, wrestling with emotion. The time for reprisal had passed. There was only time to let register what had been lost over forty years—what might have been. The hole was not researched; the hellfire was not seen. Crystal waters of restraint drowned the heat of an agonized past. Monroe returned to California an hour or two later, confused and unfulfilled.

It took a letter to express—very articulately—what it cost him to lose his father so inexplicably at the age of seven. Precise words, flowing phrases told what it is like to grow up without a father, with only the ghost of a hero, a cloudlike example, wispy and obfuscating. Only a very intelligent man can so clinically describe what it means to want identity and to look for an ideal and find only a gaping black hole. Still, the letter was delicate, careful. Oh, how I would have loved you, Father—if you had let me love you.

He'd not even had what we, his neglected plural-family children had: the example, however remote, of a life well lived, of a personage steeped in integrity, strength, and principle. That Principle.

My father had written back, another careful letter, to explain that he hadn't wished for the divorce. It was difficult to explain his commitment to the Principle, for he knew that to the unbeliever such talk sounds like the ravings of a person obsessed. My father spoke of his love and devotion to Monroe, his mother, and his sisters even now. He expressed a wish to be closer to them. He reminded the son that they had been sealed for eternity and that the covenant could not be broken without just cause. He had been just. He loved them devotedly. In his heart and in heaven, they still belonged to him.

— 275

Monroe didn't reply. My father wrote another letter, this one to Susan. She wrote back bitterly, accusing him of desertion, infidelity, egotism, even theft. To her the Principle was no more than an excuse for unlimited lust. And yet her love—her torment—was unmistakable in each agonized phrase, each jealous word, each angry jag of the pen.

He sent her three thousand dollars in child support money, long overdue. He didn't explain about his years of poverty, how the family had lived on pigweed and had moved into the white house not even knowing where the first payment would come from. She wrote him a thank-you card, conceding his integrity. The correspondence ended. Another part of my father's life, one of the beginning threads, had woven full circle. The loose ends were being tied in preparation, in preparation. . . .

I gazed into the lake, wondering whether I must follow in his footsteps to protect my own integrity. The Principle was a matter far beyond me, but the issue of divorce had hovered like a vulture, waiting for the death rattle. Could my principles, all of them fostered on a personal plane, survive alongside Brian? Or had our problems so overwhelmed me that only the death of the relationship would provide a path to salvation?

As though sensing my thoughts, his arm tightened around me. "Want to go for a swim?"

My eyes filled and I shook my head, squinting into the lake.

"What's wrong?"

"It . . . it's just the sun."

Brian cleared his throat. "Do you want to leave now?"

I shook my head. After a moment I tried to explain. "My father asked Aunt Susan to marry him here. They rowed to the center of the lake in the moonlight. He was going to ask her there, but I guess it was too frightening—no earth beneath him—because he rowed back to the shore before he gave her the diamond."

Brian gazed over the lake like a sea captain judging the weather.

"Do you want a divorce?" I asked him.

His eyes were startled, violated, the pupils dilating. "Do you?" The hurt-animal look returned to his face.

"I . . . I don't know. I have to have more room. I mean, I'm just finding out who I am. . . . I don't know if I like me, or if you like me, or if we'll like each other. And my values are . . . changing, maturing. There's my family; I have to have them in my life. There has to be room for them, both for what they are and what they represent."

Brian swallowed and stared. "I knew who you were when I married you. And these things you're finding out about yourself and your family—I knew about that, too. I don't have any trouble with that. It's . . . what if Mr. Right comes along? Where does that leave me?"

My mouth fell open. "No other man—except maybe my father—has had my loyalty. And my father's no threat."

Brian bit the side of his lip. "No threat? Huh."

Light pressed my heart. Did Brian know how much I longed for the wholeness, the roundness of my family? Did he know how I missed having many shoulders to share the weight of life's burdens, having other minds and mouths to think and speak in chorale? Did he know of the secret times, the times I hid even from myself, when I wanted him to be more like my father . . . ?

And did he understand that I knew of his nomadic yearnings and that I wasn't enough to root him to the ground or make him whole, that I hadn't been able to heal his wounds and that my arms weren't long enough or strong enough to bind the shattered pieces of his soul together. Only God could do that.

I feared commitment for fear of losing too much. But to take refuge in the cold, empty waters of divorce, to rob my life of its fullness . . .

"Moses suffered to write a bill of divorcement . . . Moses gave this law for the hardness of your hearts."

Was my heart so overlaid with fear, so encumbered with ideals that love and compassion were buried?

"No," I told Brian. My heart felt stung by a thousand honeybees.

"No?"

"I don't want a divorce."

He smiled softly and kicked a stone into the water. "Then let's get out of here."

We took our time traveling. The sense of being guided held me in an addictive kind of security. We didn't plan an hour or a moment ahead. When at last we reached Portland, night had fallen, and we would have to cross the Columbia one more time in order to sleep on the state beach. As fog clutched the windows and billowed about the car, I was haunted by a fear that I had been mis-led, or that we had taken too long and shouldn't have waited to cross at night.

The bridge was the type that opens to allow large ships to pass, perilous in theory if not in fact. Mist closed around the car as we started onto the pavement, our tires humming thinly. My heart jumped.

"This is it," I said for no rational reason.

Brian nodded and for once didn't mock my fear.

I felt suspended in space, although I knew that grids ran above and alongside the four miles of durable pavement beneath us. Fog softened the steel girders.

My father's voice played in my head, warning, "Those who do not cling to the iron rod will be lost in the mists." Iron rod—would that be the Principle? Then I was lost. But then came snatches of a hymn. "The iron rod is the Word of God."

I felt rather than heard the surging beneath. My stomach jittered. I rolled down the window, and mist reached with cold fingers to grasp my face. The roaring was incredible—almost an explosion. I was at once terrified and delighted. "Let not your heart be troubled, neither be afraid." My heart ached with exhilaration, flesh goose-bumping, hair on end. I was possessed with an unreasonable certainty that we were suspended in space, with certain death beneath us and no place to go but forward. We had reached the juncture where the two halves of the drawbridge joined; for a split second there was no backing up, no jumping over, no flying away.

In that split second I realized that this was my home, at the joining of great waters to witness the continental waters embracing the oceans of the earth. This was my place, where nature was conquered by intelligence, where intelligence was governed by principle, where principle became one with human need, where human need married environment, where thought coupled with feeling, where life bridged death's tumult, where Enoch departed heavenward and glittered from the North Star while the Gulf of Mexico deepened endlessly. This was my home, where all the earth united in a celebration of life.

My grandmother's grandmother had pulled a handcart across the plains, had left Europe to join Brigham Young's Mormons in a new Zion to begin a new way of life. She had entered the Principle in Salt Lake City, had accepted a life of accountability, human creativity, and divine order. It was up to me to take up her handcart and pull it westward, following my father's footsteps to this place where I gazed into the dark and knew that nothingness lay beyond me until the grasp of other hands, the comfort of other voices would bridge the emptiness of space and time. All the backwaters of my past poured through me and over the brink. There, God willing, they might be cleansed, merged, given shape and renewed purpose.

In that instant I knew that Brian and I were one. And that my father and I were one. And that my family and myself were one. I was one with everyone and everything. No gap stood between me and the world, between art and religion and science and nature. I knew in that instant that God and man are one and the same, one in inception and one in purpose. And I knew that I had reached the vortex, the coupling of great forces within me. I could dive into the bottomless pit and still come up riding the Milky Way.

Long after we had crossed over I sat in dazed silence, until Brian eyed me quizzically. I could only hug him and whisper, "It's so beautiful. Much too beautiful."

I didn't know until after my father was gone that Brian and I had traced the honeymoon path that he and Aunt Susan had taken, and that the honeymoon had ended nearby, when their car refused to climb the final hill overlooking the mouth of the Columbia where it joins the Pacific Ocean.

At the family home evening the faces of my family, though smiling, still bore traces of skepticism, even though my skirt was longer and my gaze no longer defiant. Some of the younger ones didn't even know me, but I could tell by the way they stared that they had heard of me.

After closing prayer I made my way through kisses and hugs and half-answered questions to my father.

"Daddy, I have to talk to you."

"What can I do for you, dear?" He said those words to everyone who approached him.

"Daddy—I've been having dreams . . . horrible dreams and beautiful dreams. Dreams that come true—some of them. And I'm afraid, for all of us, but especially for you."

He said nothing and his pale-blue eyes penetrated mine.

Aunt Gerda tugged at his arm. "Rulon, we're waiting."

I turned away, on the verge of tears, but he grabbed my shoulder.

"Come to Mother's house and we'll talk."

"My mother's?"

He nodded, then turned away.

He was waiting at my mother's, his fingers riffling a deck of cards when I arrived. "We'll talk in here," he said, moving to the living room, where he had always held serious consultations.

I told him of my dream, of my obsession to write. I described how, in a dream, I had been freed from "the authorities" and in turn had freed others.

"I . . . I don't even know who 'the authorities' are. The Church, the government, Satan. Maybe even you!" I half-grinned. "But I know it must be written down and that I must do it. I can't explain why. I only know that if I don't do it, I'll have failed, and my soul . . . won't be worth anything."

I expected him to object, to remind me of the threat of the law and my obligation to keep family secrets. I wanted to explain how I envisioned the effect of knowledge on human beings. "You, of all people, must know why I have to do what I've come here for. . . . You had your calling,"

He cleared his throat. "Don't expect the world to change its mind. The devil is god of this world, and he sees to it that the Lord's Chosen are persecuted. But in one thing you're absolutely right—the story must be told. We must stop fearing the consequences and lay the truth before the world. And you are just the one to do it."

I was astonished. I had been braced for objections, even accusations; I would explain why I had to do it anyway, and then we would part. I had hoped for understanding, but I hadn't dreamed of his approval, his blessing.

"What do you write?"

"I write about myself, about the past, about the family, about you. . . . Sometimes I write short stories, but there's a kind of truth in them. And I have this notion that the real facts have an incipient order, that they hold gold mines of truth. I need facts. I need help corroborating dates and incidents. If it's going to be true . . ."

A kind of excitement passed between us, and he interrupted. "You'll have my help and the mothers,' too. Sarah and Henni have kept journals, as have I. I can tell you about my early years."

"Your early years?" I was awed. Was I worthy of such trust? "Oh, Daddy, I've wanted to write about you, but . . ."

I held out my hands, declaring my inadequacy.

"You must begin with the foundations of the Church and with your grandfather's life. And then mine. You must trace the roots of the life-style if you are going to present it truthfully."

"But that would take volumes!"

He smiled. "You have a lifetime ahead. I can give you books on the Principle. You must read your Grandfather Harvey's journal and your Great-grandfather William Orr Allred's journal. And mine, of course. And the books that the brethren and I have been working on . . ."

He went on, listing books, references. I scribbled in my tiny notebook, trying to get down the architecture of his vision of my book, knowing that my own vision would supersede but wanting his influence and the proof that this night hadn't been another dream.

Then suddenly he broke off all talk about my writing and began telling stories—beautiful, heartbreaking accounts of his early life. Of Aunt Susan. Of their firstborn, a baby girl that had died only hours after its birth. He blamed himself for the baby's death, for in Susan's eighth month of pregnancy, he came in after a chiropractic lesson with her father and (filled with his native zeal) said, "Let me show you a correction I just learned." Lacing his arms through hers and placing his hands at the base of her neck, he simultaneously pulled and pushed, causing her spine to crackle. Susan stood blinking with surprise and said she felt wonderful. Afterward his father-in-law took him aside and explained, "I hope you haven't hurt our girl, or the unborn child. I should have warned you, this correction is not for pregnant women."

"So Susan blamed you too," I breathed, and felt I had found an important piece to an important puzzle.

He nodded sadly. "Yes, but of course I felt much worse than she imagined, for I believed that I was to blame even before she did."

He told other stories, of how his car broke down on their honeymoon and he had put Susan on a bus, then hopped a freight in Oregon and rode all the way to L.A. to meet his new wife, and how he arrived with only ten cents in his pocket. Each story had its own beauty and pain. Each story revealed the human dilemma: a propensity for greatness struggling against a tendency to err. When he stopped speaking, interrupted by my mother bearing crystal bowls of cantaloupe and ice cream, I was unable to say anything.

He smiled. "I've been blessed to heal people that weren't cured even by fine medical doctors. Some say that it's naturopathy that makes the difference. A man in Las Vegas called me at my office and described symptoms that indicated a kidney stone. I told him to go to the hospital there and have it removed, as it was the size of a peanut or larger. The hospital couldn't find the stone and was about to discharge him, along with his 'normal X rays,' when he called me. I told him that the stone had moved into his bladder and would soon pass into the urethra if they didn't get to it quickly. It would do untold amounts of damage, a stone that large, not to speak of the pain. They grudgingly took more pictures of his bladder. They found the stone and operated within half an hour."

"But Daddy, you hadn't even examined him! How did you know?" Suddenly I felt small. Perhaps he was something of a god on earth.

"I saw it."

"You mean—you're clairvoyant?"

"I'm only a vessel. The Lord does His work through me. I was given the gift of healing. But it is only a gift, just as you've been given the ability to write. We must always remember to give the glory where it belongs—to the Lord. The single biggest mistake people make is when they allow the Lord to use them for His purposes and then forget to give Him the credit. When they take the glory upon themselves or fail to use the gift wisely, it departs. Don't ever forget that."

I nodded and looked at my hands. I felt the responsibility sink in. How else to explain why I was doing what I was doing—how I had come to be here, this night, hearing my father tell his deepest secrets.

"I want you to know that I'd spend more time with the family if I could. But . . . ." How could I tell him why I stayed away, why an evening like this one required all the courage I possessed? How could I tell him when I didn't know myself?

He nodded quickly and stood. "Be patient with your young man," he said. "I think your present mission lies in this writing. Let the Lord lead you and don't worry about the future. That will insure some objectivity."

My mother came into the room, and he slipped his arm about her waist. "Your mother and I have been together almost forty years—forty wonderful years."

"A biblical number," I said. I saw the way they looked into each other's eyes—lovers still, even after all the years of pain and interference. "I'd better be getting home to Brian."

I knew that he would be waiting, the children in bed, wanting me beside him. The shift in our relationship since our trip to the coast and the confrontation of our worst fears had made space for a new intimacy. We knew, though we did not say it, that there would be a way to make it all fit together. Someday we would make our peace with Jehovah. Somehow God and man would be one.

Chapter

17

On a Sunday evening in the winter of 1976 my mother and Aunt Henni returned from meeting to find a message printed in the deep snow of their front lawn. "You're Next!" it said. Aunt Henni telephoned my father. My mother phoned me.

Everyone was certain that Ervil LeBaron's Church of the Lamb of God was responsible for the message in the snow. Other murders had surfaced in the news since Los Molinos, all linked to the strange cult that subscribed to blood atonement and stood on Old Testament scripture to justify murder.

A polygamist named Robert Simons had been missing from his Grantsville, Utah, home since 1975. According to rumor, Ervil coveted one of Simons's beautiful wives, so had him killed. (In 1978 Simons's body was discovered in a grave carved from the rock of remote Carbon County, Utah. His corpse, half the head taken by shotgun blast, was perfectly preserved by the lime the murderers had poured over him to quicken the body's disintegration. But the drought foiled them; in three years no rain fell to activate the lime.)

The death of a former "Lamb of God," Ervil's "military leader," occurred in San Diego. For failing in his duties and "apostatizing," Dean Vest was reportedly guilty of a capital offense, and the punishment was allegedly administered by one of Ervil's many "wives." Other rumors suggested that Ervil had his daughter drowned for opposing him. So we all knew there was reason to fear the message in the snow, although the police showed only passing interest in the new threat.

"Do you think Ervil's bluffing, trying to back Daddy down?" I asked my mother. "What does he want, anyway—money, Daddy's power, the group—what?"

My mother shook her head slowly. "Sometimes I get the feeling your daddy won't be with us much longer, in any case."

I had felt it too. We talked of the changes in him, of how age and responsibility pressed on him, imploding his body and drawing his spirit taut. He had lost weight and he was always tired. But he played solitaire at a frenetic pace while my mother fixed supper, as though afraid he'd be interrupted before the game was finished. My mother reported that sometimes he awakened in the middle of the night to investigate a sound or a sudden flash of light, and he'd squint through the bedroom drapes, mouth drawn, as through he feared that here, in the arms of his most gentle, placid wife, he would meet his destiny.

My mother declined Brian's offer to stay with her; brethren in the group had already arrived. My father allowed them to stay the night but soon sent them back to their families or jobs and refused to let them guard his office. Some were perplexed, even critical. "Brother Rulon, you shouldn't risk your life. You mean so much to so many."

My father nodded, his eyes closed in concentration. "The Lord has His hand in this, as in all things. He won't take me a minute sooner—or later—than He wants me."

And so his practice continued, with patients coming and going, people dropping in to discuss personal problems and to debate doctrines.

When I took Janelle in for a routine checkup, he met me with a broad grin.

"I delivered my first great-grandchild the other night. Mother Rachel's girl Renae's oldest daughter had her first child, a girl. And I delivered the baby's mother and the baby's grandmother as well."

"And I suppose you'll deliver the baby's baby, too," I said, laughing. But then we both sobered and fell silent.

He gazed for a long time at his shoes, feet a little farther apart now that he was older, searching a new balance. Still he walked quickly everywhere he went, his black oxfords pointed straight ahead, always in a hurry.

"I've tried," he stated suddenly.

I started. Tried what? Was he commenting on his errors with me? I didn't want him to speak of it, didn't want him to abdicate.

"I've tried to find someone to take my place. Andrew will take over my priesthood duties. But here . . ." He made a futile gesture. "Two doctors were brought in and trained to take my practice. I've often yearned to devote my last years to the Lord. But the good doctors had something else in mind. Even though we agreed about the Principle, they wanted to raise prices and change philosophy. My patients can't afford that."

I shivered, although the office was warm. We were talking about his death as though it could happen anytime—today, tomorrow. I wasn't ready. No one was ready—but him perhaps.

He kissed my children resoundingly and held each for a moment, murmuring endearments. Then he looked into my eyes. "Don't worry, dear. The Lord will find a way."

We left slowly, reluctantly, stepping from the dark office into the bright sunlight like sleepers pushed into waking.

For several years it had seemed that Salt Lake City no longer deserved a springtime. The weather of Zion, like the political and emotional climate, was hot or cold, no in-between. People were book burners or pornographers, Mormons or Gentiles, ultraconservative or radical. Like Nazis and Jews, they were back-to-back in their extremes, caught in disparate struggles of self-righteousness, age and youth shouting each other down, winter dueling summer.

A long stretch of cold, barren weather was at last relieved by a gray, nondescript sleet storm on my father's seventy-first birthday, March 29, 1977. Many of his birthdays had come and gone without my notice over the years, but all during this day, as I shopped in the sleet and slush, I thought of my father. I bought him a gift, although I hadn't planned to see him.

The day before, my mother and he had celebrated their fortieth anniversary. I had tried to make gift reservations for them at their honeymoon hotel in Idaho, but my father said no, he couldn't get away just now; and my mother agreed that too many questions would be raised, other wives wondering why they couldn't have a trip alone with him too, and she didn't want to add to his burdens. I couldn't shake my sadness that my mother's one small, selfish wish couldn't be granted. I felt that the two would never have another chance to celebrate their second honeymoon, and in my depression I only telephoned my mother to acknowledge the day. I didn't phone my father, thinking anniversaries were a dime a dozen to him. Later in the afternoon my mother telephoned to say that the family was holding a small informal birthday party for my father.

When the evening snow became a blizzard, Brian tried to dissuade me from going. "Stay here with me, where you'll be safe," he said. "You needn't feel bad about not going in this weather."

I shrugged and sighed. I tied a ribbon around the book I had bought for my father. I wrote on the birthday card.

I looked out the window. Snow stuck to the streets and had turned the greening lawn white. I thought of the message in the snow of my mother's lawn. I changed my clothes.

Brian came into the bedroom where I was brushing my hair. "Please don't go out in this."

I looked up in surprise. He usually promoted my outside activities, as though trying to make up for his own. He must have had a reason to ask me to stay, some premonition perhaps. I wanted to please him, but a voice spoke within me: "You have to go. This is your last chance."

"Your last chance." The voice seemed almost audible, so loud and undeniable I felt that another person in the car could have heard it. I drove with my nose near the windshield as snowflakes clung like sticky feathers to the glass. The car skidded and slid at each corner, but I drove slowly onward, praying silently and steadily across the valley until I reached the big house.

The gathering was already underway, and I tiptoed into the quiet room like an intruder, feeling typically outside the family synergy. But my father was pleased to see me. Despite the fatigue that creased his forehead and drooped his eyelids, his smile beamed approval. He knew that I wasn't there to make trouble but to honor him and show my love.

The gathering was more like a family home evening than a party. We began with hymns, then sang a few rounds. Aunt Sarah, who sat beside me on the long sofa against the west wall of the spacious family room, put her arm around me and squeezed. "So good to have you with us, Jeannie," she whispered. "Just like old times." Her eyes glistened, and an exchange of golden moments passed between us, opened by the warmth of love and shared silently, sweet and irrevocable as costly perfume.

Aunt Henni, ever solicitous of my father's health, suggested he sit in a more comfortable chair. When he was settled in the big secondhand easy chair with wisps of batting sprouting from the upholstery, he looked around at us and smiled wearily.

"I'm glad to be with my darlings. But I'm very tired this evening." He closed his eyes.

I overheard Aunt Henni tell Aunt Lisa about his difficult day at the office, how five patients showed up without calling and several others came by to chat. Aunt Sarah put down her crocheting and went to him, massaging his neck for a moment, while Aunt Henni went for his medicine and Aunt Lisa brought a pillow for his neck. They wove themselves delicately through his life, each in harmony with the other. The new wives sat looking on, watching and—perhaps—learning.

"Dear Hannah and I celebrated our fortieth anniversary last night," he commented, with a significant glance at me. I have done my best, the look said. "We went to dinner and then to a musical version of the Cinderella story. We had a marvelous time and enjoyed ourselves immensely. Things don't change much when you're in love."

"Well, Rulon," said one of the new wives reprovingly.

I was astonished, too. It wasn't like him to discuss his relationship with one wife before all the others.

Aunt Sarah leaned toward me. "This reminds me of the time he took me to Crater Lake and took my hand as we looked at it," she whispered. "It was so romantic—until he told me that this was where he had proposed to Susan." A sardonic, good-natured grin quirked the corners of her mouth. Her eyes twinkled into mine.

"Hannah's the only woman I've known who's still in her girlhood after being married forty years," my father went on, oblivious to the murmurs around the room.

My mother smiled and blushed, staring intently at her hands as they lay in her lap. I winced, wondering if he knew how truly he spoke, of the pain that her innocence had wrought.

"Tell us all about it, dear," Aunt Sarah broke in blandly. It was a secret message, an encoded warning developed long ago to give shape and balance to his life. Each of the mothers had similar, special gestures or habits to warn him of some old trouble or danger.

My father caught himself, and the poker expressions about the room relaxed and smiled again. Dear Aunt Sarah, I thought. She too had to conceal the passion of their relationship for fear of hurting others. But she hadn't closed her eyes to my father's human foibles. She had once said, while speaking in meeting, that we should strive to be children in the eyes of God, but that it made no sense to be children to one another. "Otherwise, who will rear the children?" And as my father's children grew into pubescence and the turmoils of near-adulthood, it was she who commented, "Well, raising kids isn't much like playing dolls, is it?" I thought how desperately the group—the world—needed more like her, who faced reality yet believed in God, who refused to behave like the polygamous ostrich and bury her head, who claimed the dignity of her human perspective saying, "Happiness is a do-it-yourself project."

Aunt Gerda suggested that the "party" consist of each wife sharing a personal memory of him. Aunt Henni led the reminiscence with a story of how my father had cured a man who had suffered from hiccups for three months.

Aunt Sarah spoke of my father's fishing prowess, how as a boy of fifteen, while traveling with his family by wagon to Canada, my father had caught enough fish to feed the family of eleven—the only change in their diet of potatoes and bread.

My mother was next to speak. She told of the first time she and Aunt Henni had met my father, at the cottage meeting where he'd spoken of the Principle. "I had expected to see a gray-bearded, dour old man—anything but this charming, handsome, fervent young man. I must have loved him instantly, but it never occurred to Henni or to me that we might someday be his. . . ."

Her voice trailed on, telling the story I had heard before, of how he went to my grandfather and asked for "one of your twins." I smiled slowly, with the satisfaction of knowing that the demon that had tormented my childhood had vanished, that my mother and Aunt Henni each had her own place in my father's life.

I fully expected my father to skip over me to the next mother, but his gaze lit on me. "Would you say a few words to us, darling?"

My mouth opened, then closed. I nodded involuntarily, then was horrified at myself. What could I possibly say? I thrust shaking hands between my knees and bowed my head, half-praying, half-thinking.

The barn, the rich stench of manure, the cows stomping and swishing their tails, the echo from high bare rafters and my father's long fingers and warm palm over mine, milking old Bossy.

My father's face, gritty and tired, loading and unloading truckloads of furniture, his body taunt with fatigue and fear, his long arm reaching out, pushing me aside.

The tall pines of Montana, his plaid cap tumbling between trees as an early morning breeze stole it from his head, and him laughing as we chased it down, throwing his silver-blond head to the mottled sunlight, and then setting the cap right and firm as he turned back to saw wood for the rich man's fire. The sparkling cold water of Flathead Lake beckoning and his face shining and serious above me, arm raised, a wide wet sleeve draped like an angel wing, and then the plunge of cold water and my teeth chattering, my lips turning blue and his pressed tight and almost purple, but still he seemed so white and tall and fine-looking I thought him the image of the Holy Ghost that was conferred on me afterward.

Him sneaking up the back stairs, drawing the drapes, moving steathily as a fugitive.

The memory of the sting and blush as the heated words again seared my heart. I looked up at my brothers and sisters and mothers, their faces expectant. I looked at my father. His head was bowed, his eyes squinted shut. Lord help me. I must speak the truth. But let me speak it kindly.

I cleared my throat. "I remember . . . when we were forced from the white house, and Daddy had to hide from the law. When he came to visit, he would skulk up the back stairs like a thief."

A ragged breath tore from my chest. "It seemed so unfair that we should be separated. I saw him so rarely, he was like a stranger. But when he was inside and we ran to him, it seemed he could hold all of us in his arms at once and that our house had filled with light. We lived on that light, on the hope of seeing him again, on the faith he gave us, on his strength in the Lord. We needed that more than the powdered milk and peanut butter he brought. And when he was away . . ." I pressed my lips together, unable to finish. I couldn't declare my love, how desperately I had needed him and how he hadn't been there, couldn't admit so much to my brothers and sisters, these veritable strangers who seemed so rich in companionship and love.

But I had my right to pay homage, just as they did, and to do it in my own way.

"I have lived in the world and I have loved those in the world. I have friends who are Catholic, friends who are black, friends who don't even believe in God." I looked at my hands. "And I love them . . . I love the people of this world. Please remember that God . . . created them . . . too.

"But I love my father, knowing that he is a man—a good man—and I love you, this family. I want to witness that the principles of light and love that you have been taught here are divine and eternal. They survive darkness and confusion. They outshine and outlast evil. Wherever you go, whatever you do, don't let go of the good things you've learned here. Don't forget about harmony and loyalty and family tradition. But don't forget about loving and forgiving outsiders, too."

My mouth snapped shut as if a spring had been released. The words echoing in my head, where had they come from? Sometimes the same feeling came over me as I wrote and then suddenly became aware that my arm was tired, that pages were covered with words and I had no idea how they got there.

My father was speaking in commanding, measured tones. "The Allred family is a good and saintly people. I want them to go down in history that way."

I blinked and looked up. Was he speaking to me, of my writing? Was he asking me to lie again, to whitewash everything for the good of the family? Didn't he know that the time for lying was over, that I was as committed to truth in my way as he in his?

"Saintly is as saintly does, Daddy," I remarked. "For a man who took on so much, you've done all right." There, there was my tribute.

But he would not be satisfied. "I want no black sheep among us—not one."

"That's not asking much, is it?" Aunt Sarah gibed in a whisper. "Forty-eight out of forty-eight!"

Silently I implored him to note our accomplishments, our dedication to our families and careers. Couldn't he see the good we did, have some faith in us? Perhaps we had missions that outstripped understanding, like the eternal relativity of time and space and energy. I wanted to tell him how hard it had been for us to find ourselves, impossible until we moved away from his obliterating influence. I wanted to tell him that the other side of anger is joy, that the opposite edge of envy is admiration, that the root of resentment is the terror of ineptitude. I wanted to confess, "I didn't know myself, I didn't know my mothers or my brothers and sisters, except as appendages of you—until I realized that you are a human being and not omnipotent."

But it was his birthday. It was time to be silent. I left early, before the other mothers spoke. The sky was still unloading thick flakes, but I was no longer afraid as I drove home to Brian.

The drought continued, the weather cold and steel-gray. On an occasional day when the sun shone Brian and I golfed with Danny and Dierdre. Brian's relationship with me seemed to glow with a subtle new light, the realization of what we meant to one another. Danny and Dierdre, perhaps sensing the change in me, exhibited more regard for my individuality and more respect for my marriage. In turn I was less critical of them. Despite the barren weather, too cold and dry for true spring, I felt that a cloud had been lifted and that the sun was breaking on my soul. The aching loneliness of the preceding years had diminished; each reluctant forsythia blossom, each slowly unfurling leaf bud whispered that life was suspended in a time of redemption.

We received an invitation to Deborah's wedding reception but not to the ceremony, where my father would seal the couple for eternity.

Brian and I arrived well after the program, groping across the graveled lot and into the lower story of the sprawling building where group meetings were held. The big room was decorated in powder blue and white, Aunt Lisa's handiwork making it seem as elegant as a reception hall. On the speakers' platform was the wedding line, people thronging so that I couldn't see Deborah or my father.

My mother sat at the piano in a pastel dress, playing soft music; people milled around eating and talking. Among themselves the group was gregarious enough but suspicious and sullen toward outsiders. I wondered how I would be treated—as one of them or an outsider?

As soon as we entered, Uncle Lawrence's wives clustered around, kissing and hugging me and my daughters, Uncle Lawrence himself enfolding Brian's hand.

"So good to see you, son," he said.

My dread vaporized like rain on a summer pavement.

My mother stopped playing to greet us. "I'm so glad you could come," she said, giving us each a resounding kiss, determined to make us feel welcome.

People stopped us every foot or so as we made our way to the platform. Kissed and hugged and greeted so enthusiastically, by the time we reached the platform Brian was rubbing his hand.

"I don't think I can survive another handshake," he muttered. "What is this—the firmer your grip, the more priesthood you hold?"

"They just want you to know you're welcome."

"Either that or they're trying to make sure I don't show up again." He grinned.

Deborah was lovely, her laugh full, her face radiant, yet even now restrained by the peculiar precocious wisdom evident in her early childhood.

"Shame on you for getting married and leaving your mother," I teased. "Aunt Henni waited eighteen years for you and now, barely seventeen years old, you're leaving home!"

But Deborah didn't smile. "I know," she murmured. "I can't explain—it seems so urgent."

Becky had moved on ahead of me to greet my father. "I love you, Grandpa." Her strong clear voice had the sweetness of freshly mown grass.

He took her face in his hands. "I know you do, darling. And I love you. Listen, Grandpa wants to tell you something. You must never forget who you are."

"Remember who we are." The words sounded off the walls of my lifetime, an injunction to behave properly, lower voices, giggle less, play fairly, love kindly, be chaste, benevolent, and true, and above all, keep the family secret.

Brian came up behind me, holding Janelle like a ventriloquist's puppet. He teased Deborah, kissed Aunt Henni, and verbally jousted with the groom, as though testing his mettle.

Brian belongs in this family, I thought, more than I ever realized. Then my father was reaching for me. He held me in a deep, long embrace, and for a moment I was breathless, feeling catapulted beyond space and time into a brightness beyond enduring.

"I love you, Daddy." I heard my voice, joyous and mournful. I was frightened and stepped back to look in his eyes.

"I love you, my dear daughter. I love you very much. You must never forget that." He smiled tremulously.

"What is it . . ." I began, but his eyes glittered in a strange way that begged me not to ask.

Janelle reached for him, falling from Brian's arms to grab her grandfather's neck. It amazed me that as little as she had seen him, she loved him so much and was so utterly unafraid of him.

"Do you love *people*, Grandpa?" she asked in her tiny voice.

He nodded and nuzzled her cheek. "I love you, darling."

"But do you love people?"

"Of course he does," Aunt Henni laughed.

My father's face grew serious. "What do you mean? Yes—Grandpa loves people."

"Then love my daddy—he's people too."

My mouth fell open. Brian's grin strained.

My father kissed him. "You see, I do love your daddy. And I love your mama and your sister. And I love you." He kissed her, then handed her to me and took Brian's hand in both of his, squeezing gently. "Hello, dear son." My father didn't have to prove the strength of his grip.

"Hello, Dad."

A quality of light and space like that which had surrounded us in the years before we left the white house suffused the evening. I imagined that Deborah had married just to provide us with this wonderful reason to be together, all of us married in a sense, feasting on companionship and spice cake, on love and laughter, beneath the tender auspices of the Almighty. Rivalry, bigotry, self-righteousness and fear seemed part of another, lesser world. Was this a taste of celestial bliss? Had my father's spiritual ambition, humility, and self-realization won him a heaven on earth once more?

"I haven't been so happy since I was five years old," I murmured to Brian.

He lifted an eyebrow ironically. "That's not a very flattering thing to tell your husband."

I flushed. "Well . . . there have been moments . . ."

But nothing as pure, as complete and sustained as the honeylike love that swirled around us, filling our hearts and minds with ambrosial sweetness.

The only break in my hallucinatory happiness came at one point when the door burst open and no one entered. I gazed at the door, then glanced around the room. No one seemed to have noticed the phenomenon but me. Then I saw that my father was eyeing the door, too. He quickly left his place on the platform, hurrying up the stairs to the upper story. My heart leaped after him; I wanted to follow and ask what was wrong. But I couldn't move my feet.

I nudged Brian. "My father's afraid of something," I whispered.

Brian glanced up but was drawn back into conversation.

I watched the stairs, feeling something shadowy and threatening in the room. I wanted to go after my father. Lord help us, I prayed.

He reappeared in the nook of the stairs and watched the crowd a moment, eyes darting nervously over his flock. Then he walked slowly into the room, checking the door before he began to stride in his old, rushed way. Someone had closed it by now.

I put out a hand to stop him. "Daddy, is everything all right?"

He looked at me strangely, as one who has just been awakened from a dream. "Yes. Yes, dear. Excuse me." And he continued across the room to one of the brethren.

I balked when it was time to leave. "It's too soon," I told Brian. "The girls are tired."

An ache rose in my heart until I thought it would explode, adding brilliance to the effulgence of the evening. I thought of the odd, celestial atmosphere and of the fragile beauty of my father's embrace as he committed his love to me and my family. Later I learned that others had felt the heavenly quality, speaking as though the room itself had been transported to a higher plane of being and that they too had shared a singular, commemorative moment with my father, establishing their love bonds with him.

When we pulled up before the house, I sat dumbly until Brian carried Janelle inside. I followed slowly and stopped in the living room. Suddenly I sank to my knees, closing my eyes as if in prayer. Only I wasn't praying, not exactly. I felt disembodied, the mood of the evening overwhelming my senses. My arms began to tremble, and my chest was too tight for breath and then suddenly filled. Again I had the sensation of being lifted to great heights.

I was overpowered with a soft, whirling radiance. Then I saw my father sitting on a shining throne, his silver hair grown long and full and lionlike, his eyes piercing yet benevolent. He held out his hand for me to sit beside him. I came closer. He motioned again and nodded at the figure on his left, a small person encompassed by his arm. Then I saw that he was giving the figure to me. And I saw that it was Brian, his Marine uniform stained with blood, his eyes crazed and lined in red, his face scarred by panic and terror. My eyelids opened, but the frightened face was still there, and then I realized that it truly was Brian who knelt before me in his gray three-piece suit, his face concerned, asking, "What's the matter?" And then I knew that it was 1977 and that the war was nearly over, the blood spilled there at last atoned for through some mysterious force of will or sacrifice.

Monday morning I golfed with Dierdre. I had thought to play till lunchtime, then visit my father, since I had been given leave to his time. But on calling my mother I found that he was staying with one of the new wives. He was taking Mondays off now, since Sundays afforded him no rest, an attempt at relieving his constant fatigue. As always, I didn't know whether I should intrude. These women who came to the Principle from monogamy didn't understand: one didn't bicker over or lay claim to my father's time; like the land, he belonged to God.

I struggled with myself as we returned to Dierdre's for tea. Should I go see him? What would I say, how would I justify my claim to his precious time? As I silently pondered, Dierdre embarked on one of our discussions about Mormonism and agnosticism. The conversation took the same old turns, then began the same philosophical and psychological contradictions.

"I should be going," I said, rousing slightly. I was so tired of struggling, my mind webbed with thoughts that had nothing to do with the brightening day. I wanted to see my father.

"Don't give up now," she said, flashing that smile, lips curved in a challenge, nostrils flared. "Not now when we're so close to solving all the problems of the universe!"

I fell back against the velvet easy chair, smiling weakly. Dierdre's willingness to talk was a good sign. Perhaps I could help her find some understanding for my family and my father.

Tuesday morning, while running errands, I had to pass the white house. Even before I reached it, an instinctual chill signaled the powerful pressence of the past. I turned down the lane, and my breath caught. The pine tree that had once sheltered our parlor had been uprooted; a deep excavation swallowed the front lawn, the fresh dark earth piled to one side. A strange panic gripped me, and I wanted to run to my father's office and warn him.

The grounds were poised for reconstruction, yet the houses retained their semi-tacky, semi-ornate faces. Chintz curtains bunched around window frames that bore the nicks and paint drips I remembered from childhood. The plaster crack above the east entrance had widened a fraction. The pump still leaked, and ducks splattered through its mud puddle.

I slowly stepped out of the car and crooked Janelle against my hip. The hair on the back of my neck stirred, and I sensed another presence although the yard was deserted. "Ghosts," I muttered.

We toured the grounds quickly. "Mommy was happy here," I whispered to Janelle. We gazed into the swimming pool slimed with moss; five giant gold carp swam in its murk. Suddenly, instinctively, I turned. The long-ago-buried pond where Marie was drowned had crept back! I thought then that I could see her reaching for a small duck rippling the surface.

"Marie?" I trembled violently and Janelle began to whimper.

We hurried to the station wagon. I started the car, then stared at the weatherbeaten barn, trying to calm myself. And then I sensed Grandmother Allred at the car window, her voice rasping through the glass. I felt the barrier between worlds rip like a worn-out curtain, and I shut my eyes tightly, clutching my fists against the temples. When I opened them, only the misty day confronted me, the sun veiled by ragged clouds.

That afternoon Brian strutted into the living room like spring itself. "Have you been outside? So warm! I took the afternoon off."

I nodded absently. I was thinking of my father, how burdened he was. The same burden that had primed him to wrestle with life now bent him toward the earth, compromising the ramrod posture that had once been a lightning rod to join earth and sky.

"Hey!" Brian called. "Get a baby-sitter. We're golfing with Danny and Dierdre."

We drove in Danny's car to my favorite course, the one in the mountains. Despite a kind of breathlessness and, on one green, a sharp tingle down my left arm, I played a better game than my usual dozen strokes per hole. The pale green of the mountainside was a soft coverlet over the chill of the earlier day, snuggling my fears to sleep.

As we drove down from the mountains, I gazed out at the blur of new green softening the bristle of scrub oak and realized that I was actually enjoying myself. In a single afternoon a whole winter of ice had melted, and my dreams of death had been stirred and lifted, carried away by the soft breeze. I couldn't identify the change in my relationship with Danny and Dierdre, but I no longer felt excluded. My heart was so light, it might not have been there. So much happiness in life seemed impossible, almost dangerous—like hang-gliding or parachuting. Eventually the ground must rush up to catch you.

Yet I felt nothing could harm me, that all the old hurts among the four of us had been resolved. I had been reprieved from the volcano's edge. No matter what unfolded in the years ahead, there would be salvation, redemption, forgiveness.

Brian's fingers played in my hair. Once he turned my face to his and kissed me. "I love you," he whispered. His eyes were translucent as two warm springs. My skin tingled with the knowledge that romance had returned, that my waiting had been gratified. My family would not be dismembered. My children would have a father and I a husband—someone to love and protect me in my father's absence.

A hitch in my heart. Perhaps we jounced over a rift in the road.

We descended into the valley, and it seemed that the skyline was especially vivid, the smog curiously absent from its usual haunt above the lake. The Lakeside Mountains stood distinct, giving an impression of eternity in their sharp relief.

"This place has the best hamburgers in town," Danny declared as we stopped at a diner.

"Give me a dime," I whispered to Brian, then strode across the street to a phone booth. My legs felt strong, connecting squarely with the pavement, unafraid of pain. Pain, I thought, as the metal door clicked shut, is part of living. To live, one must be willing to hurt. To live, one must be willing to die.

The phone rang only once before Becky answered.

"Have you eaten?" I asked.

"Mama! Call Grandma!" Her eight-year-old voice rang with high drama.

"What did she say?" I asked, trying to ignore the spasm in my heart.

"She needs you."

The phone went dead. I shuddered involuntarily and looked for reassurance toward the pink and gold sun now setting over the lake. I fumbled in my pocket for another dime, and my hand trembled as I dropped it in the coin slot. Becky had been so grim . . . but she was such a theatrical child, just like Grandfather Harvey who named most of his kids after Shakespeare's famous characters.

My mother sounded far away, as though we spoke long-distance.

"Mama, what's wrong?"

There were tears in her voice and a new, terrible tenderness. "Honey, I'm so glad you called."

"Something's wrong."

"Yes." Her voice came slow and deliberate. "Darling, it's Daddy. He's been shot."

"Not dead! He's dead?"

"Yes, darling."

The phone booth whirled. I could hear cries echoing. My voice. "Mama. Oh, Mama. I'll be right there."

I leaned my forehead against the cool metal, and a deep, dry cough broke from my chest. No tears. "At last it's over," I whispered to the blurred reflection trapped in steel. I had feared this for so long; perhaps now there was nothing left to fear.

I rushed across the street, not watching for cars, feeling that my heart could stop at any moment anyway. Then I was inside, telling Brian. His eyes widened, then saddened, two steady lanterns barely flickering in the storm. "Tell your brother," he husked.

"You're kidding," Danny said. Just like my father, rejecting reality when it didn't fit his view. Hadn't anyone else felt it coming, sensed this tidal wave threatening to break over us?

"It finally happened," I whispered. "Thank God we were prepared."

Danny went pale then, and we sat down. People glanced at us, then looked quickly away. Danny held his arm tight around me, as though we would both fall apart if he let go.

"Who would do it?"

"No question. The LeBarons." I had a disconnected impression of Ervil's deep-set, burning eyes.

But later, when we took the children to Brian's mother, the car radio blared the news. "Two women murdered a Salt Lake City physician in his medical office this afternoon . . ."

My mind cinched up my heart. "No! Not women!" I looked down at my hands and felt a horrifying complicity, expecting to see them stained or marked in some way.

Then it came to me. Ervil LeBaron believed himself the divine executioner of God's law. If God had His executioners, then certainly, the "One Mighty and Strong" would have his. Hadn't Ervil sent girls as well as teenage boys to bomb Los Molinos? Certainly he would not stoop to pulling the trigger himself but would send a woman to do it—sublime proof of his patriarchal thrust, making a woman cock his gun and fire. That would throw the police into a quandary, trying to determine motive.

When we reached my mother's house, Uncle Lawrence was holding my mother. His sons stood around him like sentinels, eyeing the doors and windows with red-rimmed eyes. Tall, blond, handsome young men, patriarchy budding in their faces, they were protecting their father; as part of the council he would be in danger, too. Guilt struck me sharply. Where had we, my father's children, been when he needed our help?

Uncle Lawrence had been weeping, his face gray and slick as wet clay, but his voice came gentle as ever. "It's amazing how people hold up," he said, nodding at my mother as she came to us.

Despite her breakdown she comforted us with steady strength, as though she had been willed some of my father's serenity about death. It was Aunt Henni who worried me then. She had been working with him, of course. She had watched him die.

"She called me before the others," my mother reported. "Her voice was trembling. 'Hannah,' she said, 'something terrible has happened here.' Then she broke down."

Then I broke down, and the tears came at last, gushing warmly. Dear Aunt Henni! The old reservoirs burst with love and sorrow for her, for us all. To have seen him . . . !

When at last she came from the police briefings, Aunt Henni looked beaten, imploded, the horror of the afternoon engraved on her face. Danny held her tightly, his face fatherly and seamed with concern.

"It'll be all right," he told her quietly until her sobbing calmed. "It had to happen. When you look at history, all the men who have made it happen—Jesus, Joseph Smith, Martin Luther King—they all end up martyrs. When people stand up for justice, the world turns on them. It always happens with . . . great men." The last words choked out, an admission, a recognition, a concession.

I watched him, amazed. Once he had said he didn't respect Daddy because, "ideas mean more to him than people." Danny had said that "people are what really count." But existentialists pay tribute to historical verification. And absurdists can see that the kingdoms of the righteous are "not of this world." At last Danny had acknowledged that great love can flow out of great ideas. And vice versa.

We stood around, then held each other for long, silent moments. Danny telephoned Saul, who wept openly when he was told.

"He was a fierce, proud old man," Saul said. Later we repeated the words, each comprehending in our own way. He had not conceded one jot of his faith—not to Ervil, not to Aunt Susan, not even to the Mormon Church.

When the news report came on, we clustered around the television. The first scenes showed the exterior of my father's office. Policemen and relatives clustered about as they wheeled a stretcher toward the waiting ambulance. One of my brothers was there, his face a study in grief, eyes wrinkled to restrain tears, mouth a tight line of emotion—so like my father's! More familiar faces appeared. And then the body rolled into full view on the sheet-covered stretcher. My father's feet pointed outward. My father's standard black oxfords, the same type of shoe he had scuffed twenty-two years ago while playing kick-the-can, had caked with manure while milking and wore to the office anyway after a quick scraping, shoes too pointed to be stylish, shoes no longer held straight and firm but tipped beyond restraint, without direction, without purpose. I bit my lip to still the sobbing that rose in my throat.

Then a sweetness filled my heart. Outsiders would be holding their breaths in horror, contemplating the insanity of the world or perhaps titillated by the renegade's poetic justice. But I understood that this murder wasn't some mad accident, some incomprehensible tragedy. Each step had been deliberate, each preparation profound. I for one had been delivered into this moment with sufficient strength, freed of guilt and renewed in bond with my father— the recipient of his faith and his blessing. What grace!

And what mercy for him, to be spared the indignity of old age and the outstripping of his capabilities. What providence to go quickly, to die holding a banner of freedom on the rod of uncompromised belief! My tears ceased. Perhaps Ervil LeBaron was somehow a pawn of God—not as the Divine Destroyer he believed himself to be, certainly, but still picking life when it was ripe for exalted being.

Again I listened as Aunt Henni recited the details, details she would testify to a thousand times in the courtrooms and in the vast bleakness of her double bed, trying to recapture his presence.

Five of the forty patients had still been waiting when the two women came in. One stood quietly; the other sat down. Aunt Henni glanced at her watch—it was four forty-four—but didn't stop to ask them what they wanted as she hurried to finish with a patient in the back room. My father strode past her to the first examining room to read a blood test, when the woman stepped into the office area and called to him.

The patients were not made wary by her actions, for things were always informal at Dr. Allred's office—so many wives and children and brethren going and coming! Then my father turned to speak to her and she drew from her purse a pistol, a small black handgun, and emptied it into his upper body. (Later, at the trials, I would glimpse the police photographs: six bullet holes in the head, neck, and chest. His white temple garments stained with blood, his eyes half-open, his face slack. Sometimes those photographs displace my vibrant memories of him always on the move, always working, always talking, always bringing life to life. I wish I hadn't seen them.)

My father cried out once. Some witnesses reported that he cried, "No, no!" as he fell. Others insisted that his last words were "Oh, my God!" But the witnesses were in shock. They couldn't give consistent, accurate descriptions of the assassins; they had stared at the guns, not the faces. An arriving patient saw someone depart from the office, removing a wig; police speculated that the assassin was a man in disguise. Witnesses said no, the bodies of the assailants were unmistakably female.

One man, a member of my father's group testified that he'd been waiting to talk about a ranching venture, had struggled with both women at once, trying to detain them. One struggled free and pointed a revolver at his forehead so that he released them and pushed them out the door, crying, "Please don't shoot me! I'm a husband and a father." Then, realizing that the hollow door provided no protection, he released the knob and ran to the rest room for cover. The women opened the door and shot after him; then one woman returned to the examining room, waving the gun at Aunt Henni until she moved aside, then taking aim at my father's face, which was still unscathed.

"She could have killed me too, if she wanted. She pointed the gun right at me," Aunt Henni related. She explained that she had ambled into the room, thinking that a car had backfired but confused by my father's cry. "There he was . . . on the floor. And then this woman rushed in, waving a pistol. At first I stepped in front of her, thinking I could stop her. Then I realized that he was . . . dead . . . or dying. His mouth was slack and his eyes half-open. And his hands were sort of propped up by his elbows . . . and they were vibrating like this. . . ." Her voice broke.

A cramp seized my heart; I thought of those hands that had healed so many, blessed so many heads, bandaged so many wounds, delivered so many babies. My father's hands were his focal point, his most vital connection to others. They would be the last to die, the last to relinquish power, his last energy vibrating from left to right, a palsied, frenetic plea to hold onto life.

"Why did she come back?" I mused when Aunt Henni was able to talk again.

"I think she wanted to be sure he was dead. She must have been under terrible pressure to fulfill her mission. Either that or she was trying to hit his face. But she missed. The bullet ricocheted off the floor and went through a wall and out the ceiling."

Later, when the accused murderers were brought to trial, state prosecutors revealed the possibility of both motives for the assassin's return. First, testimony indicated that Ervil considered any "military failure" to be a capital offense, punishable by death. The assassin's life, then, depended on my father's dying. Also, the Church of the Lamb of God held a strange esoteric belief based on obscure scripture that when false prophets are executed, their faces should be destroyed to indicate that in their deceit they are "faceless before the Lord." The bullet intended for my father's face had gone astray, the police said, because the second gun was heavier—a .38 caliber weapon not easily handled by a small woman. My father did not go "faceless before the Lord."

"Then they disappeared. I put my hand to my head, thinking, What shall I do?" Aunt Henni's face crumpled, remembering the terrible sense of loss that had registered with the realization of his death. "I got on my knees beside him and called, 'Darling, speak to me.' But he was already gone.

"Then I thought, I must call for help. But I couldn't remember the emergency number, I was so stunned. Another patient came in just then and asked, 'What's going on here, Henni?'

" 'Dr. Allred's been shot. I think he's dying.' " Aunt Henni clutched her head. "Then Mary said, very gently, 'Is there anything I can do?' I asked her for the emergency number and I called an ambulance."

Then there was nothing for Aunt Henni to do but telephone my mother.

After the news report I drove my mother and Aunt Henni to the big house to meet other members of the family. Danny opted to stay with Brian at my mother's house, sitting nervously on the sofa, hands twisting in the gap of his knees. "Do you think . . . would they come here, try to wipe out his whole family?"

Brian shook his head. "They're after power. You don't have any power in the group."

Danny stared at the carpet, eyes glazed. With the women gone, his strength seemed to flow out of him. He jumped up and went to my younger brother's room. From the top of the closet he took down the hunting pistol and loaded it. Brian followed him, concerned by his abrupt, irrational movements and dilated eyes.

Danny tried to grin, but his face collapsed, stuck like footage of an avalanche. "Just in case," he muttered. "You don't know those LeBarons. They're crazy enough to do anything. They believe in patrilineal priesthood. Maybe they'll try to kill off all his sons, too."

Brian gently pried the gun from Danny's white-knuckled hand. "That isn't the way to solve it even if they do come. Having a gun would only seal it—then there's no talking to them. Look, take it from someone who's been there: if you run from death, you'll wake up someday and find that you're running from yourself."

Danny nodded slowly. Brian clapped him on the shoulder and led him from the room. "Come on. Let's go sit down." Then Brian cleared his throat and said perhaps the tenderest words he had said to any man since Vietnam. "You know, you've got to pull yourself together, Allred. If you fall apart, who do I have to lean on? And I can't get along without my best friend—my brother."

After driving through the bleak night where every stoplight seemed to spill blood on to the highway, the familiar faces seemed radiant even in sorrow. Grieved smiles were beacons of hope; tearful eyes gave reflection of my own mixed feelings. We half-laughed, half-cried as we embraced, confused in our joy at meeting without him.

When I saw Aunt Navida there, I knew that our bonds were stronger than anything death could erode. Her cheeks were streaked, her glasses fogged, but I could see the refining touch of loneliness that the years without my father had etched. She had lost him long ago and now bore with us in our loss. She had learned of his clay feet long ago. Around us were those who reeled in shock, who still believed somewhere in themselves that he couldn't die, who yet believed that at any moment he would reappear and begin healing.

Faces I hadn't seen for years appeared, and our years of separation dissolved in tears; we were one family again. Love bridged the distances and conquered the unknown. Someday, I vowed to myself, I will know them all—and they will know me. Each mother and child, each aunt and uncle, that were mine through my father and yet lost in his encompassing effulgence would emerge for me. Now that he was gone, his shining just an afterglow, we would see each other in a truer light.

Uncle Andrew spoke. Already he had assumed the heavy mantle of responsibility, and his voice bore the weight of grief and unfathomable duty. Tears escaped fingers that periodically rubbed his eyes in irritation. My father's gesture, my father's place.

"The last words our dear Rulon said to me were, 'Andrew, I'm counting on you . . .' " His throat clicked and he clenched his teeth and shook his head. "That was twenty minutes before he died."

After a long, thick silence, he continued. "There will be no thought of 'getting back.' Of course we know who is responsible for this . . . vicious deed." His voice broke. He swallowed and bowed his head. Then he croaked, "The people of God do not take revenge. We know that vengeance is the Lord's."

I gazed searchingly at the crowd, surprised that such a speech would be necessary, and saw my brothers standing beside their wives or mothers. Some faces were stern, holding back tears or rage, some pinched and folded in sorrow. Couldn't they see the pattern, how everything in our lives had woven toward this completion? Our father had died for religious freedom, for the centralizing principle of his life. It was a perfect, magic circle, a completion—such a rare and beautiful thing! Dream had established itself in mythical proportion through doctrine. Doctrine had nourished faith and love. Faith and love had shored up the principle until it became a reality, spawning other realities, other lives, other dreams: my own and those of my brothers and sisters. The dream had come true, the mission had been completed, the prophecy had been fulfilled. It was a godlike quest brought to consummation.

But after I had driven my mother and Aunt Henni home and Brian and I had wearily loaded our daughters into the car, the sense of divine design unraveled as we sped along the dark pavement. The comforting events of recent years blurred and fogged into insubstantial mist. I felt empty, yet freighted with failures. Why hadn't I gone to see him yesterday? Why hadn't I gone to see him today when my feelings prompted? Why did I always let the needs and expectations of others take precedence over mine? Now I wouldn't see him again until . . . perhaps I would never see him again. I had been taught that those failing to live the higher law would be denied the higher glory. Since I didn't live the Principle, perhaps I would be trapped in terrestrial glory, unable to visit my father on his celestial throne. Doctrine stated that I couldn't travel through space and time, couldn't translate my life from one sphere to another.

I could find no argument in my own favor. I fell on the bedspread, feeling heavy and dry as an empty riverbed, and I sank into a black sleep.

It began raining the next day: the citizens of Salt Lake City rejoiced that the drought was over and called it the mercy of God. One of the brethren said that the heavens were weeping for us. It rained as I drove across town to my mother's house, where I found myriads of flowers, plants, cakes, cookies, and jello salads—typical Mormon edification for mourners, grief inextricably linked with life's processes. The heavens wept as I answered phone calls and doorbells and received mail. Friends from long ago appeared—people I thought gone from the city or that I never dreamed would know about my family. Bridges I thought had burned long ago bore the weight of my father's death, while other relationships seemed not to be bridges at all but mirages.

It rained as the family gathered at the big house to plan the funeral. Saul did not go, nor did Danny. The old family factions were still there, more poignantly than ever. In the foyer I heard a report that one of Aunt Gerda's sons, who had been "legal" all his life, had off-handedly confessed to another of the mothers that he was glad there'd be no question about his right of inheritance. Whether he was talking about my father's property or his priesthood calling or his surname, I didn't know. My brother was young and bright and handsome, liable to reckless talk. But anger rose in me that he would speak thus to a woman who had spent her entire married life and reared her children without the complacent refuge of a legal marriage. The burden had always rested on her to legitimize her children's lives, and now he had seized the source of her lifelong pain and stuffed it in her throat, leaving us all speechless.

Yet a few moments later the same young man rose and spoke to us.

"I hear a lot of talk about 'noble bloodlines' and how Daddy's natural children are his, but those who were adopted into the family through marriage aren't. Well, there's no such thing as noble blood! And these adopted children are as much Daddy's as any of us who have his blood!"

Of course Aunt Gerga's son would disparage "noble blood" since he held unshakeable legal ties with our father. By diminishing the blood-tie, his position would be securely superior over the many of us—including natural and "adopted" children!

I watched Aunt Sarah's daughter, Erin, who had gone, the day before, to my father's office and mopped up his blood so that Aunt Henni wouldn't have to do it. I imagined her there, kneeling on the green tile floor, swabbing it gently, reluctant to rinse the cloth, her tears diluting it anyway. This sacred essence was her only corporeal legitimacy on earth since her mother was the fifth of my father's plural wives. Perhaps she had thought, as I did now, that his blood was her source and the engendering of her mortal life, now so savagely squandered.

But Erin stared fixedly at her hands and said nothing. And so I said nothing.

By the time I reached the viewing room that evening most of the close relations had arrived. In a few moments his patients, distant relatives, friends, admirers, and followers would pour into the triple-size viewing room and overflow into the hall, the foyer, down the front steps of the mortuary and onto the sidewalk.

I stood in the hallway, talking with some people near the door. I glimpsed the casket flooded with light and only then realized that I was trying to avoid seeing it.

But my eyes had been open for a long time; life had cultivated me to resist the erosive running from realization. I knew that I must lean into the next moment and face it squarely, or I would go on pretending that he was only away—at the ranch or in Mexico or off visiting another wife or congregation—and that someday I would see him again and I would tell him all the things I had meant to tell him. . . .

The coffin stood alone. Others were embracing, talking, or holding hands at its periphery. I took a deep breath and stepped into the fluorescent light, feeling that I had lost the top of my head. I stood alone at the coffin, staring at my father, dead.

So much can register on the cells of the human body in a single instant. The moment of birth, the impression of the first human hand on the newborn, skull, shoulders, hips, feet, skin on skin imprinting the love-arc between bodies. An eon of light can travel that arc, can translate itself from one sphere to another throughout eternity. The two identities will always find each other, will always hold the lock and key to an immortal, nontransferable relationship of like cells with like cells, of body meeting body, of spirit knowing spirit and remembering the wholeness of intelligence, the agreement at separation, the understanding promised.

So much can register on the cells of the human brain in a single instant. The sting of a slap, the burn of a label, disseverance and fear and rejection making the mind's eye gape at the soul's night and cold. An exposed stump of relationship cauterized by the insufferable heat of true light, when all must stand alone on a corrupted, decaying planet, strangers lost in the desert, exiles from the fertile valleys of the earth, the nightmare-come-true registering suspicion for all other physical bodies, distrusting every movement as an impetus toward death or betrayal. And despite the empty socket, the phantom limb sends muted longing to become real again, a wish to splint the severed bone, to graft the cold-cracked branch back to its parent, to make whole the division.

So much can register on the cells of the human heart in an instant. Words spoken carefully, kindly. The covenants of love borne on air, the curl of tongue, pressing of lips, soft bite of each fricative, rush of each glottal, riding the wind to inscribe and circumcise the heart; an understanding reached, a love rejoined, a legend remembered, a story shared, a memory recalled, another dream hoped for then becoming real.

So much can register on the cells of the human body in an instant: The realization of ancestry and its expectations for each progeny. The terrible, terrible burden of living out the lives of those who have come before. I was my father's daughter! And he was gone.

I doubled over the coffin and couldn't look again. My voice rose from my navel and exploded in a cry as unkind and unseemly as gunshot ripping the air around and gouging the body of soft, composed voices around me. What lay before me was an empty pod, a poor sculpture of my father, however carefully the drying folds of skin were stitched together, however skillfully the clay had been molded, the putty applied to fill bullet holes and the flesh-colored paint applied and hair combed gently so as not to pull it from its dead roots. The hands that had stitched so many gaping wounds, that had rested on so many olive-oiled heads, that had delivered me into the world, were now forced into a position supposed to look peaceful, their stiffness undisguised.

It wasn't he. He had gone and was somewhere beyond us. I covered my face.

My sisters came to me, some horrified or embarrassed by my sound of grief, some understanding although better controlled than I.

"It isn't him," I tried to explain.

"Oh, Jeannie, yes it is. It's Daddy. Look—he's only asleep. His body is asleep. His spirit lives!"

But fear ruled my body; a worm in my stomach gnawed a widening hole. Resurrection remained untranslated to faith or reality.

That night, the night before the funeral, I dreamed of my father. He came to my mother's house in his shiny, secondhand black suit and gray felt hat. He hugged me, and in my sleep I could feel his body, his cells on mine registering truly.

"Daddy, you're alive!" He nodded. "Of course, darling."

I awakened with the distinct impression of his touch, feeling he had been in the room with me. I felt certain I would see him again, somehow.

Over the next four years, five people were brought to trial in my father's murder. The woman charged with firing the gun that killed my father, and her brothers and friend, charged with conspiracy, denied having a role in the murder and were acquitted. I saw it as justice, for even had she pulled the trigger, I could regard the girl as no more than a pawn of Ervil LeBaron, who was brought to trial a year later and convicted of murder and conspiracy; he died a year afterward in the Salt Lake prison.

At the funeral next day, despite my awakened faith, I sensed danger. We didn't discover until later that my father's death had been mainly a means to another's end. In the trials, witnesses would claim that Ervil had aimed to kill his brother, Verlan, in order to wrest away his power in the Church of the First Born (the LeBaron family church). Ervil (deposed from his seat as patriarch of the family religion for authoring Joel's murder) would not give up his patrilineal claim to the mantle of Joseph. He allegedly designed my father's murder, supposing that Brother Rulon, who befriended all who earnestly lived the Principle, would draw Verlan out of hiding with his death. Thus, he would kill two birds with one stone. He would throw my father's group into pandemonium, perhaps taking control of some money and some members. And he would have his "militia" gun Verlan down at my father's funeral. (Ironically, Verlan had a fatal automobile accident the same week that Ervil died in prison.)

Ervil had arranged for three men to arrive at the funeral with automatic weapons, each equipped with a pair of thirty-round clips of cartridges taped together so that each gun could discharge sixty rounds in seconds. They would fire on the crowd, killing whoever stood in their way. But they had counted on the funeral being held at the group's meeting place, not at the high school auditorium procured to accommodate the largest funeral gathering ever held in the state of Utah. They had not planned on the enormous turn-out of media and police. They had expected law enforcement officials to treat my father's murder in the same disinterested, ineffectual way to which they had responded to the threats against his life. But Murray police seemed suddenly so obsessed with protecting their peculiar polygamist segment that it preoccupied most of their forces. And the gathering evidence, the many cooperative witnesses, the strange coincidences—all coalesced into a sense of mission that compelled them to follow this investigation with unprecedented concentration. Ervil's "militia," a trio of subliterate youths, had stolen a truck and driven to the wardhouse near the funeral site. They held their weapons in their laps and watched the police milling on the lawn, hobnobbing with newsmen. Perhaps they watched, too, as Jake and Adele and Brian and I parked the car and walked into the building.

I wasn't so much afraid of dying that day as I was of living. As we sang the words my father had written, I clung to my youngest sister's hand and felt no better equipped to deal with life than she, who was only ten.

> My life is yours, oh Saviour dear
> To do Thy will through all my days . . .

Yet we shared something that would help us through the days ahead, a child's awareness that this life is a single phase in an ever-expanding pattern, that death is not the conqueror.

> I do not seek for high estate
> To walk in honor among men. . . .
> Among Thy servants I'd be great . . .
> My paths most humble, Lord.

His paths had not been humble in scope, but knowledge of their expanse and variety had made him humble. The seed dreams had been sown, and they would sprout one day and bear fruit.

Isaac read my father's favorite poems, *The Psalm of Life* by Longfellow and *Abou Ben Adhem* by Leigh Hunt. My father's sister read a poem she had written for the occasion called "The Family Doctor," mourning for the many who had believed that "the doctor could not die." Then Uncle Andrew arose and confessed that he had dreamed, some months before, that he had preached the gospel in this auditorium. He told of his final conversation with my father, how he had said, "I'm counting on you, Andrew." It was clear that Uncle Andrew didn't reach out willingly for the position, that he took it because he must. In the months ahead he would encourage the group toward "quality rather than quantity" in their lives and would warn them repeatedly, "We are only men. Don't expect us to solve your problems. Take them to the Lord."

When the funeral was finished, Isaac asked that my father's wives and children stay together in the room with his body so that we could kneel in prayer.

Brian and I sank together on our knees, facing north. Ahead of me was Jake, arm around Adele. Saul glanced uncertainly around, then knelt too. I heard the buzz of angry voices behind me and looked up just in time to see Danny and Dierdre striding from the auditorium, determination and pride on their faces.

Not until afterward, when the earth was spread over the coffin—hand carved by one of the brethren on the ranch—and someone had placed a perfect daisy in my numb fingers, saying, "Your father would want you to have this"; not until we had skipped the family gathering and luncheon to eat at a cold, formal restaurant so that the strident forces of my mother's family might yet hang together beyond the knife of judgment; not until a new, chill day had dawned did I learn what must have driven Danny and Dierdre from our midst. A woman, a complete stranger to Danny—witchlike, with gray-shot black hair and long nose and bitter smile—a woman who frequently had tried to worm her way into my father's bursting family, had approached Danny and hissed, "I want to go on record as being the one who called you to repentance." Her haunting words must have driven him from the auditorium, from this last adulation of my father.

But panic gripped me as I watched Danny's shrinking back, running like Adam from the knowledge of himself, from the responsibility for his own capacity for good and evil. He was cloaked in unbelief and fear, heading straight for apocalypse.

But then I remembered that Mormon doctrine claims that both heaven and hell must work for the Lord, that "we believe all things; we hope all things" according to the admonition of Paul. Danny owned the right to doubt, to wander and search on his own—it was circumscribed by the very religion that had spawned him. Just as I had traveled through bleak and lonely landscapes of the world and the human heart, so could he . . . and return.

Danny had the right, perhaps even the responsibility, to defy my father's connection with God until he found his own. Just as I had struck out on my own and had been led home by a tiny light that grew ever warmer, visible only to me. Just as Grandfather Harvey had followed the light of a vision through a snowstorm in marshland until he found the solid highway home. Even if the other ninety-nine must be left on their own until he was found, Danny would come home someday. For the tiny leading light of vision is love, that miraculous protoplasm that contains us through all our unions and separations. Each of us held a place in my father's family; this much was an irreducible, inalienable fact. Danny and I would not lose our space in our father's family kingdom but would go on to affect new spaces, to discover more compatriots for personal freedom and individual responsibility. Someday—perhaps not until "the fullness of times, when God shall gather all things into one"—the world itself would be free, each man holding his own spire of principle to which meaning is tethered, the same banner of faith and free will that my father had clutched so fiercely. Someday, when all the nightmares are spent and all good dreams become real in love's Christening, we will truly be One Family, One Church, One Race of Man, One World before God—our only true judge.